Astrology o
Shadow S

"There is no astrologer I trust more than Maja D'Aoust to go into the shadows with—she brings her vast knowledge in astrology, Jungian psychology, esoteric thought, and ancient wisdom traditions together in the most exciting and accessible way. *Astrology of the Shadow Self* is a sage and insightful introduction to oppositional astrology that is both a guide and a poetic meditation on the dark depths of shadow work. Beautifully written and illustrated, this book provides paths for a journey that offers an expansion of the self—and quite possibly of the collective universe."

ANDREA RICHARDS, AUTHOR OF *ASTROLOGY*, BOOK TWO OF THE LIBRARY OF ESOTERICA SERIES

"This combined work of astrology and shadow studies is the book we didn't know we were waiting for. With the aid of the birth chart, Maja challenges the reader to dig to the deepest depths to uncover the hidden and embrace wholeness. *Astrology of the Shadow Self* is a poignant and unapologetic guide to self-discovery and spiritual transformation."

NICOLETTE MIELE, AUTHOR OF *RUNES FOR THE GREEN WITCH*

"As she brings her focus insightfully into the sacred underworld of human consciousness and expression, Renaissance woman Maja D'Aoust adeptly emphasizes the gravity and strengths of engaging in exploration of the dark, rich, archetypal chthonic realms. The additional revealing of a lucid and tangible astrological process of shadow work complemented by Maja's signature writing, art, mindfulness, and wisdom has gracefully resulted in this truly charming and informative magical book."

MARK F. BARONE, MA, LMHC, HOLISTIC PSYCHOTHERAPIST AND PSYCHOSPIRITUAL CONSULTANT

Astrology *of the* Shadow Self

Working with Oppositions in Your Natal Chart

Maja D'Aoust

Destiny Books
Rochester, Vermont

Destiny Books
One Park Street
Rochester, Vermont 05767
www.DestinyBooks.com

Destiny Books is a division of Inner Traditions International

Cataloging-in-Publication Data for this title is available from the Library of Congress

ISBN 978-1-64411-917-4 (print)
ISBN 978-1-64411-918-1 (ebook)

Printed and bound in the United States by Lake Book Manufacturing, LLC
The text stock is SFI certified. The Sustainable Forestry Initiative® program promotes sustainable forest management.

10 9 8 7 6 5 4 3 2 1

Text design by Priscilla Baker and layout by Virginia Scott Bowman
This book was typeset in Garamond Premier Pro with Tenez used as the display typeface
Artwork by Maja D'Aoust

To send correspondence to the author of this book, mail a first-class letter to the author c/o Inner Traditions • Bear & Company, One Park Street, Rochester, VT 05767, and we will forward the communication, or contact the author directly at **witchofthedawn.com**.

To the soothsayers who have the courage to enter the shadow realms to confront and deal with shadow behaviors that need to be raised into awareness. The liberation of one and all depends on lifting ignorance into light, growing our branches to the sky, and extending our roots into the dark depths of atavistic vestiges.

Contents

THE SHADOW SIGNS

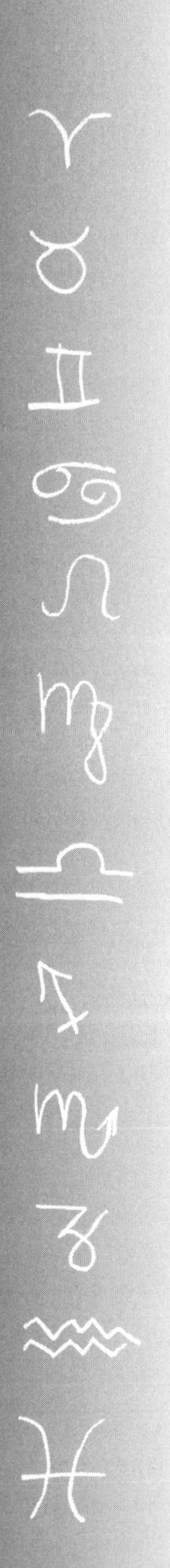

Introduction to the Shadow

> *Beware of organizations that proclaim their devotion to the light without embracing, bowing to the dark; for when they idealize half the world they must devalue the rest.*
>
> STARHAWK, *DREAMING THE DARK*

THE WORLD IS A WONDERFUL, TERRIBLE PLACE. There are the most incredible things here, as well as the darkest pockets of misery, and they all exist simultaneously together in a big stew. I have formed the habit of calling this realm the arena of terror joy. This book will probably be uncomfortable, if I am doing it correctly. Shadows cause discomfort, and this is why they are swept out of our consciousness, hidden away so that we do not need to look at them. This hiding action creates a false perception of the reality we dwell in to avoid the very real shadows present in ourselves, others, and the natural world in which we live. This book comes with a trigger warning because it covers negative energies and forms. These unpleasantries help make up reality and simply need to be included rather than focused upon in exclusion to the other dipole of positive energy and uplifting material. Presenting this work is by no

means suggesting this is all there is, nor is it a doom scroll or implying we must consume fear porn and trauma. This book of shadows examines the negative energy realm in archetypal representations for identification and preparation to transmute them.

The darkness belongs to the divine feminine. This isn't a gender statement but more about energetic correspondences. Feminine energy is negative energy, which does not mean that it is bad; Western culture has projected negative connotations on this energy, associating it with fear of death and stagnation. For the purposes of this book, negative energy refers to an energetic charge and stillness. Negative energy sinks; it is dense and goes below. Negative energy is also the reason matter forms in the universe. Things cannot grow in a positive, masculine direction forever—that creates cancer and overgrowth—and so the negative energy must also be wielded, must also exist. If everything rose forever, we would all be Icarus and be burned up in the sun. The goddess rules this area of negative energy and is Earth herself, where we shall all be laid to rest in her rocky embrace, eventually. Earth's caverns are needed for growth because no creature would ever form without stillness, without a vessel to hold space for its nurtured development in this ionically negatively charged environment that forms our blood, sweat, and tears. The goddess traditions call upon us to hold space for growth of the shadow, to nurture it, to hold it like an infant while it learns, even if it tries to scratch our eyes out in the process. This is the bass drop, the down beat, and the low vibe.

The chthonic goddesses rule our bodies, the world of the dead, what we eat and how we reproduce. These are uncontrollable things for most of us and make up our subconscious realms. Unless you have managed to consciously keep your breathing going while you slept, you are under the control of the shadow of Earth, and it is in charge of your unconscious ego. Like an iceberg, you mostly lie hidden below the surface in the caves. For every bright star in the sky there is a vastness of darkness. If we judge things by proportion of volume, then darkness, space, and emptiness win. Our ego will rebel against our mothers, against our parents, against the darkness; this is a natural part of development. So we find ourselves constantly pitted against the uncontrollable, unknowable caves of our beingness. What we cannot control or command, what brings us life and death itself, makes us uncomfortable.

Humans strive to reach the heights of greatness but are often brought to ruin by petty things: a betrayal by a friend or lover, a single blade thrust through the back. For all our huge capacities, we are all too often small and mean. Even if you achieve a maturity beyond the mud, you may fall victim to one who has not. A star might be shining and bright, at the peak of its glory, only to be sucked into a black hole through no fault of its own. Nature contains much pettiness for all its greatness. A lion might come to find it is taken from its power by a tiny germ, just as the heart of a human can be pierced forever by an insignificant insult.

Containing and dealing with shadow is a humanity-wide effort that must be nurtured, not shamed, and the shadow side needs to be raised up into awareness. This absolutely does not imply a lack of responsibility for individuals in any way. No victim of a crime committed through shadow behavior will be able to transmute that shadow nor are they responsible; they will need assistance. Shadow is a many-headed hydra, and maybe we can finally admit that persecuting or punishing individuals publicly who we deem guilty of shadow behavior will not eradicate shadow from humanity. How many bodies will be thrown into the volcano in sacrifice before we can make some evolution in the shadow realms that plague us all? We think we can shame shadow out of existence with righteousness, but feeding shame to shadow is nourishment for it, makes it strong and vindicates it. Humiliating the humiliated creates more humiliation in a cycle of imprisonment.

There is a tendency of society at large to shame and disparage people who act out violent natures, while we sit comfortably in seats of judgment, eating meat that was savagely slaughtered by someone else, not us, living on land taken from others violently, but not by us, wearing diamond rings on our fingers that were plucked from Earth by starving enslaved people—but it wasn't us who did that. We deplore the fist thrower and pay the missile launcher. The wretched individuals, unable to control their impulses, become our entertainment, as streaming sources make billions off their stories. We make a spectacle of them and string them up in the commons to throw tomatoes at them so that we feel better for our virtues and punish them, not us, for violent crimes. This is a dissociative disconnect from nature itself, but then the hypocrite is a shadow form for one and all to hold, myself included. I do not have the answer for this enormous issue of shadow; however, we can look at the contradictions and contemplate them. Perhaps you have some solutions or strategies; at least you can expand your awareness as a result of contemplating them, and that just might be good enough.

Think of this book as a private chamber you get to enter, like going into a still and empty cave, to view without fear, shame, or judgment the unseemly underbelly of the hidden nature of shadow. Take small sips or big gulps, however much poison you can stomach in one sitting. This book isn't something to engage in when you are in the wrong head space or to cause you to berate or judge yourself; it is here to provide a transpersonal bird's-eye view of some of our most difficult behaviors, choices, and actions and, more importantly, of the destructive capacity of nature and the natural world. We live in a potentially hostile, certainly dangerous reality, and if you have any doubts about this, you are welcome to go naked into nature and discover it. Nature has a million ways to poison and kill us, and perhaps through raising our awareness to these we can navigate them. There is no way out of nature; it has you surrounded and fills your belly, enters you with every breath. Let's take a peek and look around.

> *The unacceptable must be concealed. . . . For those of us who are disgruntled and who have grown alarmed at this systematic erasure of all trace of negativity, our era easily meets our objections with an impressive sampling of deviant activities, revolts, rebellions and perversions of all kinds. It could even be said that it cultivates them. In addition, everything becomes more or less subversive.*
>
> Annie Lebrun, *The Reality Overload*

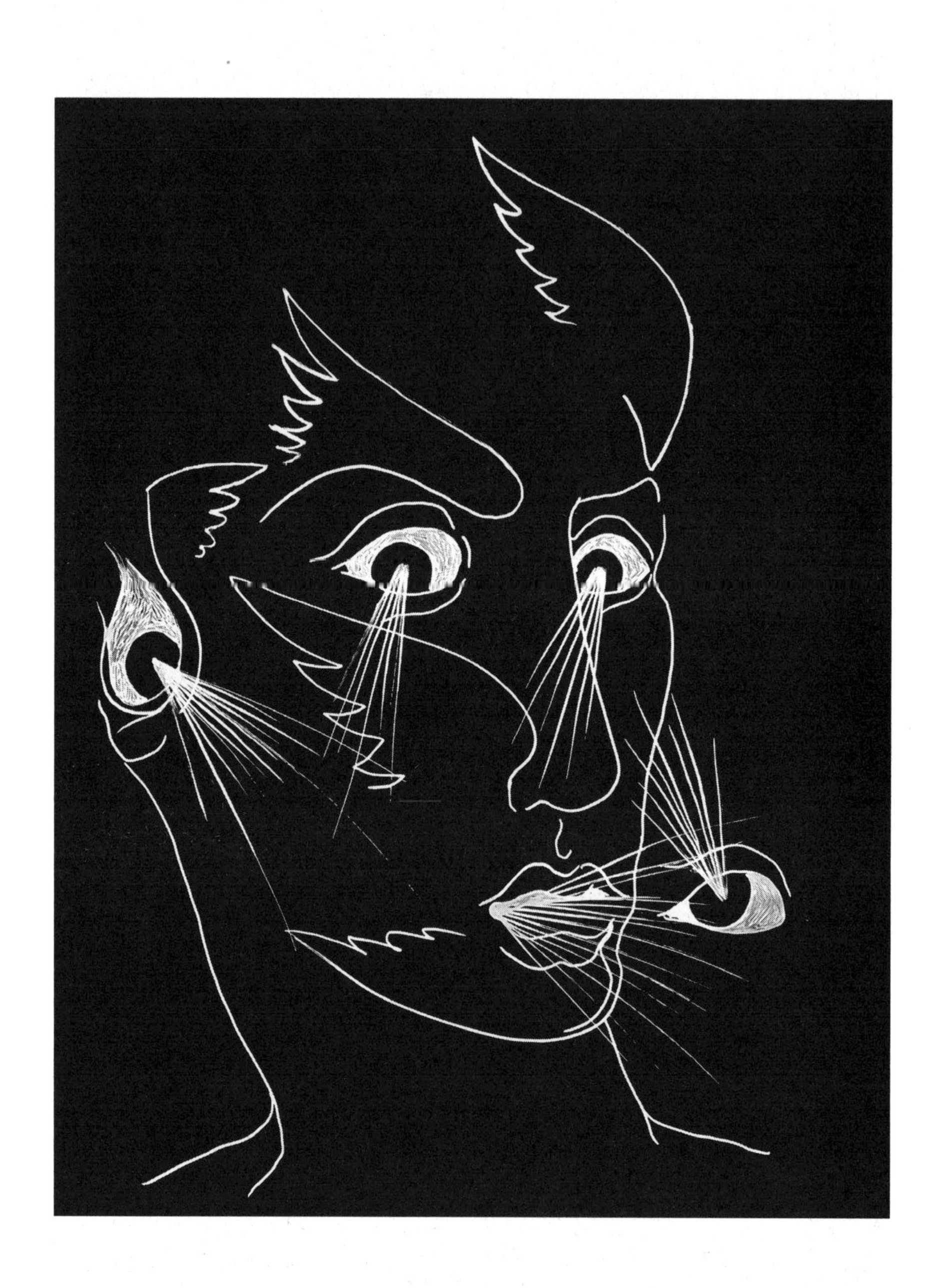

Astrology and Identity

Deepening the Natal Chart

> *So far as the personality is still potential, it can be called transcendent, and so far as it is unconscious, it is indistinguishable from all those things that carry its projections, symbols of the outside world and the cosmic symbols. These form the psychological basis for the conception of man as a macrocosm through the astrological components of his character.*
>
> Carl G. Jung, *Psychology and Religion*

Who am I? Where do I come from? Being a human means confronting the mystery of our existence at some point in our conscious awareness. Many, known as seekers, spend a large portion of their lives enthralled with such questions. Others come into a faith or religion that seems to satisfy this curiosity, while still others find the answer through arduous labor. The journey of humans to discover what and who they are remains an essential and eternal frontier of exploration. In the search for identity, one destination nearly every seeker arrives at is the heavens above. There is nothing quite like finding your place by gazing in wonder at the infinite number of stars that fill the night sky.

As unlikely as it is to find the identity of ourselves through contemplation of something as vast and unknowable as outer space, a consistent and abundant amount of insight can be gained from precisely this location. The endless abyss, when viewed from a single point, offers a perspective that can fathom the occult.

Not surprisingly, astrology dates back to prehistory, given that people only needed to look up at the night sky and observe the stars. All ancient cultures carefully tracked the stars—the Chinese, Mayans, Aztecs, Babylonians, Egyptians, Native Americans, everyone. The stars influenced human behavior: people used the stars to measure time, to determine when to plant crops, and to navigate. The stars have a measurable physical influence in our lives even if you do not apply them on a metaphysical level; for example, stars hit you with cosmic rays every time you step outside.

Astrology is a tool that can serve an impressive variety of purposes. Famously, leaders of nations, such as kings, queens, and presidents, used it as a predictive technique for events, to foretell important trends. Astrology can be a mirror for the moment in the form of horary or electional astrology, providing data for a current event. Most popularly, it can be used to explore our psychological tendencies, character, and personality to reveal the human psyche through archetype and myth. Astrology is a powerful technique for acquiring self-knowledge, solving identity mysteries, and soothing existential discomfort.

This book focuses on the use of astrology for psychological purposes, specifically aimed at identity, character, and personality. The popular use of astrology for psychological explorations need hardly be stated as it is currently experiencing a resurgence in pop culture. One could say, however, the stars never truly go out of style. Despite skepticism and every imaginable criticism, astrology has endured, to the surprise of hardened logical rationalists. Using astrology psychologically is not a recent trend, though; it was widespread among the alchemists of Europe, such as Paracelsus and Athanasius Kircher, who sought to undergo the great work or *magna opus* of transforming and transmuting the self. Astrology later attracted the attention of Western psychologists and psychiatrists. Carl Jung, who deeply studied alchemy, catapulted the use of divination tools like astrology and the I Ching as psychologically self-transformative instruments, which he touted because of their relationship with synchronicity, the simultaneous occurrence of closely related events. Working with the subconscious gained acceptance as a technique as psychology grew in prominence. Sigmund Freud, Wilhelm Reich, Carl Jung, and many others were trying to come up with new languages to approach the vast unknowns of human inner space. Roberto Assagioli, an Italian psychiatrist and pioneer in humanistic and transpersonal psychology, greatly assisted the merger of psychology and astrology. He is the author of *The Act of Will* and *The Psychosynthesis Model* and wrote additional works under a pseudonym, Clara A. Weiss, regarding the seven cosmic rays and esoteric astrology.

> *I am interested only in the basement of the human being.*
>
> Sigmund Freud, in a letter to Roberto Assagioli

Astrology, when used as a tool in psychology, expands the self's vision of itself, its identity, through including larger mythological archetypes. When an individual identifies herself solely through her vocation, for example, she can seem rather limited. Take that same individual and grant her permission to include, as part of who she is, the god Jupiter, the goddess Venus, or the very sun itself, and her self-image grows considerably, perhaps to goddess-like proportions. Affiliation and identification with gods and powerful beings has a potent effect on the psyche. Our superhero-laden Hollywood movies testify to the human *need* to consider ourselves as potentially greater than our everyday selves, even if only in our imagination. Utilizing the planets and stars to expand self-identification in this manner connects us to heaven on many levels of consciousness and sentience. When we connect ourselves and who we are to the vast expanses of space, we grow. Connecting the self-image to the stars and heaven gives the self an eternal immortal quality; doing this can help transform some of our greatest fears, such as death itself.

This is a valuable practice, regardless of the scientific complaints surrounding astrology. Most people are unaware of the potency of this method and simply enjoy getting to know their astrological identities and relating to the various character descriptions. Many feel their astrological data is unique to themselves and see it as a self-identifier. Ironically, many who enjoy astrology in modern times seem to believe astrology is presenting them with a special and unique identity rather than uniting them with larger mythological personas. The beauty and power of astrology is that it connects you with these larger identities and archetypes, which in turn are shared with others. Astrology may be used to come into larger human concepts and thereby force the ego to expand past its singularities of self-conception by connecting to the stars above.

We push the limits of identity simply by having our birth chart cast. The chart presents us with the multifaceted diamond of our being. We discover that all kinds of folks live within us: heroes and villains; men, women, and androgynes. Through the archetypes in their mythological roles, astrology presents an elegant way to break through multiple levels of identity politics. That's powerful. Sometimes getting people to envision or imagine themselves differently is downright impossible; we can be quite stubborn in our hardened beliefs.

I would like to broaden that practice of ego expansion by manipulating the birth chart to be even more inclusive. The star shadows technique deepens the chart through opposition and contracts it into a negative space, which causes a wave of novel emanations to appear. The simple technique of using our oppositional identities is vital in self-transformation as it works on our negator, our separator, our own personal Antichrist. We all have a thing we think of as "I" or self. We also have a thing we think of as not I or not self. When the I and the not I are joined, it heals such cognitive errors as oppression through justification of superiority and victimization mind-sets through a unification process into one cohesive whole. This is the alchemical space known as the marriage of the opposites and it can be achieved through the use of the psychological tool of astrology here in this book by integrating the shadow of ourselves into our conscious awareness of who we are in our own mind's eye of self-image. The practice of becoming a larger totality rather than being threatened due to arrogance actually increases our compassion, increases our interest in other human beings, increases our will to power for the purposes of growth for all. For why would we not want to acknowledge the dark self that is also us? Becoming "one with everything," as all the high-falutin' spiritualists prescribe, means doing the work of integrating everything, even what you do not like. We only trample what we view as beneath us or not part of ourselves. Just ask the serpent lying beneath your feet. Tread not upon the serpent, for it is only you, after all. Welcome to shadow work, where we come to love the thing we perceive as our anathema.

As a synchronistic aside, I wrote the above paragraph while staying in the desert, and after I wrote it, I nearly stepped on a rattlesnake. I went for a hike and as my foot landed on a sagebrush, I saw the tail, which rattled so loudly and suddenly that I nearly jumped out of my skin. Nature was forcing me to take my own advice in an unmistakable manifestation of my own words.

Many people tout astrology as a tool for self-acceptance or self-empowerment, but I would like to state exactly what that means. How does one "empower" the self? What does it mean to bring yourself power? The self grows in power in the same way as everything else—through expansion. For example, a virus becomes more powerful than the life force it is inhabiting through replicating itself so enormously it fills more of your space than you do. This is the virus's way of empowering itself through growth. We empower each other through validation, vindication, and inclusion. We help each other grow. That is power. We strip the other (and ourselves) of power through guilt, shame, and rejection from society, decreasing or diminishing. In society, people are stripped of power through shaming and ostracizing, sometimes to the point of incarceration, thus making them small or unable to expand. Here we shall try a new way of dealing with shadow, the unwanted self, the naughty one. We shall raise it up into power so that it grows and matures. The shadow within us may then ascend and become not a more powerful shadow but rather a more powerful part of our whole self. This prevents the shadow from taking over the self and hiding, lurking in our blind spots, and gives it a chance to actually heal. To become your most powerful identity, you must become all of your identities. Leave none of them out, especially not the ones that are unsavory. Begin to see yourself as large and vast as the stars *and* the darkness, including as many things as you possibly can.

> *Human beings do not seek pleasure and avoid displeasure. What human beings want, whatever the smallest organism wants, is an increase of power; driven by that will they seek resistance, they need something that opposes it—displeasure, as an obstacle to their will to power, is therefore a normal fact; human beings do not avoid it, they are rather in continual need of it.*
>
> FRIEDRICH NIETZSCHE,
> *THE WILL TO POWER*

Shadow Work

As with the prisoners in the Platonic cave, the world of ideas is a projection of shadows. In Bruno's book, On the Shadows of Ideas *(*De umbris idearum, *1582), he points out that shadows are the forms that Reason takes during the learning process, and that organize it. These shadows can be used as images and symbols to then organize the knowledge of things. Bruno suggests that there is no shadow without reflection. Ideas are described as shadows of divinity, perhaps a distant repercussion of or analogy with the Creation story in the book of Genesis; that is, first came the shadow, and consequently, an understanding of the light.*

Francisco Camacho, "Giordano Bruno: Or the Shadow of Ideas," *Carma*

Most folk familiar with the term *shadow work* are witches, spiritual practitioners, or psychologists. In many witchcraft traditions, shadow work constitutes a significant part of what witches do. It is difficult to trace lineages and identify a single source or culture for this type of work in the occult and magical worlds; one could argue that it exists cross-culturally through all of humanity if one investigates indigenous cultures and ancient traditions. Nearly all divination systems, for example, involve a good deal of shadow work in the sense that they attempt to reveal the blind spot or what you cannot see due to the eclipse created by your shadow. Simply engaging in divination is often considered a fair amount of shadow work.

I have a habit of investigating the etymologies of words and looking into language, and so I investigated the term *shadow*. The Online Etymology Dictionary listed an analogy, "shadow is to shade as meadow is to mead," and when I looked into it I found an article that traced the origin of the words *shade–shadow* and *mead–meadow*.* Both pairs were

*Oliver Farrar Emerson, "Mead–Meadow, Shade–Shadow, a Study in Analogy," *Modern Language Notes* 35, no. 3 (March 1920): 147–54.

described as *inflectional doublets*: two distinct words derived from the same source. In the case of *shade* and *shadow*, a single Teutonic word, *skadus*, had differentiated into two Old English words with slightly different spellings and meanings: *scead* (which later became the Middle English *schad* and then *shade*), meaning to "shelter and protect," as in sheltering from the heat and glare of the sun, either under foliage or behind a screen, and *sceadu* (ME *schadwe* and eventually *shadow*), meaning "dark spot due to cutting off of light, an immaterial thing." There is a close relationship between the two words, a bond or way the two interact with each other. The word *shadow* in and of itself is shadowy in that it doesn't exist on its own; it is attached to another word—and even a counterpart, in the form of *mead* and *meadow*. Without shade, there is no shadow and vice versa. This struck me, because the shadow is our double, a companion of sorts. Even the stars have been known to have companions, and many stars are binary; it is even supposed that many stars are born as twins. The double in esoteric philosophy is used to explain the hidden nature of the universe. Nearly all spiritual and religious texts recognize the rule that there are unseen doubles of everything.

> *All things are double one against another: and he hath made nothing imperfect.*
>
> Ecclesiasticus 42:24

Shade is a basic aspect of shadow. Shade not only means a place where the light doesn't shine or something that intercepts the light but is also used to express contempt or disrespect, as in to throw shade on someone. Shadow work is mostly understanding why we justify insulting or disrespecting the self and others and the dynamic and effects that occur when our words, thoughts, and actions slight, minimize, or injure another, damaging the other's ego, body, or spirit, whether we want to admit it or not.

The other aspect and meaning of the shadow is revealed in one of the old-fashioned meanings of shade. Most of us use shade to describe a spot under a tree, but shade also means ghost or disembodied spirit, the portion of the soul that goes to the land of the dead, a use of the word in English that dates from the 1610s. The world of shadow and shade is also the underworld, which is, essentially, hell. Dante uses the word *ombra*, an Italian word that means both shade and shadow, in his *Purgatory*, the second part of the *Divine Comedy*. In Virgil's *Aeneid*, Dido curses Aeneas, who has betrayed her, before she commits suicide (Aeneid 4.384–6): "Though far away, I will chase you with murky brands and, when chill death has severed soul and body, everywhere my shade shall haunt you."

Scholars have devoted much work to examining this aspect of the shade and its role within magical traditions. The shamanic work of soul retrieval often involves the shade, as has been thoroughly discussed by Mircea Eliade:

> According to Yukagir belief, when a man dies, his three souls separate: one remains with the corpse, the second one goes to the kingdom of shadows, the third ascends to the sky. . . . In any case the most important one seems to be the one that becomes a shadow. . . . It is to the kingdom of shadows that the shaman descends to seek the patient's soul.*

In psychology the examination of the shadow took over the minds of the most famous scholars in psychoanalysis. Most folks are only familiar with Jung's or Freud's analyses but they were both informed by Otto Rank's views on the shadow, which he wrote about extensively in his 1914 essay *Der Doppelgänger* (The Double). The two brothers Cain and Abel might be thought of in terms of the doppelgänger. They are in a polarity; one is the shadow of the other. As such, they are really a single individual.

The inflectional doublet of mead–meadow also plays a part in these

---

*Mircea Eliade, *Shamanism: Archaic Techniques of Ecstasy* (Princeton, NJ: Princeton University Press, 1964), 246.

esoteric truths of what it means to be a human. *Mead* is an archaic term for *meadow*, which originally meant a grassland kept for hay. But the word also refers to a fermented beverage distilled from honey gathered from the flowers of the meadow. By doing the shadow work, we distill the spirit, an alchemical process. We transform the body in the same way that hay is harvested from the meadow, a process symbolized by the ancient grain gods who are sacrificed in the fall and resurrected in the spring.

The agriculture gods Osiris and Dionysus have larger messages on shadow work to convey. Osiris must face his brother Set, who murders him and scatters his body parts, but from these parts Osiris is reborn, resurrected, to begin the vegetation cycle again. Dionysus, god of the vine, is also connected with stories of death, followed by a descent into hell and rebirth. As god of the vine, the myth of Dionysus mirrors the making of wine: plucking the grapes, crushing them into pulp, and then distilling them into wine. Suffice to say, the language used here—cultivating grain (and grape), harvesting it, and transforming it into food and drink, which are then offered communally—also describes how we work with our shadows. Digestion and alchemy are intimately linked, which is inextricable from our shadow work processes. In this book we use a system based on the natural observations of the planets, but if you would like to descend deeper into the grain gods, I will simply let you know there are caverns to spelunk.

> *"I have seen the worst," Candide replied. "But a wise man, who since has had the misfortune to be hanged, taught me that all is marvellously well; these are but the shadows on a beautiful picture." "Your hanged man mocked the world," said Martin. "The shadows are horrible blots."*
>
> Voltaire, *Candide*

Instinct and the Role of Nature in Shadow Work

How else could Nature form man's ego unless its informing life and consciousness had been given a wide enough experience, unless they had been allowed to journey through the bodies of the adder, the tiger, the cow and the horse for example, and gain the attributes and consciousness that such bodies could manifest? They were not merely useful but quite necessary in the making of the ego, the "I Am."

PAUL BRUNTON, *THE SPIRITUAL CRISIS OF MAN*

You live inside a body that is alive and has its own way of doing things that you have no idea about. Most of us are familiar with the word *instinct* but don't fully realize its implications. Knowledge is tucked away within our physical forms, a lot of knowledge, things you will never ever consciously know. Instinct is a part of the unconscious and should be included when you are trying to wrap your concepts around what exactly the unconscious and the shadow are. You are not aware of your body's ways. Even if you study the body and become a doctor or a biologist, that doesn't mean you yourself fully understand and can do the things your body knows how to do: you are just watching it do things. Your digestive track processes food, your heart beats, your brain goes through sleep cycles, but you are not consciously doing these things. The body is part of your subconscious, of your unconscious. Part of what is contained within its realm is your shadow behavior as well, along with your instinct, which does not belong to you but to nature herself. This deserves respect and acknowledgment.

Nature is something we are part of and do not own. We contain it and are contained within it, and yet seem so far away from it in our minds. You might think you can rise above certain instincts, and this may be true, but do not minimize the labor and pragmatic concerns involved there. Would you really want to completely conquer all your instincts and think you could remember to beat your own heart? You would surely die. Go ahead and try to consciously track your breathing for one hour; you will lose. The impulse and compulsion of instinct serves to keep you and all other life-forms alive. Without instinct, we would not survive; therefore instinct deserves as much respect and veneration as intelligence. If that particular egg didn't travel to the fallopian tube and if a particular sperm did not reach the egg, where would you be? Not here reading this book, that is for certain. I have never understood attitudes that seek to overcome nature as though you could rule it. Be grateful for the work your body performs for your survival.

The shadow has many definitions in different cultures, but essentially it is considered our instincts, so-called primitive biological defense mechanisms that we do not have conscious control over and can't see for ourselves without assistance from a friend. The shadow is our inner beast, our child that wants and will do whatever it takes to obtain its desire.

> *Unfortunately, although this shadowy side of the personality is usually "utterly" unconscious in the individual, it is not so hidden from everybody else; and the more repressed and unconscious it is the more obvious it becomes to others.*
>
> Liz Greene

Shadow behaviors are contained in nature, because everything is contained in nature, and do not need to be conquered or despised but brought into awareness and integrated. When the light of our consciousness reaches into the dark cave of nature, truths are illuminated. This is evolution, a dawn upon the dark. We do not need to pretend it's OK; we do not need to excuse, cover up, or repress shadow. Shadow must be dealt with and allowed to expand and heal, not ignored or just tolerated. We learn about all of nature in the things we don't want to see. When we don't like something, we tend to push it deep into the dark cave of unconsciousness in an effort to eradicate it. We don't want to look at it. The word *respect* is related to the word *regard*, which means to look at something. We are afraid to stare into the abyss, and this could be why we, and society collectively, are getting behind in our shadow digestions. The integration of shadow is very much like the subconscious process of digestion that our body does for us, except in reverse. We have to consciously integrate our shadow, while our body unconsciously digests our food. We see our food when we put it in our mouth and it disappears, while shadow comes from a dark place and rises up for us to see. When we see shadow, we have to break it down, make it less dense, dissipate it with our awareness.

The way we respond to shadow is a shadow behavior in and of itself. Just because you don't like something and it is offensive to you doesn't justify attempting to remove it from your consciousness and from your life. You may think you need to remove it, though, and that removal is the best way to deal with it. You will at the very least try and not engage with it. Sometimes getting away from something toxic is the best option for safety purposes, but we still need to acknowledge and process the occurrence. Our severe reaction to shadow is very much like an overactive immune response: we become inflamed with hate as we try to burn it out with fever, poop it out, or puke it out, to avoid becoming infected by its vile existence. Shadow will usually elicit the hate response, which serves to show us where our shadow lies. This instinctive inflammatory response to shadow causes many of us to hate each other and ourselves.

We learn from the shadow that the ego has a desire to succeed. We want to live and to prosper, not just succeed but be the best, be honored, even exalted. Our ego wants to have legends written about it and monuments erected in its honor. Shadow feels most comfortable standing as a king or queen of the hill, having vanquished its enemies, to have come through hardship and prevailed.

The shadow side of nature also wants to win, wants to succeed, wants to go into excess. Her life-forms keep striving for success; nature keeps them moving and growing, through the shadow energy. Throughout the book, I have included examples in nature for each shadow archetype to broaden our identity concepts further and penetrate into greater environments of relating to nature. It is vitally important to not take shadow personally and to see it in the reality of nature; when we see shadow in nature, not just in ourselves, we relate better to nature. There are different species of shadow, just like there are different species of animals. The comparisons between nature and ourselves are not given to suggest that all nature is shadowy and aggressive or defensive. It is merely to show that the polarity exists in nature too; that other life-forms are like us. There is a flip side to positive or constructive life-affirming emotions and behaviors in all life-forms, as well as in us. But this is a book on shadows, not nature, so the focus will be on human behaviors.

> *If humans are going to draw on nature for rationales about our own behavior, there's no obligation to look to those with clear alpha males. In fact, nothing is stopping us from drawing inspiration from spider monkeys and just trying to hug it out.*
>
> Leslie Nemo, "The Science of Alpha Males in Animal Species," *Discover*

We cannot control or conquer our own or others' shadows through force, any more than we can control nature or digest our own food with our intention or thoughts. Perhaps a precious few have the discipline to attempt such things, but on the whole, let's be real. Regardless of our most clever strategies, a hurricane cares nothing for your intentions and travels on. Understanding to flow with nature, to ride with it, is the way to proceed, rather than attempting to constrain or eradicate it. To successfully keep a venomous snake as a pet, you must learn about its behavior, respect its territorial instincts, and handle it with care. Our shadow side is much like that venomous snake: we must respect the power of our shadows, observe them and learn to work with them, transmuting shame into honor.

It is no mystery that a big trigger of shadow behavior in nature happens when a human disrespects and disregards nature and does not acknowledge her power. Snake bites in the wild happen to humans who are not paying attention, who blunder into the snake's territory and startle it or who deliberately provoke it. Nature requires respect, honor, and acknowledgment not dominance, shame, and indifference. If we can only transmute our responses when we encounter our shadow or the shadow of someone else, perhaps we, as a species that is part of a larger organism, could make some real progress.

> *In short, the ego instincts are nothing other than the sum total of vegetative demands in their defensive function. We are merely building upon well established ideas when we say that the ego instinct is the id instinct directed either against itself or against another instinct. The entire psychic process appears to be characterized by the cleavage and subsequent opposition between tendencies which functioned as a unit.*
>
> Wilhelm Reich, *Character Analysis*

Space Shadows

The dread and darkness of the mind cannot be dispelled by the sunbeams, the shining shafts of day, but only by an understanding of the outward form and inner workings of nature.

LUCRETIUS, *ON THE NATURE OF THE UNIVERSE*

The planets have real physical shadows that are perceivable and measurable. They are called the planet's *umbra* (very close to the Italian word for shade or shadow, *ombra*). You may know this word from watching an eclipse. If the word makes you think of an umbrella, which is made to shelter and create shade, you are correct in tracing that word's shared origin with *umbra*. An eclipse is nothing more than the casting of a shadow, but this event has borne a weighty significance throughout human history.

Earth has a shadow all her own; her umbra is what we call night. Night happens when the side of Earth you are on is opposite the sun; you are experiencing the shadow that Earth casts upon herself. The umbra *is* the opposition. How strange that we fall into sleep and dreaming and our own subconscious while present in the shadow of Earth. It is as if we are influenced and compelled to follow her lead and go into the night with her, to venture into the depths of our own physiology, which express themselves in the form of dreams. Earth's shadow grips us and pulls us down into the unconscious realms with a hold none can avoid for long.

Go ahead, try and see how long you can go without sleep if you have discipline, training, and safety. The longest I have gone in my vision quest training is five days and nights. Dr. Kelvin deWolfe went seven days and nights, the longest I have observed personally. My partner said that in his Marine training they went three days. Before too long, you will be pulled under; it is only a matter of time. By the end you will feel like a rock trying to float in the ocean. I quite literally felt the thing that is the night grab me and pull me under like a wave in the ocean

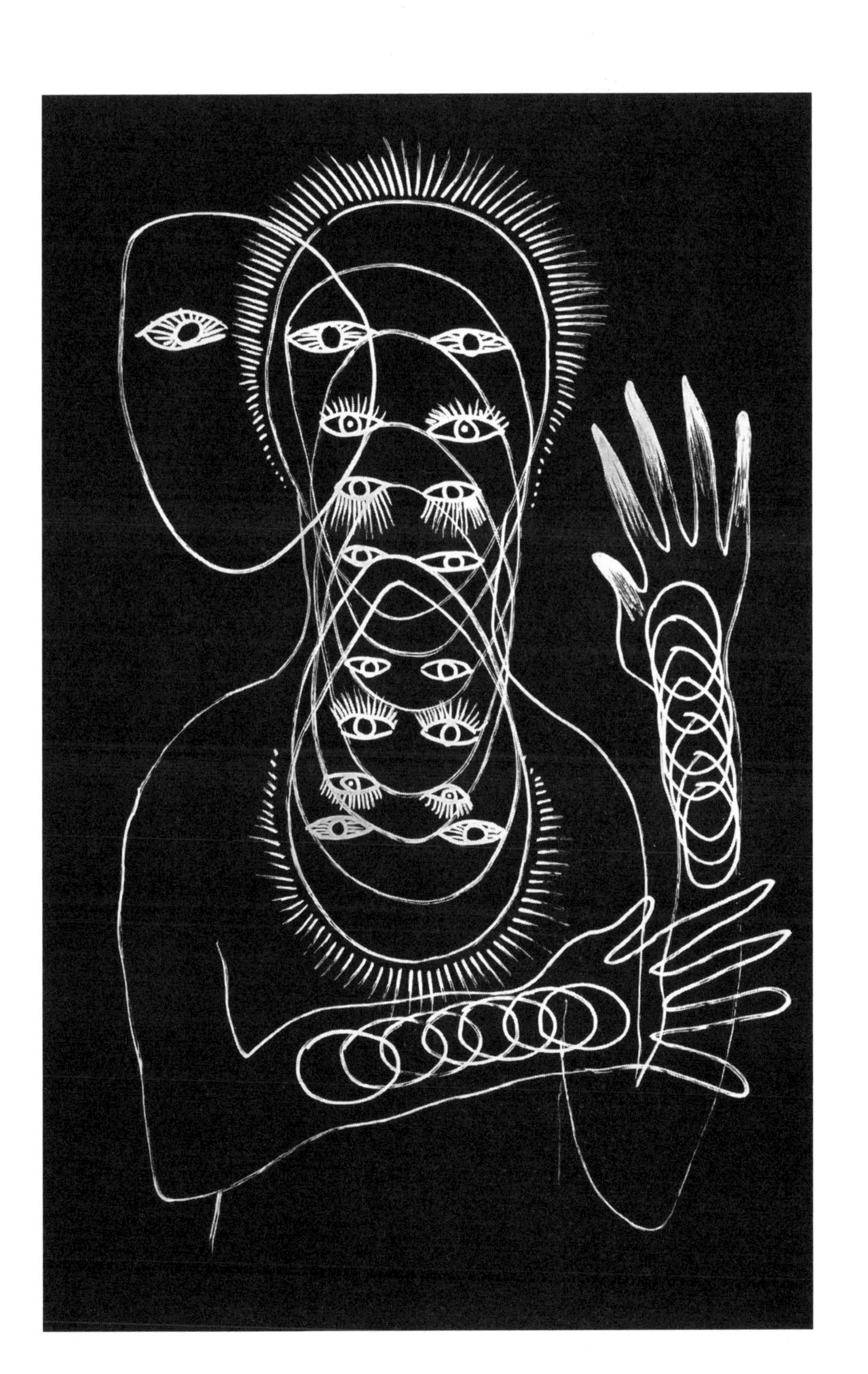

and there was nothing I could do about it, despite my best efforts. An uncomfortable feeling, to say the least.

During an eclipse, both an umbra, the darkest central area where no or little light reaches Earth, and a *penumbra*, a place of partial illumination, are cast. It is a twilight zone, an area where the light is not quite there and the shadow is not quite full. This is the liminal zone or place between the worlds where an intermingling of conscious awareness and the subconscious freely roam together.

All of the planets in space cast shadows because they have substance or matter, and these shadows affect us, as the planets themselves do; they exert a measurable influence. For instance, a fourteen-year-old was able to detect and measure the shadow of Jupiter:

> Shadows are created when a source of light is blocked. Obvious, right? Also obvious is the brighter the source, the easier it is to see the shadow cast. So you might wonder, how faint an object can you use as a light source and still be able to detect a shadow? We know the Sun and Moon cast shadows, and Venus is well-known for this as well. The entire sky is bright enough, even at night, to throw shadows under the right conditions. But what about the next brightest light source in the night sky: Jupiter? . . . Canadian "amateur" astronomer Laurent V. Joli-Coeur wondered about this as well. So he set about dreaming up a way to do it: build a rig that would allow him to set up a "Jupiter dial"—like a sundial, with a gnomon (a post) that would cast a shadow, but which he could aim at Jupiter—and take a time exposure on his camera. The hammer-shaped shadow is from his gnomon, and the light source is from Jupiter. To make sure, he rotated the rig a bit, and the shadow moved as well, indicating it was from a point source. Also, he pointed his rig well away from Jupiter and got no shadow when he took a third picture, showing it wasn't from the glow of the night sky, either.*

*Phil Plait, "Young Astronomer Captures a Shadow Cast by Jupiter," *Slate,* November 18, 2011.

Additionally remarkable about Joli-Coeur's discovery is that the shadow took the shape of a hammer. Thor, the Germanic god of war, is equivalent to the Roman god Jupiter and Greek god Zeus—all three were gods of thunder and lightning. We get the name Thursday, Thor's day, from this god. Thor wields a magic hammer with which he creates thunder and lightning. The planet Jupiter has constant lightning storms; perhaps the ancients knew more than we suppose.

Shadow forms where there is substance, or prima materia, which interferes with the free flow of light, of awareness and consciousness. Light is awareness and perception, and darkness is unconscious and mysterious. Neither one is good nor bad; they simply each cover different realms.

> *In the world of physics we watch a shadowgraph performance of familiar life. The shadow of my elbow rests on the shadow table as the shadow ink flows over the shadow paper. . . . The frank realization that physical science is concerned with a world of shadows is one of the most significant of recent advances.*
>
> A. S. EDDINGTON,
> *THE NATURE OF THE PHYSICAL WORLD*

Ancient Wisdom and the Shadow

A shadow flits before me,
Not thou, but like to thee:
Ah Christ, that it were possible
For one short hour to see
The souls we loved, that they might tell us
What and where they be.

ALFRED, LORD TENNYSON,
MAUD: A MONODRAMA, PART II

In the Hindu religion the goddess Chaya is in charge of the shadows. She is at once a personified deity and also a philosophical concept within the religion and practice of yoga and meditation. She is the consort of Surya, the Hindu sun god. Rather than being her own person, she is tied to Sanjna, the first wife of the Hindu sun god, and seems to be her ulterior persona or doppelgänger, a double. The first references to her date back to around 1200 BCE—to give you some idea of how long the concept of the shadow has been around. Chaya also plays a role in yoga, which is usually described as a yoking or union between the sun and moon.

> Chaya (shadow or reflection) has a technical significance in classical yoga. It stands for the reflection cast by the transcendental self or consciousness, in the highest aspect of the mind, called buddhi. This concept, which was first introduced by Vacaspati Mishra in his *Tattva-Vaish-aradi* seeks to explain how knowledge is possible given the fact that the mind is an evolute of insentient nature.*

Another early goddess figure depicting the tale of the shadow, dated to around 3000 BCE, can be seen in the myth of Inanna, from ancient

*Georg Feuerstein, *The Shambhala Encyclopedia of Yoga* (Boulder, Colo.: Shambhala, 2000), 72.

Mesopotamia. Her tale of traveling to the underworld to free her sister, Ereshkigal, is really just a story of how she dealt with her doppelgänger. Many seekers might be surprised to know this story is arguably the origin of the famous Hermetic axiom of "as above, so below." It refers to a goddess making peace with the land of the dead and her own shadow (Ereshkigal).

> In the Sumerian pantheon, Ereshkigal, Queen of the Underworld, is Inanna's older sister. Inanna is the Queen of Heaven and Earth but she does not know the underworld. Without this knowledge she remains immature. "From the Great Above she opened her ear to the Great Below." Thus begins Inanna's journey into a deeper life with the knowledge of death and rebirth. Ereshkigal was given the Underworld for her domain. Here she eats clay and drinks dirty water. She has no loving mother, father, brother or sister. She has no friends or companions. She longs only for her own sexual satisfaction. She is unloving, unloved, abandoned, instinctual and full of rage and loneliness. Ereshkigal can be seen as the other neglected side of Inanna, the side which feels all those feelings of worthlessness and abandonment.*

Another primary source for occult knowledge and esoterica is ancient Egypt. The subject of much cultural appropriation, a shadow behavior in and of itself, Egypt stands as a beacon of wisdom for those who begin any non-Christian spiritual tradition. The practice of shadow work in Egyptian teachings makes appearances in many of the oldest papyrus writings, including the Book of the Dead found in the Papyrus of Ani. It is not all that surprising that shadow work in Egypt is also tied to the underworld and the dead. This is clearly a cross-cultural theme: over and over again references are made to the human shadow, which eventually evolved into the *Hermetica*, spanning

*Judith Shaw, "The Story of Ereshkigal, Inanna's Older Sister," *Life on the Edge* (blog), December 12, 2012.

at least 300 BCE–1200 CE and written by alchemists of ancient Greece and medieval Europe who seemed to syncretize older Egyptian works attributed to Thoth. Any European who claims knowledge of the subconscious or shadow has gained this awareness through alchemy, which came to Europe by way of ancient Egypt and the city of Alexandria.

> If then you do not make yourself equal to God, you cannot apprehend God; for like is known by like. Leap clear of all that is corporeal, and make yourself grown to a like expanse with that greatness which is beyond all measure; rise above all time and become eternal; then you will apprehend God. Think that for you too nothing is impossible; deem that you too are immortal, and that you are able to grasp all things in your thought, to know every craft and science; find your home in the haunts of every living creature; make yourself higher than all heights and lower than all depths; bring together in yourself all opposites of quality, heat and cold, dryness and fluidity; think that you are everywhere at once, on land, at sea, in heaven; think that you are not yet begotten, that you are in the womb, that you are young, that you are old, that you have died, that you are in the world beyond the grave; grasp in your thought all of this at once, all times and places, all substances and qualities and magnitudes together; then you can apprehend God.*

The shadow in ancient Egypt and many indigenous cultures was recognized as an inseparable part of the human being, a vital and living component of who we are. It was called *shut* (pronounced "shoot"), also spelled *seut, sheut,* or *swt,* and was considered a palpable and perceivable aspect of the person. There is some scholarly debate confusing the *ba* portion of the human soul in Egyptian literature with the shadow, but most sources differentiate the two, the shadow perhaps being an

*Brian P. Copenhaver, ed., *Hermetica: The Greek Corpus Hermeticum and the Latin Asclepius in a New English Translation, with Notes and Introduction* (Cambridge, UK: Cambridge University Press, 1995).

appendage of the ba, or physical representation of the soul, but not exactly identical to it. Essentially, the human shadow expresses itself through behaviors such as projection, denial, deception, blame, and aggression, but the shadow also performs a spiritual function for human beings. The spiritual function of the shadow, discussed since ancient Egyptian times, is to provide opportunities for evolution and expansion by observing and addressing our lower natures. Perhaps there would be no enlightenment possible without the darkness of our shadows. The shadow is destructive, which seems evil, but destruction is necessary in nature so that balance is maintained and growth occurs in a healthy ratio rather than never-ending propagation, such as overpopulation, a viral overload in the body, or a cancerous tumor. Without the checks and balances of shadow energy, the continual expansion would create cancers everywhere, causing even greater disarray.

The fairy mounds in Great Britain were ruled by a fairy queen who was a dark goddess who ruled the underworld, the realms of the dead and the liminal spaces. Old fairy tales and folktales are full of dark characters and deeds—murderous dragons and vengeful queens. These often cautionary tales provide opportunities for shadow work for children. But in modern times, the inclination is to remove the mayhem and danger from stories, to sanitize them and thereby create a deep illusion. This does not serve children well; with everything presented in a positive light, lessons in ethics and morality are removed. Soon enough, children discover their experiences in the real world do not match these stories with happy endings; the stories are not true. When I was a child I watched a Japanese anime version of *The Little Mermaid* that showed her dying and turning into sea-foam while her beloved married another. This was a deep experience for me and helped me learn about the world. The Disney version of this tale has neutered the emotional labor that originally existed in the story. This is a crime to me, a robbery of youth. A pretend world is created, with a toxic tendency to ignore the reality of failure, which we all experience during our time on the planet. Sometimes things are sad; sometimes people die. We need to see it; we need to feel it, deeply.

Judaism also identifies the shadow, which it calls the *yetzer hara*, our inclination to do evil. Its opposite is the *yetzer hatov*, the good inclination. According to Jewish traditions, all humans have these inclinations, even Moses. Rather than eradicating the *hara* portion of our nature, we must create a system of checks and balances and seek to feed the *hatov* more and try to contain or control *hara*, in a process that is essentially a form of shadow work. The yetzer hara is not itself evil and can lead to good outcomes, like success in business.

> The yetzer hara has a purpose; we need to be ambitious, think of ourselves and prioritise our needs but it is also important to balance our needs with the needs of others. When the yetzer tov and the yetzer hara are working together in a seamless graceful dance, instead of constantly struggling with each other, we have balance in our lives. It is a joyful balance that allows us to pursue our passions in the world in a way that is always considerate of others, and to be of service to the needs of our family, friends, community and the planet.*

> *The ancient Sages decided that they were going to imprison and capture the yetzer hara. So they ordered a complete fast for three days. Whereupon the yetzer hara was surrendered to them. The yetzer hara said to them, "Realise that if you kill me, the world is finished." They held the yetzer hara for three days and then looked at the whole land of Israel, no one procreated, no one attended to the land, the cows did not produce milk. The Sages decided to free the yetzer hara as they realised that the world could not function without it.*
>
> Babylonian Talmud, Yoma, 69b

*Rabbi Cantor George Mordecai, "Drash on Parashat Tol'dot 2021," Union for Progressive Judaism website.

Freud identifies the two instincts fighting it out within us as the life instinct and the death instinct: we all have a deep need to live as well as a need to destroy everything. Freud called the shadow the id; Jung refers to it mostly as the unconscious. Folks who know about witchcraft, paganism, and indigenous teachings understand the long deep history of the dark self. Shadow work is ancient. Much as Freud or Jung may like to take credit for this discovery, healers, shamans, medicine workers, and witches, who were persecuted for tens of thousands of years, have all known about the shadow. The Bible itself is rife with shadow work; all one needs to do is read the story of Cain and Able to see how the humans try to hide, in their blind spot, their own misdeeds from their conscious awareness. Just as Cain buries the body of his brother, so do we all attempt to cover up what we do not wish to see in ourselves.

> *And the Lord said to Cain, "Where is your brother Abel?"*
> *"I do not know!" he answered. "Am I my brother's keeper?"*
>
> Genesis 4:9

The desperate need to keep the dark from being part of the self is shadow behavior. Shadow work is basically any set of techniques aimed at revealing or making known a part of the self or humanity that has become occulted, hidden, or repressed. These tendencies take different forms and are the *darchetypes,* as I like to call them—the dark archetypes that hide from our awareness and are harder to see.

We have to stop being angry or in denial that shadow exists in ourselves and humanity. Not because that would mean we permit it but because it is a self-evident truth and we need to deal with it. We don't need to deny that reality. It is not a moral threat to acknowledge it, any more than knowledge of something inherently corrupts us. Shadow is with all of us and is here forever. Shadow isn't going anywhere. If you can't understand why a seeming good person does something terrible or why entire nations conspire to do evil deeds, when you understand shadow work you will know exactly why this happens. More importantly, you will understand how doing shadow work will help you and others to avoid destructive behavior in the future. The shadow is transmuted through awareness and education, not through avoidance and ignorance.

Current trends in spiritual communities have highlighted a need to discourage the practice of spiritual bypassing. Spiritual bypassing is pretending everything is going to be OK, while ignoring or staying away from so-called negative energy. It's a form of gaslighting and is also known as toxic positivity. Much of the "positive thinking" and abundance or manifesting philosophies make attempts to promote positive thinking as a way to cope with negative energy and convince people that nothing is negative, or that bad things happen to them because of a negative mind-set.

After meeting several positive-thinking proponents, I critiqued this way of thinking and wrote, with Adam Parfrey, a book called *The Secret Source: The Law of Attraction and Its Hermetic Influence throughout the Ages* (Port Townshend, Wash.: Process Media, 2007) to show, through research, its origins and distortions of the Hermetic wisdom traditions for personal use and getting money. I confront and assist a lot of folks through death, dying, and loss, and I find these toxically positive views damaging, experientially and in reality. Spiritual bypassing deals with negativity through repression and shaming and discourages the expression of a negative or oppositional view. This conversation has been amplified excessively in the area of social media and for good reason. It turns out that ignoring negative energy does not make terrible things go away. A parent whose child was shot by the police did not manifest it due to their thinking. Cultures do not invite genocide because they haven't collected the right crystals or had the right focus or have bad karma. This is toxic thinking that does not serve and is offensive and outrageous to victims of shadow behavior in others. Living in Los Angeles I have watched too many individuals living off their spouses or in their parents' homes proselytize about how to get money and change their life with positive thinking to people who suffer from cultural economic wrongs done to them or who have been traumatized by domestic violence. The self-help guru is actually parasitizing you for income in many cases if you learn to see this shadow. The phenomenon of "sweeping things under the rug" is another word for this behavior of spiritual bypassing.

It was said that Gandhi had very few possessions; one was a statue of the three wise monkeys who embody the famous maxim "see no evil, speak no evil, hear no evil," which is based on Japanese spiritual teachings. These teachings have become distorted to encourage willful avoidance of negativity out of fear that if we recognize it, it will manifest. When I taught a free self-defense course for women, I had women turn me down because they were afraid that if they prepared to defend themselves against rape, they would attract it to them. Many of them were members of the positive-thinking movement. For them, it was out of sight, out of mind—until violence comes to you. Though Gandhi was a hero of nonviolence, he was assassinated by someone else who carried the violence shadow. While it's possible that miracles happen and prayers are answered, issues of negativity, violence, and inappropriate behaviors will not magically disappear without the necessary action of dealing with and confronting them.

I have had many clients who developed a neurosis, thinking they had caused all the bad in their lives because they had "thought bad things." We are responsible for some things in our lives, and for those we must hold accountability. But some things are not in our scope of control and to suppose so is an ego shadow called arrogance. Thankfully, very useful spiritual techniques are available to avoid this pitfall. Shadow work is a very good and viable way to make sure that you do not succumb to the temptation of spiritual bypassing and to assist your ability to deal effectively with negative energy. *Astrology of the Shadow Self* presents a mechanism for dealing with negative energies, with the darchetypes, without spiritually bypassing them. Remaining healthy will require that we do not feel satisfied with ignoring negativity and instead learn tools to process it in a more open, unashamed fashion. The more we assist one another to transmute, digest, and shine a light on all forms of human shadow, the better able we will be to navigate it.

We should come to realize and accept that human beings shall never stop the job of transmuting shadow. You may think you have accomplished the task in yourself, as a singularity, but it is an ongoing lifetime process. You will encounter other people who haven't accomplished much shadow work, and they can still affect you. Adjust your attitude toward processing negative energy into an understanding that it is a living process, just like breathing. Transmuting shadow is a big job. No one does it alone, but rather, each of us has been given a portion of it to chew on. How we personally create and work with shadow belongs to us and is our birthright as humans. What we put into our personal shadow is up to each individual. Tools such as astrology can help us see through and deal with our personal shadows, while archetypes and myths show what shadows the human collective holds. Transform the way you think about shadow and view it from a perspective of inclusion and assistance rather than avoidance and intolerance, and you will have already become a shadow worker.

I cast an I Ching and asked the following question: How can we best work with shadow for the good of all? The response was: hexagram 52 (*gen*, keeping still), changing line 6 into hexagram 15 (*qian*, humbleness). This was very powerful for me, because I quoted this same *gua* or hexagram in my book *The Occult I Ching: The Secret Language of Serpents* (Rochester, Vt.: Destiny Books, 2019). Alfred Huang, in his translation, uses a quote from Confucius to sum up the meaning and feeling of this line of the I Ching, which I believe deserves repeating here.

> *By knowing how to keep still,*
> *one is able to determine what objects he should pursue.*
> *By knowing what objects he should pursue,*
> *one is able to attain calmness of mind.*
> *By knowing how to attain calmness of mind,*
> *one is able to succeed in tranquil repose.*
> *By knowing how to succeed in tranquil repose,*
> *one is able to obtain careful deliberation.*
> *By knowing how to obtain careful deliberation,*
> *one is able to harvest what he really wants to pursue.*
>
> Alfred Huang, trans., *The Complete I Ching*

Essentially, the I Ching is advocating to wait, to not take the bait or act impulsively, to contemplate, to still the mind and body, to become still like the dark goddess, like the cave. The resulting hexagram 15 is about moderation and acting in the middle of things, going through the center without being too extreme. The advice in the hexagram *gen* is to be humble and act with humility. The I Ching is advocating to treat shadow not with humiliation but humility. An important distinction. This answer reminded me of a time when a painting of the Black Madonna, which I saw while in Italy, gave me a loud and clear message. Her message was a single word: *pause.* This is the wisdom of the dark goddess—to wait, to be still, to hang on for just one minute before you fly off the handle. Before you wreck everything, wait, just a minute. When we wait, things can grow in a pregnant pause.

> *A little while and I will be gone from among you, whither I cannot tell. From nowhere we come, into nowhere we go. What is life? It is a flash of firefly in the night. It is a breath of a buffalo in the wintertime. It is as the little shadow that runs across the grass and loses itself in the sunset.*
>
> Chief Crowfoot as cited in Robert S. Carlisle, "Crowfoot's Dying Speech," *Alberta History* 38, no. 3 (1990): 16–17

Prima Materia

> *Steams like black clouds, and the groves of trees growing out over their lake are all covered with frozen spray, and wind down snakelike roots that reach as far as the water and help keep it dark. At night that lake burns like a torch. No one knows its bottom, no wisdom reaches such depths.*
>
> BEOWULF

The Latin words *prima materia*, meaning "first matter," were often used by the alchemists, who were mostly also avid astrologers. In alchemy, prima materia is a substance that holds the seed of propagation for all possible forms that exist in all matter. This concept of a primal substance, a thing that contains all things, has been called many names: panacea, the philosopher's stone, quintessence, dark matter, the fifth element, to name a few. The dark matter is all inclusive, having no preferences, no exclusions; it is the mother of all matter. It might be strange to imagine that all things arise from a single thing, but we ourselves contain such mysteries. The DNA in every cell of your body contains the data and information for every other cell in your body, a storehouse tucking away potentialities, expressions, and latent memories of our ancestors.

So far, scientific ideas of the origins of matter, or exactly what this prima materia is, remain theoretical but they seem to point to outer space. Usually, we arrive at the center of black holes, when investigating such matters, or some sort of *event* like the big bang, which propelled the action of creation. Certain measurement systems locate dark matter everywhere in the universe, so it seems to be intermingled with all things simultaneously. This dark matter, containing the possibility of all things, lies in wait, just beneath the surface of the entirety of reality, including ourselves.

> *Primordial matter, forming the basis of the constitution of the human body, has absorbed influences from the stars and they nourish the elementary (physical) body and by means of these influences man's soul is connected with and united to the souls of the stars. Having three worlds in him and living in three worlds, man should learn to know the lower elements, understand the sidereal, and know the eternal.*
>
> Paracelsus

Alchemists, such as Paracelsus for example, engaged in a process to bring this dark matter, or prima materia, into personal awareness. They had steps and techniques of bringing the unknown into knowing. In order to access the prima materia, you needed to do certain things; this part of the process was called the *nigredo*, or the darkening. This would later become known in certain circles as shadow work. Before there is one thing, there is no thing. Everything starts at zero, a hard thing to comprehend really. Although this is a mind-boggling concept to wrap our heads around, like the riddle of the chicken and the egg, the importance of including empty space and anti-space when considering a body in its existence is vital in our attempts to understand the totality of reality. To know the one that is ourselves, the primordial, we cannot avoid staring back into the abyss, starting at zero. Coming into complete negation of life is an important part of the process. We cannot come into knowledge of everything unless we include knowledge of "no-thing." The more often we do this process of negation, the more complete we become, and the closer to our source, to our creator, to the positive love of life we are drawn. Life itself is renewed with each and every death; your ego is no exception. Accepting the "not I" makes us understand death on a more profound, personal level. For each and everything created, there is a "not" thing created. This is a kind of antimatter self, an uncreated self. The physical laws of the universe balance in polarities, and we are no exception. In examining the alter ego, it is important to understand the ancient alchemical laws and rules of the universe, namely that for everything there is an equal and opposite not thing. That includes you: when you were created and born, there also was created and born a not you, or shadow you.

> *If you can successfully embrace the Anti-Matter version of yourself, Time would cease to exist for You. You are God!*
>
> Vishwanath S J

Our universe has been found to contain a consistent ratio of positive and negative energy, being and nonbeing, life and death. This ratio is often called the golden ratio or the golden mean. The golden ratio has been mathematically shown in everything in nature, from atoms to planets, and demonstrates that the equilibrium of energy that we reside within is neither positive nor negative but an enduring constant of both of those energies eternally combining with each other. While the precise homeostasis of the balance of positive and negative expressions fluctuates, it continually finds its way back to center. Since we are part of nature, we also contain this ratio, this proportion of positive and negative balance. We must, in our minds and bodies, personalities and spirits, work toward keeping the equilibrium by processing or digesting the negative energy within ourselves.

Many do not seek to perform the negative processing for their psychological health because it is very challenging. Indeed, there is danger in approaching and confronting these shadowlands, but our negative qualities need not be so insurmountable for the common individual. We have many tools at our disposal to ease our way in, to take small bites here and there so that that we may digest such poisonous meals. In our successful metabolizing of these potent forces, they shift from bringing us disease and unrest to providing us with healing and medicine. One of the most powerful tools to accomplish this aim, used by humanity for eons, are the archetypes who live in the stars. The star myths and their characters have assisted more people to come to terms with the totality of their natures than arguably anything else, plants and psychedelics running a close second. I would only argue that the stars are the most effective because we are able to observe them every single evening of our lives. To plunge down into the depth of these mysteries requires only that we look up.

> *So requisite is the use of Astrology to the Arts of Divination, as it were the Key that opens the door of all their Mysteries.*
>
> Heinrich Cornelius Agrippa

Astrology is a central art in the occult. In fact, the word *occult* may itself arise from *occultation*, which describes the planetary phenomenon of one celestial body passing in front of another body, obscuring its view from Earth. When struggling to understand our hidden natures, we must look to outer space—there is no avoiding it—because outer space contains the source of all we are, and something cannot be understood, in a whole fashion, until you return to the beginning. This desire and need to return to the source is what drives human beings to recount creation myths, over and over again. To know what *one* is, you must return to *one*—and to even before one, which is zero. You must return to the primordial source of void, the prima materia, to find yourself, your source, and that requires engaging negating energy.

> *Man is a microcosm, or a little world, because he is an extract from all the stars and planets of the whole firmament, from the earth and the elements; and so he is their quintessence.*
>
> Paracelsus

Subconscious Influence

A responsive influence exists between the heavenly bodies, the earth, and animated bodies.

Franz Anton Mesmer, *Propositions Concerning Animal Magnetism*

It is really pretty odd, but human beings can create other versions of themselves in their own minds. We can also create versions of others in our imagination, which may or may not be anything like them. This might sound a bit like child's play and silly, but it is a phenomenon of the human psyche. The mind is like a strange womb, conceiving and giving birth to things that emerge into reality. This is the realm of the Hermeticist and the alchemist, the mind creator. The strange chameleon that is the *self* is a shape-shifter, creating forms and selves at whim that change depending on who is in front of the self. The prima materia can take on any persona because it contains them all.

Obviously, limitations exist on just how much our creations of the imagination can translate into physical reality. It's true that though we can imagine ourselves to be a unicorn, we cannot literally become a unicorn, and yet, we can imagine ourselves differently and then become different. There are many who feel that the human mind does not influence, inform, or shape reality at all. Some feel that we are just along for the ride, participating in a reality that our thoughts and feelings do not affect, do not have a relationship with. To me this seems rather simplistic: when you look around, all you can see are productions of the human mind unless you are in the middle of some wilderness. What we imagine can be made real through work. Levels of ability to influence the world certainly exist: some are masters of reality, shifting it substantially, while others cannot move it an inch, no matter how hard they try. Humans build cities, technologies, machines, rocket ships, and infrastructures that affect the entire planet; that is a measurable sway that our minds have on this place. Human beings alter the environment by making their thoughts substantial through work. Our words create influences that move each other and drive events of human history. Our artistic endeavors lift and carry the human spirit through unimaginable terror. Imagine what power lies hidden within the shadows of the human psyche if we can see what we are already capable of.

Take a moment and examine what influence means, how it can be used in the context of this book and how it is the driving mechanism for the use of the alter ego, or hidden self. The word *influence* arrives thanks to astrology. When we examine the history and meaning of influence, we find it is rooted in subconscious portions of the ego responding to cosmic rays among other things.

> influence (n.) late 14c., an astrological term, "streaming ethereal power from the stars when in certain positions, acting upon character or destiny of men," from Old French *influence* "emanation from the stars that acts upon one's character or destiny" (13c.), . . . of fluid or vaporous substance as well as immaterial or unobservable forces. Meaning "exertion of unseen influence by persons" is from 1580s (a sense already in Medieval Latin, for instance Aquinas); meaning "capacity for producing effects by insensible or invisible means" is from 1650s.*

If you are not familiar with cosmic rays, and maybe you are thinking that it sounds suspicious, I implore you to investigate further. We are surrounded, infiltrated, and penetrated by all manner of energetic rays from space.

> cosmic ray, a high-speed particle—either an atomic nucleus or an electron—that travels through space. Most of these particles come from sources within the Milky Way Galaxy and are known as galactic cosmic rays (GCRs). The rest of the cosmic rays originate either from the Sun or, almost certainly in the case of the particles with the highest energies, outside the Milky Way Galaxy.†

*Online Etymology Dictionary.

†Michael Wulf Friedlander, "cosmic ray," *Encyclopedia Britannica,* updated June 2, 2023.

Neutrinos from our sun pass through our physical bodies every moment, sailing about on the breeze to come and go as they please. The planets also are permanently exuding continuous oceans of vibrations that assault our physical bodies constantly.

> [A] fraction of the cosmic rays detected on Earth come from Jupiter. This result draws attention to the idea that magnetospheres of astrophysical objects could contribute to the sources of cosmic rays. . . . The cosmic ray fluxes are larger on average when the Earth orbit intersects the lines of the measured interplanetary magnetic field connecting Jupiter with Earth.*

Many people make fun of ideas that the planets and objects in outer space could somehow influence human beings here on Earth. They seem to think that nothing so far away could make us operate outside our own will. Perhaps if they knew they were swimming in a soup of particles from stars and celestial spheres, they would open their minds to include this possibility. If planets can hold such sway over us, it becomes less of a stretch to imagine the push and pull of the tides of ourselves and how we come into affecting each other. If the moon can cause women to menstruate, and women being around other women can influence an onset of menstruation, imagine what other physical and psychological drives are being pounded into us each time we cross our thresholds. This is the secret of the magicians throughout the ages, to push and pull, as the heavens above.

> *There is an attractive power in the soul of man, which attracts physical, mental, and moral diseases from the Chaos. The planetary influences extend through all Nature, and man attracts poisonous qualities from the*

*G. Pizzella, "Emission of Cosmic Rays from Jupiter: Magentospheres as Possible Sources of Cosmic Rays," *European Physical Journal.*

moon, from the stars, and from other things; but the moon, and the stars, and other things also attract evil influences from man, and distribute them again by their rays, because Nature is an undivided whole, whose parts are intimately connected.

PARACELSUS

Alter Ego

All those qualities, capacities and tendencies which do not harmonize with the collective values—everything that shuns the light of public opinion, in fact—now come together to form the shadow, that dark region of the personality which is unknown and unrecognized by the ego. The endless series of shadow and doppelgänger figures in mythology, fairy tales and literature ranges from Cain and Edom, by way of Judas and Hagen, to Stevenson's Mr. Hyde in the ugliest man of Nietzsche; again and again such figures have appeared and made their bow before human consciousness, but the psychological meaning of this archetype of the adversary has not yet dawned upon mankind.

ERICH NEUMANN,
DEPTH PSYCHOLOGY AND A NEW ETHIC

The alter ego can be interpreted in a few different ways and so can be a bit confusing. It can be another person we are good friends with, an identity we create, or another personality occupying our body, including an invading intelligence such as an angel or demon. The concept of the alter ego can be seen in ancient cultures, and using a power double, or *alternate form*, is a human practice throughout the globe. The daimonic practices of the pagans all made use of this technique. The modern era attributes the concept first to Cicero then to Roman philosopher Seneca, and then it was more intensely investigated by one Anton Mesmer, who later influenced the psychologists of Vienna with his discoveries.

A huge source of shadow work, especially in astrology, is *On the Influence of Planets*, a thesis written by Anton Mesmer while he was in school in Vienna in 1766. It should be stated many have claimed he heavily plagiarized Dr. Richard Mead, a shadowy behavior indeed, but nonetheless this thesis formed the basis of modern work with the subconscious and was astrological in nature. This work informed the development of mesmerism, which led to the practice of hypnotism. Some challenge whether the connection of hypnosis to mesmerism is valid, but the work of mesmerist James Braid makes the link plainly clear. It could be that some modern practitioners have attempted to distance themselves from Mesmer, fearing their reputation will be sullied, which is in fact a shadow behavior itself. Mesmerism and hypnotism were so effective they were used to spare people physical pain while undergoing surgery until anesthesia was invented. Imagine being hypnotized and feeling no pain while a scalpel is inserted into your abdomen. To exert such influence upon the body and its instincts is no doubt a master of shadow. Regardless of personal skepticism, this is an impressive feat. While I'm sure many are skeptical and would challenge such statements, I suggest that, instead, we respond with a sense of wonder in our pursuit of shadow work and what the alter ego, as explored and defined by people such as Anton Mesmer, can offer to humanity for the growth and service of one and all.

Astrology has long been used as a technique to enlarge our identities and personalities by incorporating archetypes, gods and goddesses, from the myths of ancient cultures who, through their stories, attempted to explain and understand the stars. When we create an alter ego, we make a vessel within which we may forge a new way of viewing our character and personality, thus altering and shaping them in the process. The best way to transform something is to put it in a pot and cook it.

These days people create alter egos in the blink of an eye. The musician Eminem famously made a shadow alter ego, appropriately called Slim Shady. Every avatar we make to engage in online culture can contain the power to become an alter ego of life-changing proportions. Because these online avatars are mostly anonymous, their human creators may feel free to use their avatars to engage in shadowy behavior, but their online alter egos may end up bleeding into reality when they are held accountable for destructive behavior.

> *Natural selection is not the wind which propels the vessel, but the rudder which, by friction, now on this side and now on that, shapes the course.*
>
> Asa Gray

Influences and Shadow Projections

> *Most people are other people. Their thoughts are someone else's opinions, their lives a mimicry, their passions a quotation.*
>
> Oscar Wilde, *De Profundis*

Let us imagine what might be needed to come free of the unseen and unknown influences affecting you right now—planetary, human, or otherwise. Do you think it might be possible to stop the cosmos from influencing you? You are quite small, and the cosmos is quite big. How might you be able to identify and fend off such an onslaught? You will not be able to, but you *are* able to become aware of it. We are swimming in an ocean and so will be influenced by the tides. What we *do* have for ourselves is a boat, a vessel to navigate these waters: this vessel is the ego. The waters of the world are constantly trying to breach your hull and fracture your ego so that their influences can get inside of you. Do not ignore all the waves hitting you. Watch the winds, see the seas.

Imagine if people became completely responsible for their own energy and how they are influenced and could see, in a clear and untainted light, when they or anyone else was engaging in projection, projecting undesirable feelings onto others. A transparency would arise in human life that would prevent many shadow-influenced blunders. If individuals could reconnect with their own energy source—their own sun, their own identity—shadow projection could be decreased considerably. Many lose touch with their own innate ability to create energy and become vampires on others because they fear they will die if they don't draw vitality from someone else.

If our awareness of this shadow projection is raised, either through conscious techniques, such as provided in *Astrology of the Shadow Self*, or forced through crises, we begin to become aware of other people's behavior toward one another—among our friends and family and in our community, and even nationally and internationally. When we are able to perceive our own shadow, we can then shine a light on all shadows; we become like a crystal, refracting the light of this awareness and shooting out rainbows everywhere. As horrifying as it is to realize that, when a deep emotional response overwhelms us, we are being possessed and influenced by a primal shadow, it's best to just rip the whole thing open so that we can see the shadow and accept it. The time has come. Rather than being shocked when someone does something shadowy, see and understand what is happening.

When we practice divination techniques, such as tarot, astrology, runes, Erindilogun, or the I Ching, we learn all about the characters and archetypes of old and how everyone is rolling through the archetype pantheon, as in a parade. Once you become familiar with the stories of the archetypes, you will begin to raise these subconscious titans up into your own awareness and, thus, free yourself from repeating mistakes due to their subconscious influence. This isn't humanity's first rodeo, maybe watching some reruns could help us all avoid age-old mishaps.

Relationships and how we relate to one another happen not only on an atomic level, with electrons and protons, but on a larger level, through the archetypes of the planets. Under unification theory, if you are not conscious of it, you might fall victim to disaster, which literally means "an unfavorable position of a star or planet." Astrology raises your conscious awareness of the planets' influences. Be aware of your influences and you can consciously take action to use them in a positive, more beneficial way. Keep your influences in mind, do not leave them out of your awareness.

> *O keep not captive my soul. O keep not ward over my shadow, but let a way be opened for my soul and my shadow, and let them see the Great God in the shrine on the day of the counting of souls, and let them hold converse with Osiris, whose habitations are hidden, and those who guard the members of Osiris, and who keep ward over the ba, and who hold captive the shadows of the dead, and who would work evil against me, so that they shall [not] work evil against me.*
>
> Papyrus of Nebseni

Using This Book

The ridiculous arises out of a moral contrast, in which two things are brought together before the mind in an innocent way.

JOHANN WOLFGANG VON GOETHE,
"THE SORCERER'S APPRENTICE"

THE PURPOSE OF THIS ASTROLOGY BOOK is to assist you in becoming aware of the ways in which the planets and constellations relate to your subconscious shadow. By using the negating technique of oppositional astrology in *Astrology of the Shadow Self,* you shall come into your alter ego, your Antichrist, your "not I," which then can merge with the astrological signs you have been identifying with in your birth horoscope. When your Christ (conscious solar identity) and Antichrist (oppositional destroyer) merge together, you expand. In being liberated from influences, we can become whole, completely our true self, without any externalization; we emerge as our *own star,* to shine brightly as our *own sun* and no other. It is beneficial to, at some point, undergo this process of removing and negating external influences. Why not do it now? If you are using astrology to identify yourself, you are only the sun as it moves through the zodiac, you are not yourself. If you could truly be a sun in and of yourself, unleashed from the zodiac ring, what would that look like? Who would you be?

Astrology of the Shadow Self seeks to explore this adventure.

In this system, you will take your commonly calculated birth chart and investigate the oppositional chart, in other words the "antichart," that is created when the positions of all the planets and stars present at your birth are reversed or opposed. It happens to be my personal opinion that we cannot remove our oppositional counterparts even from our astrological identities, so we must become aware of them, lest we meet them over and over again in the form of an "enemy," or outward embodiment or projection of our shadow.

By accepting more factors as part of our identity and gathering unto ourselves attributes and qualities we once distanced ourselves from, our true self and full nature emerges, and our grand potentiality comes round full circle, like a planet in orbit, rather than us remaining stuck in some incomplete moment in time and space. Here we truly transcend our ego limitations by annihilating what we had thought we were in favor of examining what we *could* be.

You can use both Western and sidereal systems with this book. In many of the shadow planet placements presented in this book, I have given examples of well-known people who have that particular placement, based on the Western system. There is no reason, however, why you can't use this book as reference in the sidereal system. For example, perhaps you are a jyotish astrologer practicing in India; the sun sign of someone with a Scorpio sun in Western astrology would be a Libra under the sidereal system, which essentially is moved to the sign preceding the Western zodiac due to the precession of the equinoxes. You can simply look up the Libra sun in this book and still find efficacy.

For a deeper perspective, you can also look at the house placement of the shadow. Look at the house your planet is located in your birth chart and then look up the shadow sign for that as well. For example, supposing in a birth chart Mars is in Libra in the second house. The shadow location for the planet would be Mars in Aries in the eighth house. Aries is opposite Libra, and the second house is ruled by Taurus, which is opposite Scorpio. So you look for the house ruled by Scorpio, which is the eighth house.

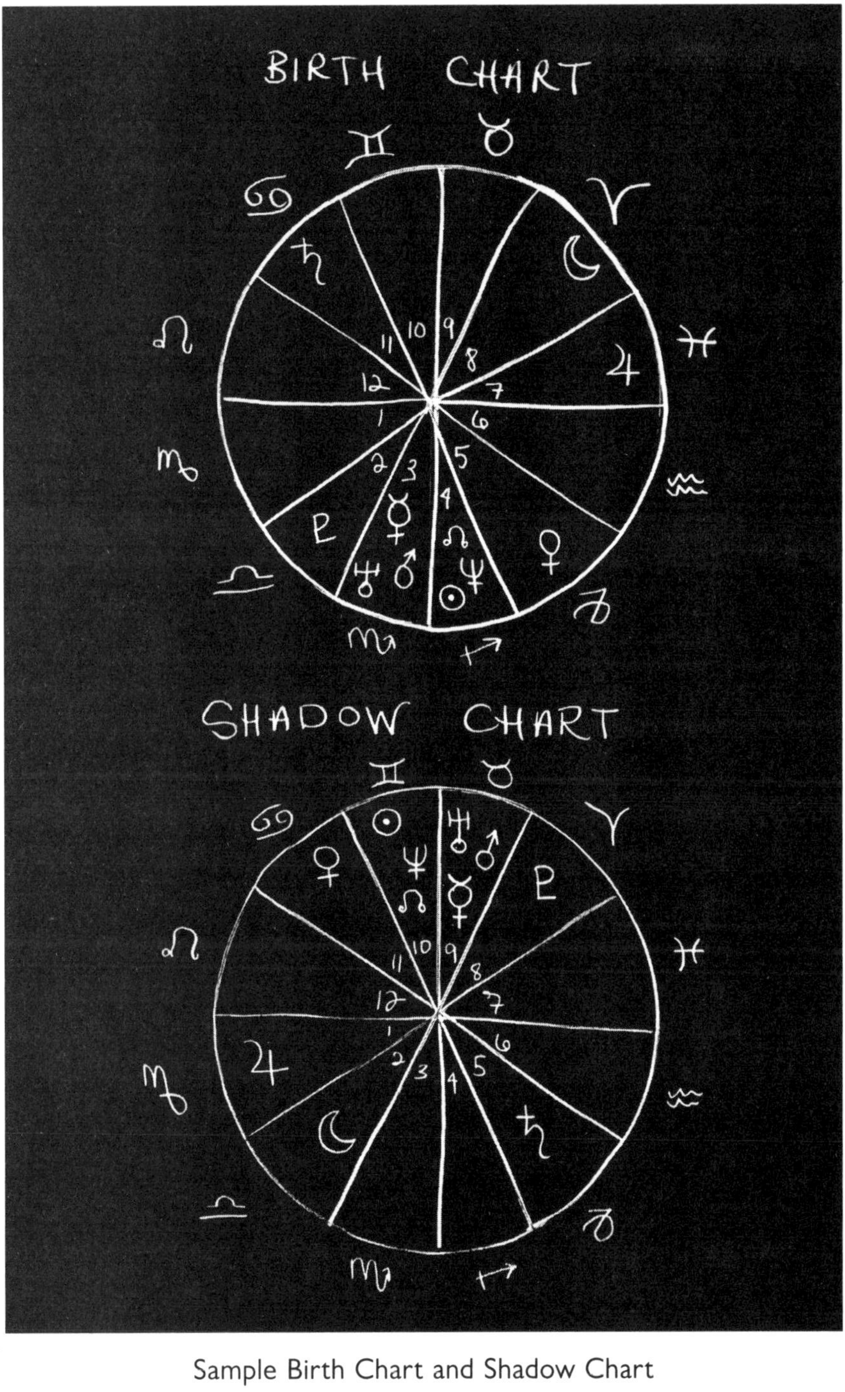

Sample Birth Chart and Shadow Chart

House Rulers

First house: Aries
Second house: Taurus
Third house: Gemini
Fourth house: Cancer
Fifth house: Leo
Sixth house: Virgo
Seventh house: Libra
Eighth house: Scorpio
Ninth house: Sagittarius
Tenth house: Capricorn
Eleventh house: Aquarius
Twelfth house: Pisces

This book can also be used to examine transits occurring in real time. Wherever the planets are located in a particular moment in time, you can look up their opposite positions in this book to gain insight on the influences affecting a current period of time. For example, when I finished writing this book, Saturn was located in Aquarius, about to shift into Pisces, so the shadow influence would be that of Saturn in Leo, about to shift into Virgo. You could read the chapter on this position to see the shadow being cast over that particular moment in time. To see what transits are occurring now, you can find these easily online, and then look up each shadow influence in the relevant chapter. In this way, this book can be used to understand and analyze the prevailing influences of the collective, beyond an individual's birth chart. For information on how to look up transits, I highly recommend Robert Hand's work, and all the current transits can be found at astro.com as well as your favorite astrology app on your phone.

Please keep in mind that all the following listings will be the opposite of the planets in your chart. You will need to first check your planet location (such as moon in Gemini) and then look up its opposite shadow placement (which would be moon in Sagittarius).

Instructions

The phoenix must burn to emerge.

JANET FITCH

1. Make your astrological natal chart in the same way you normally would. If you have never seen your chart or made one, the process is fairly painless now, using online resources that will do this for you at no charge. My favorite website for making free astrological charts is astro.com. Consider making a donation, as one of this site's authors is Robert Hand, whose work I greatly admire and who has made such a huge contribution in the field of astrology. I am forever in awe. You will want to print the chart so that you have a physical copy of it.
2. Get yourself a red marker and a ruler or straight edge.
3. For each planet in your chart, line up the ruler as level as you can with the planet or star you would like to shadow scry so that the ruler cuts the circle of the chart cleanly in half from the starting point of the planet in question.
4. Take your red marker and make a symbol or circle where the completely opposite point in the circle is; you can place it on the exact opposite degree to be precise.
5. Look at the zodiacal symbol in the space where you made a red mark: this is the shadow sign of the planet you are investigating. For example, a line that begins with sun in Aries should land at some degree within the Libra constellation, when the circle is halved by the ruler. Libra is the opposer of Aries and its shadow sun.

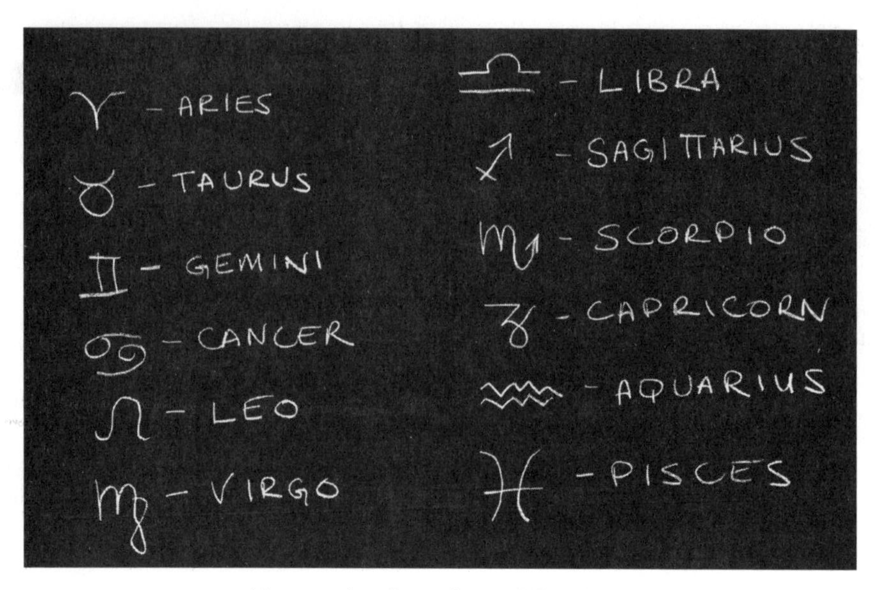

Key to the Astrological Symbols

Finding the Oppositional Shadow

Zodiacal Opposite Pairs

Aries–Libra
Taurus–Scorpio
Gemini–Sagittarius
Cancer–Capricorn
Leo–Aquarius
Virgo–Pisces

Trigger Warning

This is a book of shadows that discusses negative behaviors in humans and nature including: violence, racial violence, family violence, sexual violence, suicide, substance abuse, death, and abusive mental patterns, including gaslighting. Be advised these topics are covered from the perspectives of perpetrators, victims, and observers. Examples used are not meant to equate or match the reader with them, but rather to educate on where shadows may lead, as a cautionary tale. Shadow work is a study of danger that is real in this world and in ourselves.

Note on Historical Astrological Charts

The majority of natal astrology charts of historical and celebrity figures referenced in this work were found on astro.com's Astro-Databank, which is a fantastic source and reference.

THE
SHADOW
SIGNS

Sun Shadows

I Against I

> *The enlargement of the light side of consciousness has the necessary consequence that the part of the psyche which is less light and less capable of consciousness is thrown into darkness to such an extent that sooner or later a rift occurs in the psychic system. At first, this is not recognized as such and is therefore projected—i.e., it appears as a religious projection, in the form of a split between the powers of Light and Darkness.*
>
> CARL G. JUNG, *THE SYMBOLISM OF THE SPIRIT*

THE EGO IS A WONDERFUL, terrible thing that is simultaneously our best friend and worst enemy. Many are inclined to shame and disparage the ego, and ego haters abound everywhere you look, but try for a moment to imagine a world with no ego. Looks pretty boring to me—no Prince, no Nelson Mandela, everyone the same and gray. The ego is not perfect, but it's what we have in this world to navigate.

The shadow sun is the negatively charged, hidden expression of our sun sign *ego identity,* which rears its head when push comes to shove. The shadow sun is in a polarity relationship with the outward expression of our sun sign, which expresses itself through the ego specifically. The shadow side of our ego will harbor all its failures, all the negative identity behaviors that have gone unfulfilled in its outward expression. These behaviors have most likely been judged or shamed, causing the ego to think that it is not worthy or that it is undeserving of these failures and so the ego does not include these realities, thoughts, or actions in its personality. Quite a shame to not include our failures, for failures often are the best path to a future success. The ego is the part of our personality that likes to think highly of itself in terms of who it is as a person and how it fits into society. For most people, having a healthy ego is about healthy relationships, self-worth, and healthy self-esteem. When our self-esteem is damaged, either due to a real event, such as mistreatment in childhood, or through a misperception or insult, the ego starts to slink into the shadow sun. The shadow sun provides a protective mechanism for the damaged ego, trying to spare it from the pain of being subpar. Ironically, the best way to realize our full potential is by embracing and incorporating our shadow sun and expressing our identities through it rather than focusing solely on a positive self-identity; in this way our totality shines through. The reality is we will all fall in and out of our shadow sun personalities at different times throughout our lives. The most important thing to do is to raise our awareness of our shadow sun's characteristics so that we may bring it into the light of our consciousness. Exposure of our true and complete self seems threatening until we understand that only through permitting the veil to drop and come into the full view do we stand in our full power.

To find your shadow sun, simply find your sun sign based on the day of your birth, in either the Western or sidereal system of astrology, whichever you prefer, and then look at the zodiac sign that falls exactly opposite that sun in the ring. For example, if you have an Aries sun, your shadow sun is Libra because it lies on the opposite end of the cycle.

> *The human body is vapor materialized by sunshine mixed with the life of the stars.*
>
> PARACELSUS

♈

Aries Sun Shadow

The Shadow Boxer

Birth Sun: Libra ♎
Mask: Passive aggressive

Your birth sun in Libra makes you concerned with fairness, partnership, and peace by way of avoiding conflict and escalation. The positive expression of this sun is diplomat, negotiator, lawyer, justice advocate, artist, musician, and peace maker. That means your shadow sun is war itself and the drive to not only confront conflict but take it all the way to an ambitious and, if necessary, bloody victory. Vladimir Putin is an example of this shadow sun who is known for his diplomacy, but also exerts his ego behind the scenes, as evidenced by his invasion of Ukraine, which he has insisted is not war, per se, but a "special military operation."* You really want to fight about it, but you won't. Instead, the fight burrows deep within you, smooshed into a hidden ball.

The main expression of shadow sun Aries is that you need to become comfortable with confrontations. Engaging in battle in a confident, straightforward manner, rather than being passive aggressive, will unite you with your darkness. This does not mean you need to be overtly aggressive, in fact quite the contrary: it means settling into the confrontation while being calm, cool, and collected. You will find that when you master your shadow sun, the shadow boxer, you will be able to avoid fighting altogether because the argument will dissipate in the confrontation itself. You are truly at your most powerful when you are able to be at war, making peace during an active conflict. Did you just relax a bit even while you read these words with a sigh of relief? Until you are able to breathe into the fight, you will find yourself placed

*I wrote this entry in 2020, before Putin invaded Ukraine to the extent that has occurred, which obviously now at the time of publishing has blown into full-on war, in full shadow form. Perhaps the implication could be to see the full evolution of the shadow behavior. My wish is that it serves to raise awareness.

in situations where you should have had a direct confrontation but instead everything went sideways because you subverted your instinct that needed to have it out then and there. You ran away with your tail between your legs. Come clear of this through habituating methods of strategic and decisive articulation of your thoughts and feelings during a heated argument. Stand up for what you believe in, even when other people disagree with you. Don't wait till later to let your mind have it out in battle as you are trying to fall asleep. Show yourself; do not be afraid. Say what you are and put aside your deep need to make sure the other approves. Do not be so concerned with the other that you dismiss yourself. No one wins when the chips are stacked in one person's favor; this is unfair and you know it. Aries warriors need no other and can stand on their own two feet. Once you stand here, then you can come into interdependent partnerships free of the knot in your gut that keeps silencing your voice and sweeping everything under the rug. Your destiny, once your Aries shadow sun is integrated, is that you will be the ultimate partner due to your excellence in fairness, diplomacy, and negotiations—but to get there you will have to hash it out. Get into it, don't mitigate self for other; you are creating the bias you hate in this behavior. You will leave countless partnerships because you avoided all the decisions, leaving them up to the other entirely because you did not speak up, then you resented their unfair advantage. Raise awareness to this and begin the shadow work now.

Example in Nature

Bucephalus the Horse. Bucephalus was the famed steed of Alexander the Great. As legend has it, Alexander broke the wild horse when no one else dared go near—not by force but by turning the horse's head toward the sun, understanding that Bucephalus was simply afraid of his own shadow.

— Katy Steinmetz, "Top Ten Heroic Animals: 2. Bucephalus the Horse," *Time*, March 21, 2011

♉

Taurus Sun Shadow

The Sensual Security Seeker

Birth Sun: Scorpio ♏
Mask: Possessive

Stop hiding and sneaking your physical pleasures late at night. Just let yourself have healthy treats while keeping up your concentration and focus on your discipline. Leonardo DiCaprio is a notable with this shadow sun. If you put in your hard day's work, then you can eat whatever you want and lay about like Ferdinand the bull. Want to drink? Fine, just openly have a minimum and don't be ashamed of it. Your permission of your shadow sun in Taurus, the sensual security seeker, to occasionally indulge shall give you quite a bit of relief from unhealthy behaviors. Bring up all your body shame and thinking into awareness and the full light of day, and you will rise up out of indulgence and into a healthier relationship with your earth element and its needs. Restraining or taking away physical and earth-based luxuries or indulgences will not serve you; it will only be subverted into guilt and shame.

It is also really obvious you have a deep need for security. We all see how jealous and possessive you are in your fear of loss or not getting the reward. Just relax. It is OK to be afraid of losing what you have. It just means that you are very, very loyal and want to keep the things you appreciate or feel like you have earned. Your deeply dominating and controlling nature hidden within the folds of your shadow sun is trying to show you how very admirable you are if you just let your heart plunge into the true depths of its own love, even if the price of this is feeling the pain of grief. Scorpio sun hates being vulnerable so avoids taking on possessions, but once you do give in and accept this, pay close attention to your shadow sun Taurus trying to secure and control every breath you take. Jealousy isn't actually a Scorpio trait, contrary to most astrology sites, it is a Taurus fear state caused by a need for security. True Scorpio energy is self-reliant to the extreme. If you feel you are afraid of losing another, you may be slipping into shadow.

The ultimate negative expression of this shadow sun is hoarding, so please make sure that you are finding your security within yourself and not your possessions. Once you are able to master the shadow sun of material possession, you can rise to the eagle expression of Scorpio, which is transcendence of the physical world. Ownership isn't everything; if you love something, set it free. This may sound like a threatening suggestion until you apply it to yourself and bring yourself to liberation by stepping into the full realization that you are not what you possess. You are much more than that and require no possessions, people, or objects to achieve your own growth and destiny. You may attract haters as you rise into this position, but it is just their own shadow projection of jealousy of your mastery of this shadow sun.

Example in Nature

Among the crustacea there seems to be a high degree of emotional life. Pliny credited the pea-crab with jealousy. Lobsters are known to monopolize a special corner of an aquarium and jealously to expel intruders within a certain sphere of influence. Crabs fight vigorously for the same morsel of food, and show a tendency to clutch the morsel and swim off with it, guarding themselves with the free mandible. Hermit crabs often make disturbances in aquaria, because of a sort of restless jealousy which impels a strong individual to leave an apparently good shell and evict perhaps a half dozen of his neighbors from their domiciles, in succession, after as many encounters.

— Arnold Gesell, "Jealousy," *American Journal of Psychology* 28, no. 4 (October 1906): 2

♊

Gemini Sun Shadow

The Two-Faced Tongue Twister

Birth Sun: Sagittarius ♐
Mask: Jekyll and Hyde

Get your facts straight and mind your gossip. Loose lips sink ships. Your ever-expansive Sagittarius sun can run into trouble with your shadow sun in Gemini when you stick your foot in your mouth. Mind your words. Singer-songwriter Nicki Minaj is an example of this shadow sun; her controversial words have at times threatened to eclipse the light of her talent. Shadow sun Gemini is quite a creature, running its mouth, then changing its mind later, leaving those who were subject to its wanderings reeling in its wake. Geminis learn and process through talking, so in the shadow, this energy takes on the form of speaking in vain. Just because you think and say things does not mean they are true. The Gemini shadow sun creates a mind thirsty for knowledge and a deep need to know, speak, communicate, and discover at all costs. The voracious appetite of the mind and tongue here makes for a competitive attitude that ignores personal boundaries.

This shadow gives the Sagittarius sun its qualities of high mind, higher thinking, education, and wisdom, due to the force of the need to know things, but only after the shadow sun of Gemini has been integrated will the data transform to wisdom. The lower aspects of the animal mind, Mr. Hyde, must be addressed for the ascension to occur, and Dr. Jekyll will be celebrated for innovative discovery. If you have an ability for science, worldly knowledge, physical knowledge, or philosophy but have been ignoring your animal nature, your Gemini shadow sun will betray you in an outburst through your mouth at the worst possible moment. For the Sagittarius sun, the shadow is in what comes out of your mouth, so mind your p's and q's. Don't take the temptation to fracture into dualistic arguments, include all the views when you speak to others. Sagittarius wants to see the whole picture, but their shadow sun in Gemini wants to tear things in two. Right and wrong, black and white dualistic thinking does not apply to knowledge and wisdom. You do not need to be correct; you only need to have a sincere expression.

For Sagittarians who are athletes or body minded, this shadow sun appears in the form of competition for achievement and a deep need to be the best, creating a poor sport. Feeling you are in the right in all you say and do can prevent you from ever obtaining that, so release it and just play. Once conquered, this shadow sun can arguably have more fun than anyone on the planet, infecting all around them with a childlike exploration of mind and body that expands even the most hardened cynic. Sagittarius aims high; shadow sun Gemini will paralyze its flight through analysis of the details. Watch where you are going as you shoot off into space, and don't aim any arrows at others in self-righteous vanity that creates a monster out of your mouth.

Example in Nature

New research published in the journal Animal Behaviour *has revealed that lemur vocalizations have specific uses other than general communication, including improving the bonds between favored friends and family members within a clan. Since lemurs are a distant relative of humans, this implies that our ability to gossip could be a social bonding tool passed down from our very ancient primate ancestors.*

— Robin Andrews, "Lemurs 'Gossip' to Improve Social Bonding, Just Like Humans," *IFL Science,* December 15, 2015

♋

Cancer Sun Shadow

The Master Manipulator

Birth Sun: Capricorn ♑
Mask: Pessimist

If you do not feel your emotions, they will devour you. For most of the Capricorn birth suns I have met, their emotions are embarrassing, and they would rather not deal with such a mess. The Capricorn hates unstructured feelings and so represses them, creating the shadow sun of Cancer. Jim Carrey is an example of this shadow sun native, who battled his depression and shadow and came out the other side by committing to feeling.

Cancer is completely emotional, feeling everything, empathizing with everything. When Cancer emotions become stagnant, they gather into swampy dark energy, which draws in negativity with an impressive force. The Cancer shadow sun absorbs and holds on to negative energy like a sponge. This causes symptoms such as depression and feeling like everything you do will fail. The dark cloud this creates could prevent you from obtaining the success that you so desperately long for and deserve from all your hard work.

Shadow sun Cancer will afflict you with a state of melancholy, but rather than take responsibility for this state, you will project it onto everyone around you and subconsciously manipulate those around you to work for you. People influenced by this shadow sun are often the boss, placed in charge of huge corporations, banks, or businesses. They will throw themselves into their work in an effort to overcome the blockages presented by their negativity and try to solve it through sheer force of labor, when really they just need to sit down and cry for a while. Refusing to do their own emotional work, it then becomes the burden and fault of anyone who happens to express an emotion around them. Dark feelings belong only to them, and this shadow sun will dominate all the sorrow in the room. Shadow sun Cancer will win the prize for best cynic. Often the stress of this shadow sun will lead to coping mechanisms such as alcohol or escapism.

To master this shadow sun, you must come into your emotional nature despite your displeasure of it. It is far easier for the earthy Capricorn to be comfortable with sensual feelings than to feel negative emotional energy. Once those dark melancholic feelings are acknowledged, accepted, and celebrated, the shadow sun moves to the side, and the Capricorn native steps into the ruler position of the dark comedic satirist. Your most arrogant emotions are actually very hilarious, and you will begin to be able to see the humor upon reaching maturity through feeling all those icky sticky waves of emotional energy. Your self-acceptance here will nourish everyone because your sardonic jokes are the best medicine a human being could ask for. If you cry hard enough, you will start laughing, and if you laugh hard enough, you will cry.

Example in Nature

> *In farming ants, some workers will specialize just in shepherding and caring for the aphids! There's even some evidence that ants build pastures of a sort, to keep their herded aphids in. When the colony departs one nest site to form another at a new location, they will carry an aphid egg with them, to establish a new herd and maintain their resources. Ants certainly are the world's oldest, and smallest, farmers.*
>
> — Ada McVean, "Farmer Ants and Their Aphid Herds," Office for Science and Society Weekly Newsletter, McGill University, August 16, 2017

♌

Leo Sun Shadow

The Attention Hog

Birth Sun: Aquarius ♒
Mask: Arrogance

Pride secretly waits at the doorstep of those born under the Aquarian sun, watching their every move. Behind all their well-intentioned humanitarian endeavors, they really just want their name in lights. They want everyone to see who it was that so generously helped others. The Aquarian birth sun will invent something that helps everyone, and wants everyone to know who it was. Those born under Aquarius are made to assist their fellow humans; they cannot escape this destiny. The twist of fate placed within them is that they have been given a nature that makes them entirely unique non-followers. How is someone who is entirely self-contained, happy and aloof from others, living in self-created very special ideas, supposed to relate to other people? Openly sharing a personal perspective with friends, one can't help but notice how valuable the ideas are and how much people are benefiting from them. Would it be so hard for a nod or a wave of appreciation? asks the Leo shadow sun.

Under the influence of the Leo shadow sun, Aquarian natives will help us all, make no mistake about that, but they will also ask you to erect a statue of them in your yard, commemorating the moment for all time. The need for validation that erupts from your Leo shadow sun is the repressed pride thrust upon the Aquarius birth sun because you want to be a selfless assistant to the human race; but really, you don't. Admit it, you want the attention, and why not? You deserve it. The less you exclude your own involvement, the less negative energy your shadow sun will harbor and inappropriately project onto others. You only want to get all eyes on you in classic narcissistic fashion because you aren't letting yourself take credit for your greatness.

Paul Allen, cofounder of Microsoft, had this shadow, and although he indeed performed many philanthropic acts, he always made sure his name was on them; perhaps this was exacerbated standing in the shadow of Bill Gates. The key to mastery for this shadow sun is to bask in the light of your own self-appreciation now and then; the power of Leo is to love the self in pure innocence. This will melt away your inappropriate compulsions to seek attention that only seems to push the spotlight further away from you. When you work with your shadow sun and allow yourself to take pride in yourself, you can emerge as truly selfless and offer up all your amazing contributions to your fellow beings. The Aquarian insight is invaluable, and no one else can see things the way you do; that is your source of pride. Master your shadow by seeing things through your own unique eyes, releasing the need for other eyes to look at you. The individual is as important as the community; one is not better or worse than the other. One can help the many. Be fully and freely yourself as the alpha that contributes to the omega, and don't be shy about giving yourself some pats on the back. You are amazing: take credit for that, and your shadow will dissolve in the light of the rising sun.

Example in Nature

> *All in all, giving and searching for attention-seeking displays can be an evolutionarily stable strategy in extensive form games. These signals may or may not reveal the quality of the signaller, may or may not be costly; however, they are expected to be highly detectable in the natural environment of the given species. Attention-seeking displays might be more prevalent in nature than their current weight in the literature suggests. Extravagant traits previously interpreted as costly signals of quality might turn out to be ASDs. Highly detectable signals given even in the absence of receivers or given at the "introductory stage" of the interaction that transmit low or no information on the quality of the signaller are prime candidates for this function.*
>
> — Szabolcs Számadó, "Attention-Seeking Displays," *PloS One* 10, no. 8 (August 19, 2015)

♍

Virgo Sun Shadow

The Self-Flagellator

Birth Sun: Pisces ♓
Mask: Doubt

Pisces natives are known for their egoless sacrificial nature, and the shadow sun in Virgo is the resentful martyr. Pisces natives seek to expand the ego into formlessness and undergo an ego death; they seek to be amorphous and unidentified. The Virgo shadow sun seeks to classify and articulate the ego, to find order. When this ego sun shadow in Virgo takes over, there will be a big struggle to control how much of the identity is lost and how much of it needs to be archived for the records. When you are under the influence of your Virgo shadow sun, you are in danger of being overly self-critical and of suffering because you cannot bind the self to certain identifiable characteristics that are stable and dependable. Your sun shadow becomes angry at your Piscean inability to formulate a logical, pragmatic role for yourself, and so you browbeat yourself and fall into self-doubt because of your constant shape-shifting. A classic accusation from the Virgo shadow sun would be: Why can't I be more like my sister (brother)? The perspicacious ability of Virgo to analyze gets turned on the ego, the self, and becomes an inner critic, an enemy of the self. This can cause a debilitating pity party and push you into seeking oblivion from the ego altogether. You need to disrupt your inner critic and permit yourself to exist with an identity that remains as fluid and deep as the ocean. Self-acceptance is the power tucked within this shadow sun, which can only be accessed after it defeats that critical devil in the desert of mind.

According to many scholars, Jesus was a Pisces, making him a shadow sun Virgo. Jesus had to release all the ego identifiers that he placed on himself and that were thrust upon him by others to conquer this shadow sun placement. Society identified him as a thief, which he had to break through to find the depths of his Pisces sun. Jesus makes quite a few identifying statements or "I Am" declarations in the Book of John, trying to expand them each time. In these identity statements, he relates himself to things obviously much larger than himself, which annihilate his ego identity.

> *I am the good shepherd. The good shepherd lays down his life for the sheep.*
>
> John 10:11

> *I am the way and the truth and the life. No one comes to the Father except through me.*
>
> John 14:6

The ability to analyze and find self in everything could be a beautiful thing. After all, isn't the ability to relate to everything and become one with everything the ultimate ideal? But this can become creepy when, say, your roommate starts to dress like you, talk like you, and thinks she is you. Mirroring here is mere copycat shadow behavior and seems more sociopathic than enlightened. When you are everything, you are also nothing, so try to find some places where you are unique and yourself and can feel your truth within the depths of your heart. When you keep it small, you might just become rather great with this shadow sun placement.

Example in Nature

Over the last decade it has become apparent that consistent inter-individual differences are ubiquitous across the animal kingdom. Animals often differ consistently from one another in a wide range of different traits, often referred to as "animal personalities." But the role such differences may play in the emergence of collective behaviour remains unclear.

In a new paper in the journal Current Biology, *a team of researchers from the University of Konstanz, the Max Planck Institute of Ornithology, and the University of Cambridge now present compelling experimental and theoretical evidence that suggests that individual characteristics play a fundamental role in the dynamics and functioning of social groups. This research shows for the first time how the behaviour of groups can be predicted from the characteristics of the individuals that make them up and takes an impressive step forward in predicting how individuals in groups will behave based on their personality.*

— University of Konstanz, "Individuality Drives Collective Behavior of Schooling Fish," phys.org, September 7, 2017

♎

Libra Sun Shadow

The Codependent

Birth Sun: Aries ♈
Mask: Indecisive

The ego of an Aries is self-focused, striving, and singular. Aries are able to be themselves and obtain a definable identity. The Libra shadow is cast upon this well-formed idea of the self and introduces the other. If you are under this shadow, you may sneakily seek codependence, despite your claims of self-reliance. But your need of others and lack of independence may anger you, and you may attack the other that you need so badly. Here the ego tries to hide itself in another through projection and blame. The Libra sun shadow can easily make everything about the other person rather than the self. Housing your ego outside your own self is uncomfortable and soon grows intolerable. Insecurities arise, and there is a bit of a confidence issue. The ego will protect itself by blaming its lack of confidence on its need for the other.

A person with a healthy ego will speak up for herself in a confident calm fashion and take responsibility for self-caused actions, expressing them openly. Someone under the Libra sun shadow must justify personal existence by finding someone to fight with. It's the child who shouts "They started it!" when asked to take responsibility for his own actions. If something is another's fault we can justify taking action against her and ignite a battle; fault is the perfect excuse for violence.

One of the key reasons a country goes to war, under the natal Aries sun, is to cast a shadow on the other. The Libra sun shadow is unable to contain its own shadow and so will constantly look for someone else to throw it upon, even if it is an entire country. We seek justice for wrongs done unto us. The Libra shadow sun is the soldier who stands up for law and order in the name of greater things that have absolutely nothing to do with personal ego; those under the Libra shadow sun love to hide their ego behind values that justify war mongering. Libra seeks to balance the scales, and the Libra shadow sun seeks justice for its own ego by blaming the other.

Dietrich Eckart, who became a spiritual mentor of Hitler, is an example of this sun shadow. He belonged to the Thule Society, whose members included many Nazi sympathizers. The society sponsored the German Workers Party, which Eckart founded and which later became the Nazi Party. Eckart is a classic example of the shadow nature of codependently blaming the other for all the evils rather than being a true warrior and being responsible.

Racism itself contains a shadow behavior of competition and blame.

Racists attempt to justify themselves at the expense of another group; they can only lift their self-image by heaping derision on others. Why accept any failure or negative perceptions of self at all when you can unload it on your neighbor? We can find one of the roots of racism in the shadow need to project blame onto some target that can absorb and retain all the failings to keep the projector from feeling uncomfortable. What follows is often an insane justification to permit total annihilation and pillaging of the target and a theft of their resources.

To come clean and evolve from this shadow, you need to accept failure and defeat without justifying yourself or blaming others, especially entire groups of people. Once you can own your shadow sun Libra without feeling threatened, you will cease needing to codependently treat others as a toxic waste dump. This comparison is not to accuse anyone holding this shadow of participating in racism; it is simply to show an extreme example of where this shadow behavior can lead when we project it onto others.

Example in Nature

It's a common (but evil) survival strategy in zombie movies: Injure somebody else and run like hell while they get eaten. But humans aren't the only bastards who do this. Some shoaling fish also use this selfish tactic when they're being chased by predators, according to new research. . . .

[G]roup living gets difficult when "selfish" individuals come into the fold. Scientists often see passive, or indirect, selfish behavior in animals—for example, they may see an animal hide behind its neighbor to escape from a predator. "That's common to observe," says Robert Young, a biologist with the University of Salford Manchester in the U.K. "They may be hiding behind someone else, but they're not actively pushing someone forward." . . .

A few years ago, Young and his colleague Flávia de Oliveira Mesquita thought they observed such behavior while doing research on behavioral barriers. The scientists were trying to figure out ways to keep fish out of areas of risk, such as turbines, by using different deterrents, including strobe lights and mock predators. To their surprise, they saw group members become aggressive towards one another in the presence of active (chasing) predators.

— Joseph Bennington-Castro, "These Fish Are Evidence That Humans Aren't the Only Evil Animals," Gizmodo, July 10, 2013

♏

Scorpio Sun Shadow

The Paranoid Possessor

Birth Sun: Taurus ♉
Mask: Scarcity

We arrive at the shadow sun in Scorpio with the birth sun in Taurus. The Scorpio ego shadow of the Taurus sun seeks to possess rather than secure. The need for security rises to an obsessive controlling dominance over the object responsible for the safety of this ego shadow.

There is a difference between ownership and possession. You may have a lover, but you do not possess your mate. Do you own your things or do your things own you? We are possessed by our possessions and identify with them in the Scorpio shadow, placed firmly in our root, and are terrified to let something go. You might purchase a house and feel secure within it, but you will still need to venture out into the world and interact with danger. Understanding this you might cease to leave your house and stay within the safety of its walls, refusing to interact any more, and now the home owns you, rather than the other way around.

The farm of a certain rich man produced a terrific crop. He talked to himself: "What can I do? My barn isn't big enough for this harvest." Then he said, "Here's what I'll do: I'll tear down my barns and build bigger ones. Then I'll gather in all my grain and goods, and I'll say to myself, Self, you've done well! You've got it made and can now

> *retire. Take it easy and have the time of your life!" Just then God showed up and said, "Fool! Tonight you die. And your barnful of goods—who gets it?" That's what happens when you fill your barn with Self and not with God.*
>
> LUKE 12:16

This is the entrance of shadow where the fine line of ownership and possession is crossed. With possession comes paranoia at the threat of loss. Once you have a thing, you are always fearful that it can be taken away. An old friend from Vietnam, Hong Nguyen, once told me some wisdom his father imparted to him: "Never get a fancy car or a beautiful girl, because someone will always try to take them away from you." In this shadow sun we learn the hard lesson of nonattachment. The world and time teach us how little we truly own here, as the Scorpio fact of death is always waiting just around the corner. Death and loss will, ironically, free you from the shadow sun in Scorpio and its possessive clinging as you realize the truth "you can't take it with you." Rather than dropping down into your root chakra, flailing to maintain your gains, seek meaning within what you are given. Under this shadow sun, you must learn to give as much as you get and to adapt an "easy come, easy go" attitude. When you make this adjustment, a feeling of gratitude may enter your awareness, which may be the best part about having things to begin with—the feeling of happiness.

The late queen of England had this sun shadow, and she placed a good portion of her focus on protecting her kingdom and guarding it violently if need be. Hoarding jewels, taking land around the world from the indigenous who live there, and squirreling away riches and artifacts taken from other nations are wonderful examples of how this paranoia can get the better of us. When she passed, I doubt her cold dead hands were able to grasp even a single gem that had been placed within her crown.

Example in Nature

Pack rats pee all over their nests, and in arid climates (like deserts), the urine crystallizes as it dries. This preserves the items inside the middens, but it also presents a challenge to scientists studying the finds. "They have very highly concentrated urine, and once it crystallizes, it's rock hard," says Buffalo State College ecologist Camille Holmgren. "In order to collect middens, we often need a rock hammer and a big flooring chisel to hammer away at these things because they're often cemented to the rocks." Holmgren's research on vegetation and climate change involves collecting amberat, the ancient pee-hardened middens of pack rats, which she has to soak for at least a week to break down the urine and extract leaves, seeds and twigs from an ancient world.

— Sadie Witkowski, "From Ancient Seeds to Scraps of Clothing, Rats' Nests Are Full of Treasures," *Smithsonian Magazine,* November 15, 2019

♐

Sagittarius Sun Shadow

The Party Never Ends

Birth Sun: Gemini ♊
Mask: Indulgent

The shadow sun in Sagittarius creates an ego that hides within itself the expansive nature of Bacchus or Dionysus and Jupiter or Zeus, the party gods of excess and debauchery. Those born under the Gemini birth sun are social creatures by nature, so when this shadow gets the better of them, the danger is that the party will become their entire life, eating everything else. Everyone wants to be the life of the party with a lampshade over their head; the shadow sun Sagittarius might actually achieve this archetype. The attention can be addictive, and the party may become an ego identity, which can be hard to shake. At celebrations people feel good and euphoric, and when we provide this feeling to people through the party, the ego swells to Sagittarian proportions.

Sagittarius in mythology is associated with the centaur Chiron, who provided healing and doctored people back to health; one might say he, and the sign Sagittarius, is the original Doctor Feelgood of the zodiac. The shadow sun in Sagittarius seeks the high vibe of the endless summer and wants to be the go-to for the good times. This shadow placement can be used to the advantage of its holder as there are many successful careers built on creating never-ending parties. Festivals and entire cities could be said to be inhabited by this shadow ego placement. The shadow ego in Sagittarius argues that every day is a celebration; *carpe diem* is this placement's motto. But when limits and boundaries are disregarded, when we overstep the healthy limits of imbibing and participating in celebration, the so-called party foul comes into play. Spirit told me once through the I Ching that parties are for celebrating special occasions, not for every day. Dionysus, known to the Romans as Bacchus, haunts this sun shadow placement, and while Dionysus deserves veneration, if permitted to dominate, the morning after is like a bomb went off. Actor Colin Farrell is an example of this sun shadow; the party god usurped him and nearly claimed the focus of his entire being. Known as a party-boy lothario, his bad-boy reputation threatened to overshadow his acting career.

Transmutation of this ego shadow is going to require discipline and limiting good times. You need to learn to wax and wane, to take care of your physical body and avoid an engorged ego, your head full of substances. Once you release the party identity, your own unique personality will shine through.

Example in Nature

> *New research shows that spider monkeys routinely consume fermenting fruit, backing up the notion that humans inherited our proclivity for alcohol from our primate ancestors—the so-called "drunken monkey hypothesis."*
>
> *It's well known that certain non-human primates enjoy a drop of the hard stuff. Chimpanzees are known to raid stocks of palm wine brewed by villagers and feral vervet monkeys in the Caribbean are famous for stealing alcoholic drinks from bars.*
>
> — Stuart Blackman, "Do Monkeys Get Drunk? Scientists Find out the Truth," *BBC Wildlife Magazine*, May 4, 2022

♑

Capricorn Sun Shadow

The Conqueror

Birth Sun: Cancer ♋
Mask: Ambitious

The ego in the shadow of Capricorn needs to be successful in worldly pursuits. Those with this shadow sun seek to dominate and focus on success above all things in an unrelenting constant fashion. Individuals who hold this shadow sun will go through many failures only to reach huge success. Egos like Elon Musk, Richard Branson, and Ariana Grande are examples of this shadow. Here the instinct and will to live becomes the will to succeed. Think what you might about those with this shadow sun and the means they use to attain success, they get there nonetheless. The Cancer natal sun placement highlights keen instincts and the ability to meet the needs for survival. When these natives focus their needs on the material world, they set their sights on accruing great wealth or business success to ensure they will never be needy again. A common backstory in the lives of these natives is beginning life in poverty, which triggers their shadow sun into overdrive, pushing them to avoid failure at all costs.

They often shift from survive to thrive due to their forceful and powerful connection to their survival instinct. This ego's relentless ambition to climb ever higher has fueled Richard Branson and Elon Musk to rise higher than most, exemplified by their travels to outer space; they have extended past the boundaries of almost all other egos. The shadow of this earth ego pushes them to rise higher than Earth itself, which has its own special kind of beauty and comes at its own price, draining resources from Earth to enable such a climb. Here the ego will use Earth itself as a step stool to its own accomplishments, like a pharaoh building a pyramid to touch heaven on the backs of the slaves. It is true the pyramid is beautiful, but the shadow ego broke a lot of eggs to make that omelet.

The danger of this shadow ego is the loss of self through ambitious pursuits. Don't forget you have your own special identity and ego outside your worldly gains; do not ignore the child inside yourself at the expense of securing your needs. Your heart will suffer as a result of the imbalance of this shadow sun taking you over. Transmute this shadow through self-discovery and spending time connecting to your feelings and emotions. Listen to your heart; it is just as valuable as those riches you seek.

Example in Nature

Horseshoe crab blood is bright blue. It contains important immune cells that are exceptionally sensitive to toxic bacteria. When those cells meet invading bacteria, they clot around it and protect the rest of the horseshoe crab's body from toxins. Scientists used these clever blood cells to develop a test called Limulus Amebocyte Lysate, or LAL, which checks new vaccines for contamination. This technique has been used all over the world since the 1970s to stop medical professionals giving out jabs full of bad bacteria that could make humans very sick. It's great for humans, because vaccines save us from all sorts of unwanted diseases, including measles and mumps. It's not so great for the horseshoe crabs: thousands of them are rounded up and bled every year.

— Katie Pavid, "Horseshoe Crab Blood: The Miracle Vaccine Ingredient That's Saved Millions of Lives," Natural History Museum, December 3, 2020

♒

Aquarius Sun Shadow

The Loner Leader

Birth Sun: Leo ♌
Mask: Validation seeking

The ego of shadow Aquarius seeks to experiment with identity. This is the shadow of those born under birth sun Leo who want to express their identity in total confidence. The Aquarius shadow sun forces the ego to lose confidence so that the individual can come into union with the community and become a team player. Leo sun natives need to be honored by others as valuable leaders and influencers, but their Aquarius shadow asks them to be part of a larger collective. The key to resolving this is to find a collective of individuals who all agree on the same values. When the force of the individual meets the force of the community, we have some of the most exciting moments of history. To break away in a fashion that assists the many to become empowered as individuals is the destiny of those with the Aquarius ego shadow. How are the self and society reconciled? Truly a problem humanity has faced since the first rogue member of a tribe left the group to form a new group. This shadow requires that you cannot break all ties with society for you need them desperately to realize your goals. A general isn't much of a general without an army to back him. How do you experiment with identity and yet maintain some identity as a leader with followers?

The key to integrating this shadow is relationships. As the natal shadow holder of this space, you must not alienate yourself from others and even if you only have a few friends; you must have intimacy, integrity, and closeness within those relationships. Finding sincerity of heart among your fellows will guide you through the difficulty of this ego placement. Napoleon Bonaparte carried this ego shadow and struggled with it as evidenced by history. Many focus on the negative shadows of Bonaparte, but there were huge community gains and service he provided under his leadership. Napoleon constantly oscillated between his own ego and service to his nation and ultimately died in exile, a prime example of the loner leader.

> *History is a set of lies that people have agreed upon. Even when I am gone, I shall remain in people's minds the star of their rights, my name will be the war cry of their efforts, the motto of their hopes.*
>
> Napoleon Bonaparte, quoted in Count Las Cases, *The Life, Exile, and Conversations of the Emperor Napoleon*

It is a fine line between self and others. Even though a leader may act for the greatest good, the crowd can turn on a dime, so leadership is a precarious position to fill. Remaining authentic while trying to please the many might just be impossible, no matter what benefits you offer the many. If, for example, the crowd thinks you betrayed them, suddenly all your past assistance is forgotten and the focus is only on your perceived betrayal. Within all empires are both shadow events and benefits. The British Empire punished Napoleon and caused his downfall, while his French soldiers remained loyal to him and his empire, showing he was able to earn true friends, regardless, and in the end mastered this shadow placement.

Example in Nature

Dozens of goats and sheep brought for slaughter escaped from a New Jersey livestock auction house Wednesday night—and the facility's manager believes another goat who had bolted to freedom more than a year ago helped them to make their getaway.

The animals escaped through an unsecured gate at the Hackettstown Livestock Auction House on West Stiger Street around 9:30 p.m. . . .

Locals jokingly point the finger at another goat nicknamed Fred that escaped from the same auction market more than a year ago and sporadically pops up around the town. In fact, cops received reports that Fred was in the area a couple of hours before the escape.

On Thursday afternoon, after the escape, Fred showed up at the facility and headbutted the gate holding newly corralled animals multiple times, in an apparent effort to let them back out.

— Jennifer Bain and Amanda Wood, "Rogue Goat May Have Helped Dozens of Farm Animals Escape," *New York Post*, August 9, 2019

♓
Pisces Sun Shadow
The Martyr

Birth Sun: Virgo ♍
Mask: Follower

Pisces shadow sun is a Virgo birth sun. The Virgo is the taxonomist of identity who loves to perceive and discern what makes them who they are and what makes others themselves in contrast. Seeking and finding patterns, analysis, and understanding make the Virgo sun feel the most comfortable, so of course, the shadow nature of Pisces wants to wreck all articulations and force everything into unidentifiable chaos. In the face of its shadow of murky, swampy, irrational dissolution, the Virgo panics and tries to find something for its logical nature to cling to while the Pisces shadow keeps piling on more chaos. When the ego is faced with the shadow of total ego death, it may react with a panic attack typical of the sun sign Virgo, needing to analyze and organize to make itself solid again. The ego does not want to die; the shadow sun in Pisces wants the ego to die. It will seek to annihilate things the ego identifies with. You will need to be cautious of self-sabotage with this placement as the shadow here seeks to destroy the ego.

Werner Erhard (John Paul Rosenberg) has this shadow sun and founded the EST movement, which later got integrated into Landmark Worldwide. The nature of this shadow is to create an organized analytical system of breaking down the ego in a group setting and making it succeed in a Virgo earth-based way. The key to avoiding abuse with this shadow sun is to understand that you will never destroy the ego. Being the destroyer of ego becomes another ego identity. To try and escape the thing we hate we become the thing again. Rather than attempting to achieve oblivion by losing the ego, the thing that makes the self, perhaps attempting to include selfhood in oblivion could be more useful? Trying to annihilate the egos of others also invites such shadow behaviors as mind control and loss of cognition or will for individuals. While working in groups and achieving hive mind can be powerful and potentially a wonderful thing, mindlessly following in zombie hordes could be problematic.

To claim mastery of this shadow, do not seek to vindicate your ego by hating all manifestations of ego; this would be like throwing the baby out with the bathwater. Perhaps some celebration of identity and ego is in order, so that you may learn how ego serves the self, how it is beautiful in its own right, how it remains an aspect of our nature, and how it doesn't really need to be perfected or annihilated but can be permitted to simply exist. The same quality we permit to the stars in the sky, simple acknowledgment of existence, can work wonders on our judgments of humans holding an ego.

Example in Nature

The lemming became the archetypal suicidal animal in the twentieth century precisely because of its lack of intelligence, foresight and consciousness. Lemmings were used to describe the senseless devastation of global warfare and to warn of the violence of totalitarian political systems. As the century progressed, the collective impulse became more prominent, and the lemming became less a self-destroyer and more of an automaton. The lemming became the totemic animal in an age of cultural pessimism, a symbol of an unconscious and mindless urge towards mass self-destruction, and references to its suicide are legion.

— Edmund Ramsden and Duncan Wilson,
"The Suicidal Animal: Science and the Nature
of Self-Destruction," *Past Present* 224,
no. 1 (August 2014): 201–42

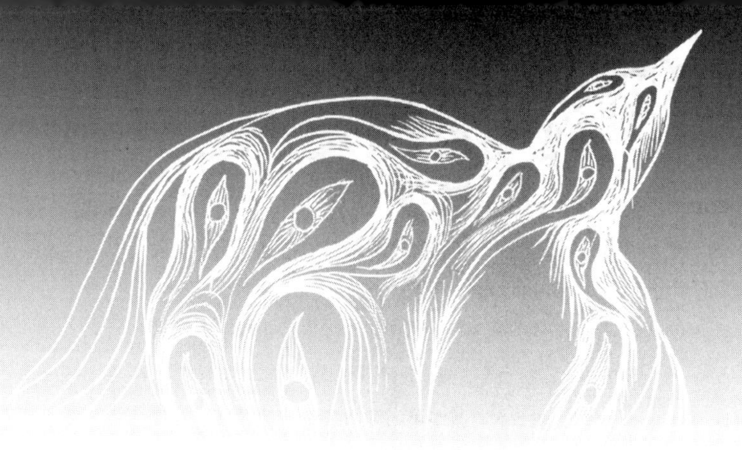

Moon Shadows

The Tell-Tale Heart

> *You may not yet be able to bring your unconscious mind activity into awareness as thoughts, but it will always be reflected in the body as an emotion, and of this you can become aware.*
>
> Eckhart Tolle, *The Power of Now*

The shadow moon in our chart represents the emotions that we most need to express. The shadow moon has been tucked beneath the surface, buried in an unmarked grave, and requires a resurrection. This side of our emotional nature has become hidden, unknown to us, because we have not acknowledged it. Mastery of the moon shadow comes through integrating the emotions that take us out of our comfort zone. Integrating the moon shadow is a major key for coming into our instincts, our physical bodies, so that we can combat disease and discomfort. Clarity of mind unobstructed by the muddy waters of our latent emotions can liberate our movements and free us from deep stagnation. The way we integrate our shadow moon is through challenging our boundaries and creatively expressing the negative emotions that the shadow moon represents. Only through a reunion of the two moons,

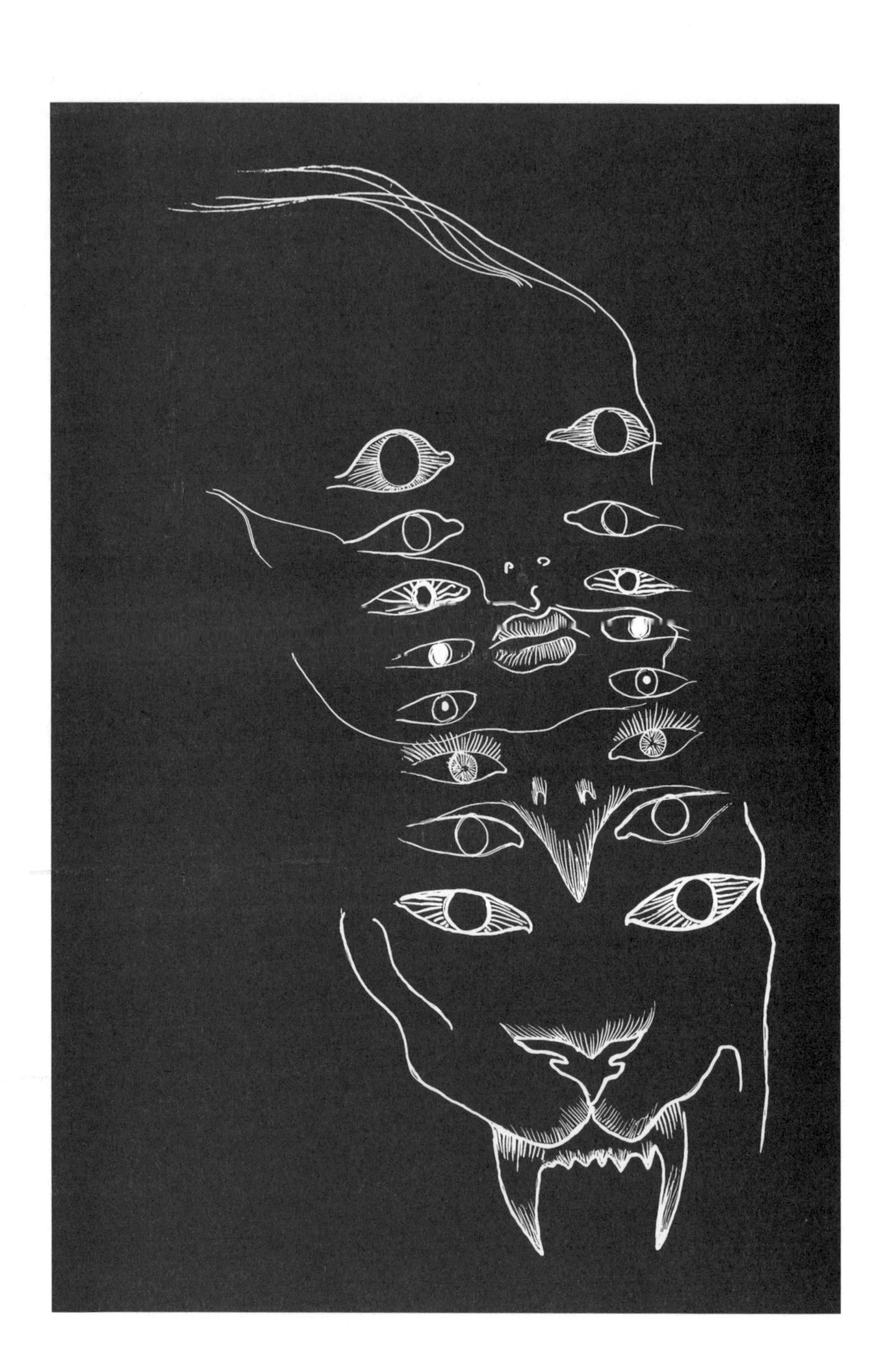

our birth moon and our shadow moon, can we master the emotional lessons of our current incarnation. It is not enough to embody the emotions of your birth moon, you must also feel and accept the emotions of your shadow moon, even though you will not like it one bit. Indeed, you will revolt against it. A rash may break out on your skin the first time you permit such emotions to flow through you. But the purpose of such a rash is to clear something that has festered beneath the surface.

The moon and our emotional nature is best represented by the term *instinct*. The philosopher Immanuel Kant called this a priori knowledge, or things you know without ever having learned them. Our instincts are an extremely valuable asset to all of us, part of our nature as Earthlings. The knowledge contained in the shadow moon unfolds the potentialities of our instincts so that we may use them for our greatest good. To say that you have instincts that are yours alone is an ignorant statement. All things in nature have instincts, and they belong to all as a birthright.

> *I explained to him, however, that my nature was such that my physical needs often got in the way of my feelings.*
>
> Albert Camus, *The Stranger*

Our instincts are expressed through emotion. The emotional expression can be a natural response to our instincts, or we can fight against our nature or work against ourselves in a self-sabotaging manner. Your moon in your birth chart represents your natural way of responding to your instincts: this is the way you outwardly express instincts through your emotions. Your shadow moon represents the way you attempt to destroy or repress your instincts. Through mastering this level of our subconscious, we may shed no small amount of insight into places where we become paralyzed by our fear response or mired in aggressive behavior—responses that may make no sense to our rational mind.

Here the power of astrology as a tool can be physically felt directly as we free ourselves from the hidden chemicals we release within our deepest trigger levels. Emotions, as they occur inside of our bodies, release chemicals into our biological system; much research has been performed scientifically examining this. Joy and love release endorphins, stress and anxiety release cortisol and adrenaline, dopamine and serotonin are released from emotional responses as well as substances, foods, and drinks. These chemical releases dictate our response whether we like it or not. When you see someone break into a sweat or shake when feeling nervous, they cannot hide that they feel nervous. The more you hide your shadow from yourself and others, the more your nature will expose itself to one and all without your conscious permission. Any tool that may assist us in remedying this is immensely valuable.

To find your moon shadow sign, simply look up the location of your birth moon and follow the zodiac ring to find the directly opposing constellation.

> *Identity confusion . . . is as if somebody lost their mental road map and has no appreciation of who they are or what is going on in their life. They may know they know but become blustered or baffled as to why they don't. The information is inaccessible and likely would remind a person about things that have gone on in their life that are simply unacceptable and unknowable, in a given moment, because of the emotional gravity involved.*
>
> Richard A. Chefetz, *Intensive Psychotherapy for Persistent Dissociative Processes: The Fear of Feeling Real*

♈

Aries Moon Shadow

Temper Tantrums

Birth Moon: Libra ♎
Trigger: Confrontation
Boundary Needed: I do not need to threaten to confront

Your shadow moon in Aries means you need to master the anger that arises when you have a confrontation. You must learn to neutralize the fury you feel when confronted, which you use to justify your aggressive actions. Alec Baldwin, who was involved in the now infamous accidental shooting on a movie set resulting in a death, is an example of this shadow moon and has been arrested for violent behavior in the past. Like a blowfish that puffs itself up and forces out its spikes to appear threatening, someone with the Aries shadow moon becomes so antagonistic that people get scared of the confrontation and run away.

Looking deeply into this, we see you aren't actually having a confrontation at all. Scaring the other into thinking you are more powerful is only another shadowy way for you to avoid the confrontation. Have you been using your anger to scare away the people you need to actually have a diplomatic confrontation with? Do you think it is strange that people back down from having a conversation with you when you threaten nuclear war? Do you think this means you have won that battle? When two roosters prepare for the cock fight, the first thing they do is ruffle their feathers as far away from their bodies as possible, making illusions of grandeur. Swelling up in anger, like a cat puffing up its fur and rising into an arch to look as big as possible, does not replace the fight itself. Here we see only another tactic of avoidance. Yelling in self-righteous fury while blaming and shaming the other may have saved you from some fights by intimidating your opponent, but do you feel a sense of fulfillment and accomplishment afterward? Was the problem solved at all? Or do you deeply understand you will only need to defend your territory again and again, slipping further into distrust and defense.

To master this shadow moon, you need to become aware of how you are extending your fear mask. You shall come into your true emotional power when you find that you no longer need to threaten, justify, or intimidate but can sit quietly in your stance as you whisper your truth with pure confidence. The boundary that shall set you free is when you forbid yourself from engaging in threatening tactics rather than taking the time to explain the depth of your feelings in the disagreement. Do not give yourself permission to attempt to destroy the person making the confrontation. Who cares if the other doesn't listen to you? State your case calmly without taking a single thing from your opponent. The prize you win at the end of this fight is your dignity. Self-implosion might make the confrontation avoidable, it is true, but the cost is too great; calm down and dig your heels in. You do not need to be in harmony with everyone; it is OK to disagree without negating your whole existence. Notice how you become angry that someone has denied you and give them the space to be themselves while giving yourself the space to also be what you are. There is no threat in disagreement. Don't be mad; be articulate and diplomatic. You are only angry because you are removing your rights to feel things as an individual. Remedy this immediately through self-inclusive emotions rather than becoming destructive.

Example in Nature

> *Pop superstar Shakira says she was the victim of a random attack by a pair of wild boars while walking in a park in Barcelona with her eight-year-old son. The Colombian singer said the animals attacked her, before seizing her bag and retreating with it into the woods. She shared her bizarre tale in a series of Instagram stories on Wednesday. Holding the now recovered but torn bag towards the camera, she said: "Look at how two wild boars which attacked me in the park have left my bag." "They were taking my bag to the woods with my mobile phone in it," the singer continued. "They've destroyed everything."*
>
> — BBC News, "Shakira: Singer Attacked by a Pair of Wild Boars," September 30, 2021

♉
Taurus Moon Shadow
The Green-Eyed Devil

Birth Moon: Scorpio ♏
Trigger: Competition
Boundary Needed: I have all I need

The shadow moon in Taurus of the birth moon Scorpio must permit their emotional nature to feel jealous. Jealousy serves a specific purpose.

When we are jealous of another person it is only giving us a feedback mechanism. The data conveyed in the biology of the feeling of jealousy is: "I want that." Rather than being consumed by the fact that someone else has something that you want, try acknowledging through the feeling of jealousy that you want that thing. It is OK to want what someone else has, and you can find your own. The song I think about with this shadow moon is "Jessie's Girl" by Rick Springfield. If you want what someone else has, that is only your heart trying to tell you what you need, it does not mean you need that specific one. Elizabeth Taylor was born with this moon shadow and fought both sides of its expression. Taylor was consumed with jealousy for Sophia Loren regarding her spouse and his interactions with her while also being a target of jealousy by Marilyn Monroe and Jackie Kennedy.

Try and broaden this shadow sun out to include that you also can have what other people have. It won't be theirs; it will be yours. Open up to include options. Birth moon in Scorpio feels things deeply. Maybe more so than anyone else may feel something; this will be obsessive and compulsive due to its intensity. The shadow moon of Scorpio moon will *need* that thing they have been obsessing about in order for them to have emotional comfort. Without the obtainment of the thing they have decided that they need, often as a result of seeing that someone else has it, they will become very unhappy indeed.

If you want a thing in order to possess it, the universe has set up a trap for you, because you are not able to own anything at all. Everything shall slip through your cold dead hands eventually. In order for you to rule your shadow moon in Taurus, be comfortable with death and loss and the ability to own nothing at all. When you lose something, does it mean you are not wealthy? The truest answer is no. You don't actually need to own that thing in order to obtain the truth of your shadow moon. Overcoming shadow moon in Taurus requires a boundary focused on a relinquishing of materialism and ownership altogether. This does not mean you get rid of everything, it means you stop focusing emotionally on your stuff.

The liberation obtained through the release of your needs for creature comforts affords you more wealth than you could have ever imagined. Here your emotions will expand to depths you never thought possible as you are welcome to feel without owning, touch without grasping, and have without holding. Truly one of the highest states of enlightenment comes when our emotional and instinctual nature comes free of any earthly needs at all and this is the destiny of the Taurus moon shadow, to need nothing at all. God bless the child who has its own, and when you see all that you have, you will never again long for what someone else possesses; this is a type of freedom most can only dream of but that shadow moon Taurus is destined to achieve.

Example in Nature

> *Among invertebrates, only terrestrial arthropods are well known to hoard food for future consumption (Vander Wall 1990). For example, bees hoard food for their young, carabid beetles hoard seed (Alcock 1976), and orb-web spiders wrap prey for future consumption (e.g. Eberhard 1967, Champion de Crespigny et al. 2001).*
>
> — Tae Won Kim, "Food Storage and Carrion Feeding in the Fiddler Crab *Uca lactea*," *Aquatic Biology* 10, no. 1 (June 2010): 33–39

♊

Gemini Moon Shadow

Deception

Birth Moon: Sagittarius ♐
Trigger: Shame
Boundary Needed: I do not need to justify myself

The birth sign Sagittarius moon is very good at seeing emotions objectively through a larger lens, almost like a psychotherapist. They can remove the person from the emotion fairly adeptly. In the moon shadow of Gemini, this ability becomes maniacal. The removal of the person from the emotion is an invitation to shadow land as the attempt to cover over and exempt the person's involvement in negative emotionality grows to dangerous levels. Without accountability and responsibility for our negative feelings we might just drop into a state of denial. Seeking to remove self from drama and gossip, the moon shadow of Gemini fractures the emotional self into those who feel such terrible things and those who do not. Donald Trump is a famous person with this placement and has had to deal with gossip, shame, and mud-slinging throughout his lifetime on both sides of the coin. While blaming others for low behavior he himself may have initiated at times, he embodied the two-faced aspect of this shadow moon. Interestingly, for Trump, his birth sun is in Gemini and his shadow moon reflects a hidden side of Gemini nature with this combination. Pressure he faced to justify many of his actions and decisions became a steady presence in his life. Recognize that all of us feel such things, including yourself. By removing yourself from the melee of human emotion, you will not be doing yourself a service. Instead you are shoving something into the darkness that you will only have to acknowledge in yourself later. You will lie and try to justify why you are more exempt than the other if you are unable to see those emotions as part of yourself, so the deception shall spread.

No one *wants* to be petty, but we *are*. The Sagittarius birth moon wants to grow much larger than the inferior feelings of root-level emotions, it wants to raise them up into higher thinking and virtue, but the only way to do that is start from the bottom and build up. You are here, down at the level you want to avoid, so don't pretend otherwise. There is no getting around your petty nature. Look at it deeply, and see how you diminish and trash talk others, if you do not include these behaviors in yourself you will find yourself guilty of slander and liable without even being consciously aware of your misbehavior. Pretending to be a king while we act like a schmuck won't fool anyone. The key boundary to mastering this shadow moon is to let yourself be catty and rude. Accept that sometimes you can get a thrill out of using your words to put someone else down in front of other people. If you are able to release people from contempt you will cure yourself of this predicament and not lose nearly as many friends. Make fun of yourself also and admit to others when you are in your lower, less virtuous nature. Your ability to see the person outside of the emotion will grant you the superpower of humility if you just understand that you also are part of this dichotomy. We all say and do things we don't mean sometimes. Just apologize when you goof up by taking the negative emotion into your own hands rather than trying to shove it into your pocket. You were rude too; it's fine, just admit it.

Example in Nature

[C]ases of "social rejection or exclusion" have been observed in three different behavioral contexts. Most frequently, a chimpanzee is the target of hostility as the result of competitive interaction within the community; in such cases, social cohesion counterbalances rejection, typically leading to integration within a relatively stable pattern of dominance and social interaction. The occasional departure of an individual who has been the target of aggression . . . seems due to persistent hostility by a few males rather than general "ostracism" by the group as a whole. A second form of exclusion concerns outsiders found in the home range of the group: in these cases, hostility is more generalized, particularly in response to the attempt of an adult female with offspring to join the community. Finally, there are the rarely observed instances of shunning a group member whose behavior seems abnormal the social rejection of Pepe and Old Mr. McGregor after they suffered from polio.

— Jane Goodall, "Social Rejection, Exclusion, and Shunning among the Gombe Chimpanzees," *Ethology and Sociobiology* 7, no. 3–4 (1986): 227–36

♋
Cancer Moon Shadow
Defensive Withholding

Birth Moon: Capricorn ♑
Trigger: Emotional responses
Boundary Needed: Everyone has feelings

An aversion to feeling emotions at all is the shadow here in this placement and so holders become protective, isolated, and defensive of their emotions, trying to protect themselves from feeling. Emotional irritants are avoided and repressed.

Those with the shadow moon in Cancer will protect their emotions and their heart at all costs. The heart here will grow a protective shell. This protective response also happens when others engage in emotional outbursts; people with the Cancer moon shadow will instinctively close off to those who are expressing strong emotions because they perceive this as a threat to their own feelings, which they will hide, withhold, deny, and protect. Those with the moon shadow in Cancer will withhold love as a defense mechanism and will give love only when they feel they have control or are in control of how the other feels, which makes them feel safe.

This can obviously lead to being emotionally manipulative, either with oneself or with others. Control of emotional displays becomes calculated. This is difficult to sustain and could lead to an eventual explosion of repressed emotions: earth moons tend to be volcanic, feelings collect underneath, like deep magma pools, until pressure forces them up to burst forth. Celebrity chef Anthony Bourdain had this placement, and it would seem his ability to control his emotional nature served him well in his career but not so well in his personal relationships. Obviously having a superpower of emotional control is highly valuable in entertainment. The repression and control of emotional energy that was so deep could have contributed to Bourdain's dysregulation and suicide. The danger here is an issue with true intimacy of feelings that are sincere and not merely contrived to receive a response that is desired.

In order to transmute this moon shadow, permit yourself to let your feelings show even if they are negative or uncomfortable, but even more, hold space for others to express negative feelings and expressions without trying to place a need or outcome on their expression. If you are unable to achieve this, consider communicating boundaries and providing resources to assist your loved ones to find this space to honor their emotional needs. It also might benefit you to find spaces you feel safe to connect deeply to your true feelings with no one around to perform for.

Example in Nature

Most of the time, Black Herons look like your typical wading bird—long legs, long necks, long beaks. But when it's time to eat, this jet-black African species has a pretty nifty trick up its wings: It turns into an umbrella.

Not literally, of course. But while fishing, the bird will tuck its head down, spread its wings around its body, and create a sun shade of sorts.

But what exactly is the purpose of this behavior? There are several possible advantages to canopy feeding, says Kenn Kaufman, a bird expert and field editor for Audubon *magazine. One commonly accepted theory is that small fish looking for places to hide are attracted to the shade created by the heron's wings, he says.*

— Shweta Karikehalli, "Watch a Black Heron Fool Fish by Turning into an Umbrella," *Audubon*, January 17, 2019

♌
Leo Moon Shadow
What about Me

Birth Moon: Aquarius ♒
Trigger: Identity theft
Boundary Needed: Intellectual property rights

The natal moon is in Aquarius for this shadow. The emotion of pride presents to the natal moon in Aquarius that would rather view itself as magnanimous and egoless. Aquarius moon rebels against its own emotions and projects them onto others and so the Leo shadow moon forces these emotions in upon their own feelings. Despite all the imagining, all the observing and all the dissociation, the heart feels what it feels and the moon shadow in Leo is going to reflect that into a confrontation for the holder of this shadow. The further into outer space the Aquarius moon projects itself the louder the Leo shadow roars it back down into the shelter of its emotional nature. Leo shadow moon is the heart of the hero; the emotions placed here form idealized concepts of what it expects to feel versus what is real.

This shadow moon reflects the ego and causes the emotional defenses to focus on protecting its ego and identity at all costs. There will be tendencies to ignore others and the bias will lead to self-defensiveness rather than team work. Because the moon in Aquarius often will love to lose itself in community, the beauty of this moon shadow is that the individual must find out who they are in relation to the community, come into self, find out how they feel about things, and separate from others. The Aquarius force will cause them to need another again, and the power to transmute this moon shadow through protecting their unique being allows the community to benefit from their creative self, and they can keep themselves safe at the same time. Here the compromise is through feeling safe in their own identity and not needing external validation or being told who they are from someone else. To transmute this moon shadow, protection of the person's creative ingenuity is needed, things like filing for patents, getting trademarks, or publishing their unique thoughts will help them have their ideas protected and then they can move forward into community once they have themselves established. Muhammad Ali had this moon placement and his Leo shadow forced him to declare himself and his identity to the forefront loud and clear for everyone to hear. As soon as he had his ego clearly shouted he was able to do things on larger levels that represented entire communities of people and represent his fierce heart for the love of others as well as himself, becoming an embodiment of this shadow relation.

Example in Nature

> *We all know the type—pushy people who elbow their way to the front of the line or cut in on us when we are driving. And then there are those who have less assertive personalities, and happily defer to others. Animals show similar behavioral variety, according to biologist John Shivik. In his new book* Mousy Cats and Sheepish Coyotes, *he explores the science of animal personalities and how it helps balance nature's necessary tension between individualism and cooperation—and underpins important aspects of evolution.*
>
> — Simon Worrall, "How Diverse Personalities Help Animals Survive," *National Geographic,* January 5, 2018

♍

Virgo Moon Shadow

Blaming and Shaming

Birth Moon: Pisces ♓
Trigger: Emotional responsibility
Boundary Needed: I can share my own feelings instead of judging yours

People with birth moon in Pisces are empaths. This forces those with this Virgo moon shadow to analyze, nitpick, and criticize the feelings that others are having while luxuriating in never sharing how they feel themselves. This isn't their fault, since they are literally inundated with the feelings of others to the point that they have no idea how they feel about it. It is much easier to pick apart the others' obvious emotional responses than to take a look in the mirror.

I have found clairvoyant gifts usually accompany this moon shadow. The ability to perceive others' emotional data is a hugely valuable skill but difficult to wrangle boundaries. This shadow moon can be well placed for, say, the art or literary critic who can make a living off his shadow behavior; however, in their day-to-day lives those with Pisces moon will find that they run into issues in their interpersonal relationships until they are able to peel their eyes and opinions away from what other people's emotional responses to things are.

Observing responses from an objective and analytical position could be helpful here, and only giving those observations when solicited will be very important. Your analysis of someone's emotions really isn't healthy behavior, unless you are being solicited for it or if the other is abusing you and causing damage. Perhaps if you find you default to this behavior, if you find you engage in it often and are unable to avoid it you could benefit from being a therapist, psychic reader, or something of this nature.

Prince had this placement and in classic emotional martyr sense, once he quit critiquing and rebelling against the abuse he faced in the music industry and made his own label, he transmuted this moon shadow and created his own empire. He conquered this shadow moon placement in an amazing victory of an individual expressing against the larger entity influencing his behavior and attempting to dominate him. In his personal relationships there were allegations of abuse and violence by several women in his life, so there seemed to be patterns of justification or substances causing him to engage his shadow in terrible ways.

Example in Nature

Emotional contagion involves matching the perceived emotion of a nearby individual, positive or negative. It is found in all sorts of social species suggesting its importance as a mechanism of coordination. . . .

The reviewed studies show that certain animals seem to be affected by the emotional displays of others, suggesting that the sharing of emotions could be widespread among social species capable of emotions. Emotional contagion seems to be related to the ecological circumstances and socio-behavioral traits of the species and thus present a great variability across the animal kingdom. Therefore, depending on the species, it could be triggered by a great variety of stimuli, modulated by different factors and be based on distinct mechanisms. This phenomenon thus could be far more complex and flexible than previously thought, and we should be cautious when generalizing about its functions and mechanisms between species.

— Ana Pérez-Manrique and Antoni Gomila, "Emotional Contagion in Nonhuman Animals: A Review," *Wiley Interdisciplinary Reviews: Cognitive Science* 13, no. 1 (May 5, 2021)

♎

Libra Moon Shadow

The Emotional Litigator

Birth Moon: Aries ♈
Trigger: It's not my fault
Boundary Needed: My feelings are justified

Those with a birth moon in Aries never have a problem telling you how they feel. When someone is able to state their feelings, from a purely personal perspective, this usually solicits an argument because it does not include the other person. Disagreements arise since the feelings are coming from the Aries moon individual at the exclusion of the other, so the person left out feels a need to stand up for themselves against the Aries moon, which is what forms the Libra moon shadow here. Libra natal moons have difficulty finding their feelings in relation to others and tend to be overwhelmed by mirroring others' feelings, while those with natal Aries moon have only their own feelings and often cannot feel the other. The Libra moon shadow, in an effort to reach equilibrium, forces the Aries native to recognize and discuss the emotions of the other as well. Under the influence of the Libra shadow moon, you may find you must litigate, articulate, and justify with explanations why you feel the way you do to the other in order to remain in a relationship. Otherwise, you may fear you will lose the other if you are too dominating.

While feeling our feelings ourselves can be viewed as arrogant and narcissistic, whose feelings are you feeling most of the time if not your own? Is one better or worse or just different? The quandary of the Libra moon shadow requires that no one person gets to be the only one feeling things, and there will constantly be differences in how we feel. If this is your shadow moon placement, rather than seeing your justifications as a domineering battle, view them more as an explanation and plead your case. Provide evidence and express your core feelings rather than temper tantrums and force. Your feelings belong to you, and you have that right. Don't let anyone bully you into feeling their feelings.

Alexandria Ocasio-Cortez, American politician and activist, has this moon shadow and seems in her career to constantly be placed in a position of justifying her personal opinions and views to include her opponents. Her own Libra sun and Mars oppose her Aries moon, which casts its shadow on these other planets in her chart. This creates a dynamic where her personal emotions will be required to be related to the greater good whether she likes it or not.

This shadow will require practice at dialogue and discussing feelings rather than a "my way or the highway" attitude. With your moon in Aries, you will find yourself in the position of the scapegoat (the ram, symbol of Aries, was a sacrificial animal to the new moon), and you will feel the need to prove that you are not to blame for other people's feelings and that you deserve to feel the way you do.

Example in Nature

Although positive reciprocity (reciprocal altruism) has been a focus of interest in evolutionary biology, negative reciprocity (retaliatory infliction of fitness reduction) has been largely ignored. In social animals, retaliatory aggression is common, individuals often punish other group members that infringe their interests, and punishment can cause subordinates to desist from behavior likely to reduce the fitness of dominant animals. Punishing strategies are used to establish and maintain dominance relationships, to discourage parasites and cheats, to discipline offspring or prospective sexual partners and to maintain cooperative behaviour.

— T. H. Clutton-Brock and G. A. Parker, "Punishment in Animal Societies," *Nature* 373, no. 6511 (January 19, 1995): 209–16

♏

Scorpio Moon Shadow

You Belong to Me

Birth Moon: Taurus ♉
Trigger: Jealousy
Boundary Needed: I respect your lack of interest

With the moon shadow in Scorpio, you will be emotionally triggered if your survival needs are threatened. If you have identified a resource, person, or situation as something you need to survive, this moon shadow will influence you to retaliate and defend your territory. If you experience loss or feel abandoned or like someone is trying to take your resources, the shadow will respond by prompting you to immediately engage in retribution, and you may be overwhelmed with feelings of jealousy. I feel like jealousy is a healthy emotion and is the heart's way of communicating a desire to the holder of this emotion. It is nothing to be ashamed of and need not lead to coveting. The key to this moon shadow is to listen to your feelings of jealousy to know what the heart wants. When you see something you want, you don't need to take it for another, but you do need to seek it for yourself.

If your feelings are strong enough to control another to be with you, listen to your feelings without projecting them on the individual. This is your emotional way of communicating what kind of relationship you need for you to feel safe and comfortable. If another will not provide you with that, you need to listen to your feelings and explore more secure territories. I once made a promise to myself never to fight to be where I wasn't wanted; if someone makes me feel insecure, I'll move on to more secure territories. Don't impose your needs on someone who won't provide for them; instead, seek those who respect you and would love to fulfill your survival needs. Then both parties are released and liberated.

Singer Chris Brown has this moon shadow. Whether or not allegations that he committed domestic violence are correct, it is apparent he is holding this shadow given his emotional responses in general and his tendency to express territoriality. Constant court reciprocity for Brown has attempted to assist him with this shadow by imposing boundaries and limits upon it where he could not, but repeated incidents show this shadow is still prevalent, and the court was unsuccessful at bringing it into healing for him. The best antidote is staying in one's own lane, and sometimes several years of celibacy will effectively remove the attachment to controlling other people. When you disengage your base need to control someone you are with by willingly being alone, you can come into mastery of this shadow. Step away entirely to gain perspective and release toxic behavior patterns, especially where consequences from the justice system and society aren't getting the message through.

Example in Nature

Territoriality is a link between social behavior (competition and dominance) and population control in many animals. Communities regulate their own numbers by the use of "conventionalized" competition, usually among males, for territory and the accompanying rights to food and (sometimes) mates. The winners are dominant animals and acquire social status, but since they are a fraction of the population, only a few community members get access to space, scarce resources, and females, thus limiting the size of the next generation. The next generation is also guaranteed food, because winners of territory spread themselves thinly over the terrain. Thus the habitat's food sources are not exploited beyond regenerative capacity, and a reasonable supply is ensured for the future.

— Julian Edney, quoted in Jason G. Goldman, "Defending Your Territory: Is Peeing on the Wall Just for the Dogs?," *Scientific American*, March 7, 2011

♐

Sagittarius Moon Shadow

The Drama Queen

Birth Moon: Gemini ♊
Trigger: Emotional restriction
Boundary Needed: I am included in the story

Gemini birth moon throws the Sagittarius shadow on its emotional face. Under the influence of the Sagittarius moon shadow, you may try to be philosophical about your own feelings and counsel others to avoid their feelings. This is the therapist or mythological scholar who wants to find emotions in stories, religions, or fables rather than her own heart. The Gemini moon seems fickle and polarized so natives can get uncomfortable with their emotional instability. A great way to deal with this difficulty is to place it outside the self and become fascinated with tales of those who have intense emotional outbursts. You may enjoy drama and soap opera; you may even try to force others or their partners into emotional displays so that you can watch them and then relate stories of interpersonal power struggles rather than acknowledging your own role in what went down.

The danger of the Sagittarius moon shadow is in seeking to transcend your own emotions and becoming the therapist friend who advises everyone in order to vicariously deal with your own issues. This causes dissociation and a neglect of your personal needs and emotions. The best way to transmute this shadow is connecting deeply to and expressing your personal feelings, not going around them and ignoring your heart to deal with the hearts of others. When you neglect yourself, and your own emotions finally rise to the surface, you may seek negative attention from those you previously helped deal with their emotions, in an effort to finally get some reciprocity. For example, if I constantly assist my sister with her breakup and speak with her about it, but I do not tell her that I am also going through a breakup and mention none of my feelings and then blow up and call her insensitive for ignoring what is happening in my life, is it her fault or mine? My shadow made me deal with my breakup vicariously through her and then I engaged another shadow behavior, the guilt trip, to make her feel bad for me even though I was staying hidden the whole time. You don't need to be everyone's parent, especially if you orphan yourself.

Sigmund Freud had this shadow moon and obviously became a therapist for others, owning this aspect of his shadow and making it serve him. He did not, however, care for his own feelings and emotions and died from inoperable cancer of the jaw, a cancer that may have grown due to lack of self-care. Obviously, the use of therapizing is beneficial, but find the limits and boundaries of your own emotional needs in your pursuits for amassing the puzzle pieces for others.

Example in Nature

An orangutan mother will stay in close contact with her baby for up to nine years—longer than almost all mammals other than humans. Much like humans, orangutans rely on their mothers to learn life skills—such as what to eat and where to find it—before they finally reach independence almost a decade after birth.

— Caroline Schuppli, "Orangutan Mothers Help Offspring to Learn," Max-Planck-Gesellschaft, December 8, 2021

♑

Capricorn Moon Shadow

Aloof and Breezy

Birth Moon: Cancer ♋
Trigger: Emotional responsibility
Boundary Needed: I can share my feelings

The emotions are very uncomfortable for sensual Capricorn, so this moon shadow tends to focus on feeling good and repressing bad feelings. Those with natal moon in Cancer deeply need to feel all their emotional range, which is considerable, and repression of negative feelings by this Capricorn moon shadow can lead to volcanic eruptions. When Earth keeps a lid on things, it can only last for so long before the liquid magma surfaces. Many repressive Capricorn actions can also lead to dysregulated coping mechanisms through hedonism, which is fine and often a good idea but not when habituated or in excess.

With your shadow moon in Capricorn, you can become controlling of others' expressions of negative feelings because you don't want to feel them; you want to feel good. Uncomfortable with your own and others' emotional expressions, you can become something of an emotional dictator, taking it upon yourself to punish others for displays or call them childish. The hermit, taciturn nature of Capricorn shadow moon can quickly make you feel gloomy and pessimistic due to an overabundant storage of unexpressed negativity. Purposeful expression in a contained or creative fashion can do wonders to transmute this moon shadow. Setting a space where it's OK to be angry, to be sad, to have grief is essential for this moon, as well as finding ways that allow the free flow of feelings to prevent an overwhelming emotional eruption. By allowing channels of intimacy to flow, the holder of this shadow will feel less isolated and be better able to hold space for the emotional expressions of others.

Sacagawea who assisted Lewis and Clark had a Cancer moon and a depth of feeling and emotion. She was only a teenager at the time; she had been kidnapped and had her first child, which she brought along. She put aside her own emotions and did what was needed and pragmatic according to most accounts, providing incredible service to the mission. Famously in their journals, Lewis and Clark noticed that they never saw her show any emotion, with the exception of when she was reunited with her family.

Example in Nature

In J.D. Salinger's Catcher in the Rye, *the novel's troubled antihero, Holden Caulfield, gets into a strange discussion with a cab driver in New York City. Wondering what happens to the fish when a large pond in New York's Central Park freezes over for the winter, the agitated cabbie informs Holden that the fish freeze right along with the pond. When the ice melts, the fish thaw out and go on their way.*

Can fish and other aquatic creatures really survive in a state of suspended animation until spring? The surprising answer is yes, sometimes. It is true that some fish can spend the winter frozen in ice and come out swimming once the ice melts. Not all fish get caught in the ice, of course. Ponds and lakes freeze from the top down, meaning that beneath the icy surface there is usually a layer of liquid water where fish swim. . . .

Moreover, some fish contain a kind of antifreeze substance that allows them to survive very cold conditions.

Much like bears and other hibernating animals, some ice-bound fish are able to shut down basic bodily functions, slow their metabolism, and enter a dormant state. Cold but not frozen, these fish bide their time until spring, when the ice disappears.

— Don Glass, "Frozen Fish," *A Moment of Science,*
Indiana Public Media, September 27, 2003

♒

Aquarius Moon Shadow

Spare Me

Birth Moon: Leo ♌
Trigger: Leave me out of this
Boundary Needed: I can come back from dissociation

Those with birth moon in Leo are very emotional and fiery by nature, seeking an ideal self or ego. The shadow in Aquarius is very analytical and intellectual, needing to serve others. This shadow moon forces the Leo moon natives out of their comfort zone of deep feeling and into the ambiguity of outer space and total imagination. This combination can make for some delusions of grandeur, with projections that blow emotions out of proportion.

The moon and Aquarius energy have a hard time with each other. The moon wants to feel, as does Leo energy, but those with Aquarius moon shadow must use their intellect to pick apart emotions and create a critical theory through which they can observe emotions from a distance. This traps the self and the emotions away from each other, with the mind's eye in the middle, watching them both. By not being immersed in emotions you can learn much from them, but the physical body can feel disconnected, and you can become stuck in your head and cynical, rather than living life and experiencing things on any level of depth.

This moon shadow is a very good placement for writers and artists as the emotions can lift them to great heights of imagination, but it can completely remove them from objective reality. Here the shadow can link the native to the muse in a dramatic Shakespearean psychodrama way that is undeniably powerful and very much like a soap opera that pulls you in.

Kurt Vonnegut Jr. had this moon shadow, and it served him well in his writing, to great acclaim. One might think this was all his own doing, but upon inspection his mother had tried to be a writer and passed away from suicide. In a way Vonnegut's Aquarius shadow served him well by taking up his mother's passion and serving her and the community by sharing his thoughts.

Example in Nature

Patients with complex dissociative disorders remain in alternating psychophysiological states which are discrete, discontinuous, and resistant against integrative tendencies. In this contribution, a parallel is drawn between animal defensive and recuperative states that are evoked in the face of severe threat and the characteristic responses of dissociative disorder patients as displayed in major dissociative states. Empirical data and clinical observations seem to be supportive of the idea that there are similarities between freezing, concomitant development of analgesia and anesthesia, and acute pain in threatened animals and severely traumatized human beings.

— Ellert R. S. Nijenhuis, Johan Vaderlinden, and Philip Spinhoven, "Animal Defensive Reactions as a Model for Trauma-Induced Dissociative Reactions," *Journal of Traumatic Stress* 11 (1998): 243–60

♓

Pisces Moon Shadow

Hungry Eyes

Birth Moon: Virgo ♍
Trigger: Neediness
Boundary Needed: I will mind my own business

Pisces shadow moon is born from a Virgo moon natally. The Virgo moon articulates and analyzes its emotions, seeking to bring them to a perfected state. The Pisces moon shadow seeks to bring the emotions into oblivion through total connection with others and a loss of articulation. Those with this moon are empathic, due to the Pisces shadow, and tend to hyper fixate on the emotions of others. The need here is to expand the emotions past the self, not focus on other people's shadows. We all have shadows; the purpose of this work isn't to encourage anyone to go about eyeballing everyone's shadows and imposing on them. The purpose is also not to get all judgy on your own shadow and be ashamed of it. The Pisces shadow can cause an individual to identify with the shadows of others and take them on as her own, consequently experiencing a strange mix of guilt and shame.

With this Pisces shadow, you may mistake, empathetically, a behavior that is subconscious in someone else as belonging to you, or caused by you, and find yourself relating to the other in a strange milieu of guilt and shame. You are seeking, ultimately, to harmonize with the other but may find yourself in a codependent dance. Emotions can take on a contagious property for empaths. Those with this shadow who are trying to resolve conflict in a group may, in their effort to manage the emotional energy, take on more damage than others.

The current Dalai lama, Tenzin Gyatso, has this shadow moon placement, and one might say he has taken on the shadow of his entire nation as an empathetic leader. One of the meditation techniques he utilizes is analytical meditation, which engages the Virgo aspect of his lunar energy, while his other practice of emptiness employs the Pisces need to obliterate the self and all feeling. Gyatso identifies as communist in a testament to the emotional shadow here, which seeks to serve and unify with one and all in an amorphous and ambiguous egoless place.

Example in Nature

Cannibalism usually occurs when the birds are stressed by a poor management practice. Once becoming stressed, one bird begins picking the feathers, comb, toes or vent of another bird. Once an open wound or blood is visible on the bird, the vicious habit of cannibalism can spread rapidly through the entire flock. If you notice the problem soon after it begins, cannibalism can be held in check. However, if the problem is allowed to get out of hand it can be very costly.

— Phillip Clauer, "Poultry Cannibalism: Prevention and Treatment," Penn State Extension, April 22, 2016

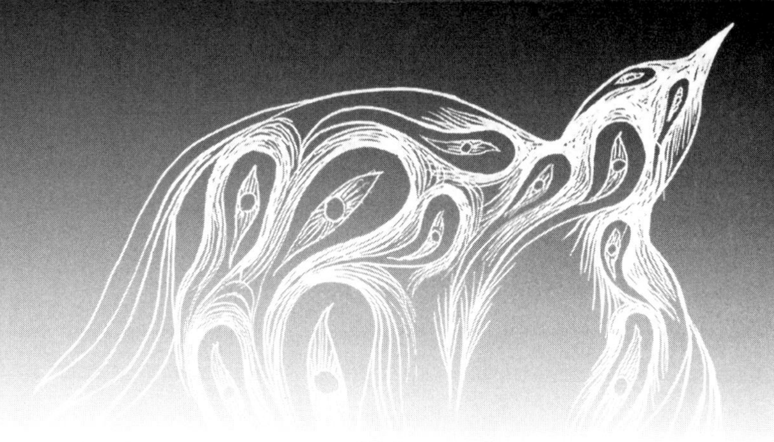

Mercury Shadows

The Mind Parasite

> *Any attempt at using logic as a tool (organon) in order to extend and expand our knowledge, at least supposedly, can end in nothing but idle talk, where one can assert or, if one prefers, deny, anything one likes, with a certain semblance of plausibility.*
>
> Immanuel Kant, *Critique of Pure Reason*

In astrology, Mercury represents the mind, how we think and the forming of our awareness. In most pagan and indigenous creation myths, all matter is formed from mind and consciousness. The mind and mental state are heavily involved in our ability to receive input and data from our surroundings as well as in forming the paradigms we use to interpret the data gathered through our senses. The majority of paradigms are formed from ideas, and so depending on our worldview, we can have vastly different interpretations of the data we receive as we journey through the earth plane. Most of our behavior is based on our ideas, which influence us more profoundly than we realize.

Holding a false concept or untrue idea and relying on that to guide our actions can be as dangerous as a violent reactionary impulse or

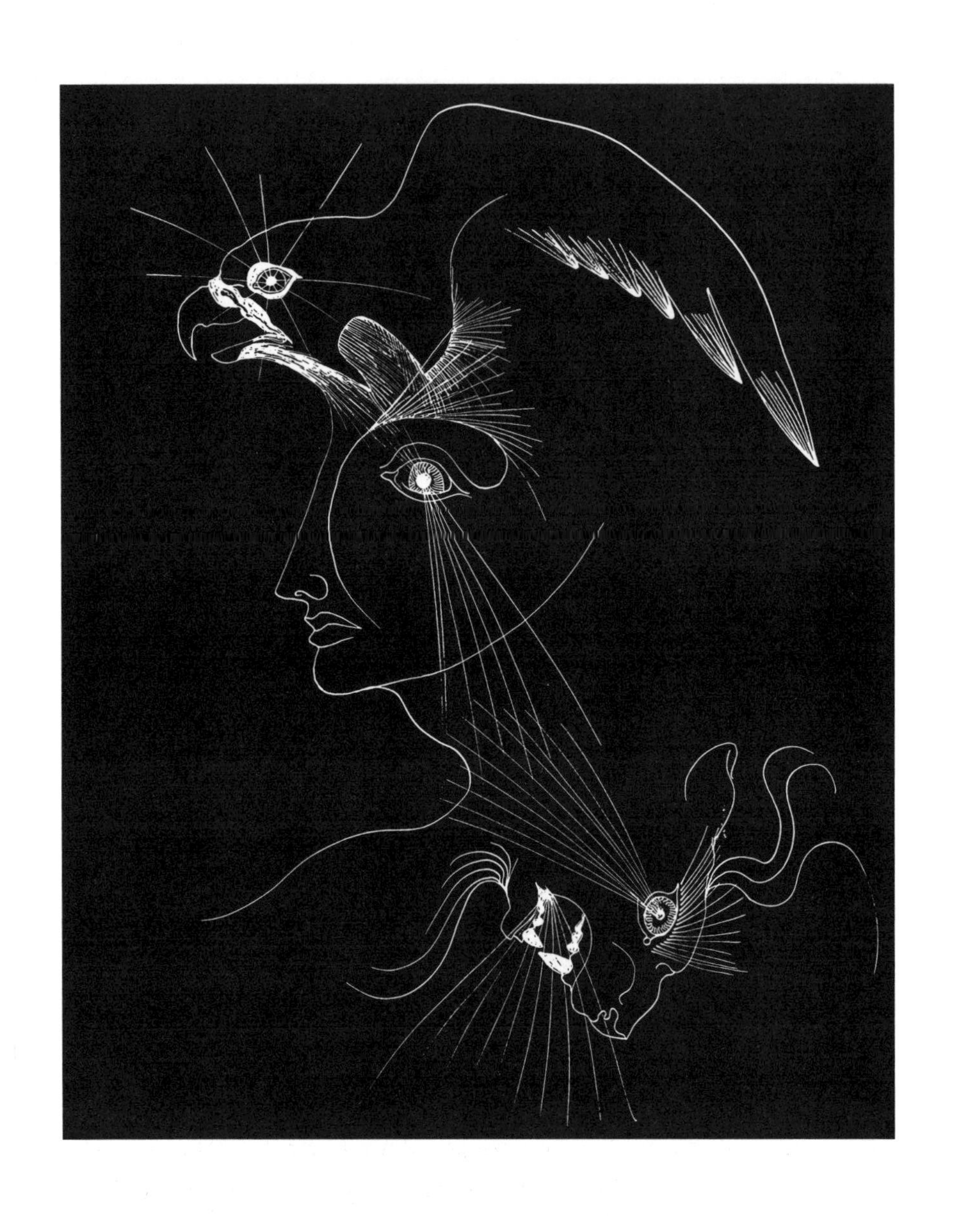

action. Western philosophies, as they spread throughout the world, propagated the idea that human beings were the only life-forms in the natural world gifted with intelligence and self-awareness. This tragic error overtook humanity and has taken years to correct, and we are still under the sway of this ignorance in many places. Placing human beings above nature (by our own mind, simply because we decide it is so) is a shadow form. Separating ourselves from the natural world, as something different and superior to it, creates disease (ecological disasters) in the same way that seeing the mind as separate from the body is harmful.

Parasites are organisms that infect or live symbiotically on other life-forms and feed off their vitality. In the mind, a thought can drain and siphon all the energy from a perfectly good intelligence to the point of destroying it. The mind, especially for the intellectually gifted, or those who engage in thinking pursuits, can become host to a plague of locusts, ceaseless swarms of parasitizing thoughts that force the mind into madness. Parasites in nature can exert an influence upon the life-forms they inhabit and can compel them to act, or think thoughts that are not their own. Mice infected by *Toxoplasma gondii* lose their fear of cats, for example. The *cordyceps* fungus when it infects an ant first causes it to become hyperactive, foraging night and day, and then sends the ant away from its colony; the ant then climbs onto a twig and becomes the paralyzed host for the fungus feeding on its insides. This fungus compelling an organism to a suicidal action through mind control exhibits a terrifying power over the natural instinct of that creature to live and stay alive. In a similar way, parasitic thoughts can compel someone to do things without his or her conscious awareness and manipulate the instincts unnaturally on a depth we can barely fathom, all from a thought or idea.

Nature is intelligent, so smart that it made that mind within your skull, and many life-forms other than ourselves think, have self-awareness and an ego, and have creative, complex, and recursive abilities. There is no reason to think we are unique in this. Everyone knows dolphins, elephants, and chimpanzees have exhibited varying degrees of intelligence, and research has shown that even songbirds have self-awareness. But take a moment to consider the intelligence of the cosmic bodies—the sun, the planets, the stars—and expand your concept of thought to include these phenomena. If an amoeba can exhibit a decision, if a photon can be seen to make a choice, understand that many entities are capable of such gifts. Let's see how our minds mirror them and how much of our thinking is not our own. What thought have you had in your life that you can truly claim is *your* thought? Take a moment to contemplate this. Who is doing your thinking? You may just find that it is mind itself thinking your thoughts, and that those thoughts do not belong to you any more than the oceans do.

The Mercury shadow is the mind realm of thought forms, imagination, and egregores—esoteric concepts representing nonphysical entities. The planet Mercury is conscious and able to communicate. Mind is knowing and seeks knowledge in its love affairs and refuses to see itself as ignorant or uncertain; here we find the mind's shadow—in its doubt. The shadow of Mercury rears its head when we do not know; when we fall into doubt and uncertainty, we go into this place of shadow. The flip side of mind is the influence of delusion, which invariably leads it to a labyrinth of mirrors that every adept must navigate as they attempt to unify with the creator, or source.

Mercury, the heavy metallic element, is a very reactive and volatile substance, meaning it easily evaporates. It is the only metal that is liquid at room temperature. This fluid element is ever moving, never standing still, and likes to adhere to anything that touches it, clinging to it and becoming part of it. Your mind is like the element: it will easily attach to every thing, just like mercury. Raise your awareness to this. Mercury is restless, flitting from place to place looking for something to cling to and merge with. Mind can carry you, when used as a focused fuel, to the outer reaches of consciousness itself or spiral you into a never-ending whirlpool of useless thoughts that repeat ad nauseam.

When we approach the Mercury shadow it is important to note that the mind can be thrown into disarray at the negation of itself, so it is good to employ systems to help us in our calculations. Using Socratic techniques and astrology can provide helpful parameters if we are stuck in one-sided thinking or need to know the mental issues we deal with are much larger than our own limited perceptions.

> *The idea of self-emancipation through knowledge, which was the basic idea of the Enlightenment, is in itself a powerful enemy of fanaticism; for it makes us try hard to detach ourselves or even to dissociate ourselves from our own ideas (in order to look at them critically) instead of identifying ourselves with them. And the recognition of the sometimes overwhelming historical power of ideas should teach us how important it is to free ourselves from the overpowering influence of false or wrong ideas. In the interests of the quest for truth and of our liberation from errors we have to train ourselves to view our own favourite ideas just as critically as those we oppose.*
>
> KARL R. POPPER, *IN SEARCH OF A BETTER WORLD: LECTURES AND ESSAYS FROM THIRTY YEARS*

As human beings, our minds remain a mystery to us, on the whole. We struggle to understand consciousness, but despite thousands of years of attempting to explain it through myth and scientific experiments, we have yet to wrangle or lasso the thing that does our thinking. At once a planet and a metal, the mysteries of Mercury present us with some clues to the shadowy entity behind all of the thoughts we will ever form. The shadow of an astute Mercury are things such as arrogance, insanity, madness, cognitive fallacies, and many traps in imaginary perceptions. The realm of mind takes down many otherwise perfectly stable human beings. We approach the Mercury shadow and explore the treacherous realities of the mental realm, without stigmatizing or judging mental illness.

> *To rule by fettering the mind through fear of punishment in another world, is just as base as to use force. . . . Reserve your right to think, for even to think wrongly is better than not to think at all.*
>
> HYPATIA

In my practices I see how certain Mercury placements can contribute to tendencies and habits of thinking as well as pointing to how to ameliorate these thought patterns. In modern psychology, techniques are used to interact with many mercurial events such as hypnosis, cognitive behavior therapy, EMDR (eye movement and desensitization and reprocessing), and counseling, to name a few. If you are suffering some severe Mercury and mental challenges, please seek help from many sources and do not feel shame. If anything, I wish to communicate the level of this shadow is large and ancient; it isn't personal. It is no failing on your part to struggle with this shadow. Take a look at the patterns your thinking may be taking due to the shadow cast by Mercury.

Love conquers all—intellects.

George Hammond

♈

Aries Mercury Shadow

A One-Sided Argument

Birth Mercury: Libra ♎
Parasite: Arrogance

Mercury shadow in Aries places the birth Mercury in Libra. People with Mercury in Libra are loathe to make a decision, preferring instead to see possibilities, and so the shadow in Aries is there to force them to one side. A decision that comes from deliberation or a fear of that deliberation can grow and become more forceful in the mind, such that the decision-maker justifies to himself or begins to think that the decision is good for everyone or that it is good for him to make the decisions for everyone. The mind projects the need to make a choice, even if it is a bad one, to solve the problem of not being able to settle on a side. The Mercury shadow in Aries can grow into a beast that feels it must make all the choices and take all the action and becomes fearful of considering options presented by others: this is the "my way or the highway" attitude. Making decisions becomes a coping mechanism to hide the insecurity that arises from careful thinking and including others in the decision-making. The difficult process of deciding on one or the other option may haunt Mercury in Libra natives for all their days, so they are often relieved to let the shadow Mercury in Aries step in and take control.

Often, due to the arrogance and lack of consideration, the decision that this Mercury shadow makes is not met with praise and adulation, or may not even be what the decision-maker wants most of the time. Now she is embarrassed and not sure what to do as a result of backlash from poor decision-making. Mercury in Aries will cause a fight in this way and blame the terrible decision on the other, finally including the other in the process at the end to make it seem like it was all the other's idea, now that the outcome has gone south.

Actor Will Smith has this Mercury shadow and is no doubt haunted by his decision, influenced by his partner, to assault comedian Chris Rock in front of an audience, regardless of his partner's needs.

The courage to voice personal opinions is what the Aries Mercury shadow is trying to achieve, and leading with that can cause fewer arguments and misunderstandings for this placement. To heal the shadow Mercury in Aries, make more decisions and execute them based on deliberation rather than forcing your voice through, and don't be shy to let your mind think its own thoughts for a while. Consider what thoughts are yours and what thoughts are coming from your partner, which you may be becoming dependent on. Be cautious about only reaching a firm personal decision in retaliation for not liking an earlier decision that was made under the pressure and responsibility of choice.

Example in Nature

Primate grooming interactions thus represent an ideal opportunity for examining the flexibility of the decision-making process underlying partner choice. . . .

Here, we look at partner choice as a decision-making event, where an individual has multiple potential partners before deciding

> *to groom one of them. At the same time, all potential partners who were not chosen witness the choice as bystanders. . . .*
>
> *In grooming, bystanders can impact the outcome of interactions by actively disrupting or joining grooming, or by inciting partner switching by either of the groomers. . . . Partner switching of the groomee could be more likely if attractive bystanders are around, leading for example chimpanzees to invest less in a grooming bout if high-ranking bystanders are present.*
>
> — Alexander Mielke et al., "Flexible Decision-making in Grooming Partner Choice in Sooty Mangabeys and Chimpanzees," *Royal Society of Open Science* 5, no. 7 (July 11, 2018)

♉

Taurus Mercury Shadow

Curiosity Killed the Cat

Birth Mercury: Scorpio ♏
Parasite: Intrigue

It's a good thing that natives with Mercury in Scorpio seem to have nine lives because their snoopy, nosy nature will get them into a lot of sticky situations. These natives are like Nancy Drew or the Hardy boys, eager detectives addicted to solving mysteries. The shadow Mercury in Taurus will introduce fear, scarcity thinking, fear of loss, and suspicion to the mind in an obsessive-compulsive fashion, creating puzzles for the mind to solve. Thoughts will stray toward tracking motives and connecting dots; they maniacally want to solve the puzzle of why others, and the world at large, act the way they do. This Mercury shadow can be conducive to conspiracy theories, conjecture, and speculation. Laugh all you like, there is a deep need for this type of cognition as it is closely related to scientific theories and inventiveness, thinking outside the box. When the Taurus Mercury shadow interferes in this mind, creating suspicion and paranoia, the mental waters grow too muddy to be navigable, and the native Mercury in Scorpio needs to slow down and gain perspective.

Mercury in Scorpio wants to get to the bottom of things, to find things kept secret and hidden, and those with this position usually wind up solving some of the greatest mysteries of reality, or at the least they become good detectives. But when the Taurus shadow steps in, the individual can place the focus in the wrong direction of accusation and intrigue rather than on wisdom and knowledge. The Mercury shadow in Taurus will tend to concentrate on resource-based intrigue, involving loved ones; nevertheless, this focus can certainly extend into larger areas. The key is to understand others rather than target them and come into realizations and achieving wisdom rather than trying to expose some criminal underpinning. It may very well be that this shadow assists to uncover a criminal case, and that is a beautiful thing, but to avoid becoming consumed and lost in the chase, the holder of this shadow must expand out of the drama.

I have this Mercury shadow in my birth chart, and I can attest that I am drawn to intrigue like flies to poop. I share this placement with Hedy Lamarr, whose mind was equally focused on solving problems and ended up basically inventing the internet as a result of her tireless mind. Investigating and researching secrets and taboo drives my mind to a fault. If I am unable to find an answer to a query, I admit it takes over my mind, like a parasite, until I am able to find satisfaction, sometimes through years of compulsive research. While serving me greatly, my mind can also tend to keep going far beyond where it is needed, to both accomplishment and detriment. The key to transmuting this Mercury shadow, I have found, is to leave well enough alone and find satisfaction when you come to a reasonable conclusion. I am a bit of a gumshoe in terms of snooping into things that are beyond my scope, and I am also a professional secret keeper for my clients, being employed to solve their mysteries.

Example in Nature

*An international team of researchers have now found evidence for the existence of a "curiosity-gene" in a songbird, the great tit (*Parus major*). The gene (Drd4) carries the building instructions* *for a receptor in the brain, which forms the docking station for the neurotransmitter dopamine. Birds with a specific variant of this dopamine receptor D4 gene show a stronger exploratory behaviour than individuals with other variants (Proceedings of the Royal Society London B, 2 May 2007).*

— Bart Kempenaers, "'Personality-Gene' Makes Songbirds Curious," Max-Planck-Gesellschaft, May 2, 2007

♊

Gemini Mercury Shadow

The Minah Bird

Birth Mercury: Sagittarius ♐
Parasite: Plagiarism

With this Mercury shadow, the focus of the mind is drawn toward parroting data rather than understanding or knowing something through intensive study or wisdom earned over time. All the knowledge of the ages, all the secret teachings, are turned to serve the vanity of the individual, who completely misses the meaning of the words repeated and certainly is not the originator of any of these teachings. Often we will see this placement in public speakers, writers, and singers, who are saying words written by others and do not live the words they speak. There is a giant chasm between what they say and what they do. Often, they will steal words from others to seem wise, when they are really an empty shell.

Britney Spears has this placement, and as someone who grew so much, so fast, extending around the globe and becoming a star, who can go bigger? But the ungrounding nature of shadow Mercury in Gemini spread her mind too wide and thin. Spears has been accused several times of stealing her songs from others, and her mind has destabilized more than a few times. When a native of this Mercury shadow does come upon some wisdom, the ego will seek to own the wisdom and present it as original. Albert Hoffmann also had this Mercury shadow, and we might be convinced that it was he who discovered LSD, according to him anyway. But anyone familiar with the Eleusinian mysteries and the drink *kykeon* knows that goddess worshippers long ago spoke of the psychedelic fruits of the ergot, and it was well known to be drunk by initiates, long before he claimed to "discover it."

Example in Nature

Apparently, cuckoos have evolved the ability to mimic the eggs of certain other bird species, and those are the species that they seek out when invading nests. Secreting pigment in their oviducts, the parasitic birds can closely replicate the host birds' eggs. A cuckoo can dart into an unattended nest, snatch up an egg, lay a close copy and be gone within 10 seconds. After hatching, some cuckoo chicks (though not the great spotted) instinctively shove their foster siblings and remaining eggs out of the nest, so as to have all the food to themselves.

— Frank Kuznik, "Bullies of the Bird World," National Wildlife Federation, August 1, 1997

♋

Cancer Mercury Shadow

Doomsday

Birth Mercury: Capricorn ♑
Parasite: The unnecessary destroyer

Cancer shadow of Mercury is born from a natal Capricorn Mercury. Too much focus on needs by Capricorn stifles the emotions, which burble up in irrational thinking and controlling thoughts. Some fear and paranoia can result if emotional thoughts do not receive expression or at least acknowledgment. All work and no play makes Jack a dull boy, as we know. The shadow of Capricorn Mercury is instinct itself, and the danger is that the impulse will begin to drive the individual. Emotional impulses can gain the better of this native in desperate decision-making; when instinctual emotional needs are ignored, they take over actions and thinking.

The heavy weight of negative thoughts can create a downward spiral that can consume Mercury shadow in Cancer into depression. Negative mind-sets can make or break thinking activity. The ability to negate things is very important for any thought, which is the main purpose of this book; however, having a mind-set of "no way out" and total failure will cause the mind to destroy all possibilities. Reaching a negative state that erases everything, including real occurrences, is an illusion. This parasite becomes a kind of useless delusion that does not contribute and poops on everyone's party; it becomes a contagion of negativity, infecting all who step across its path. Here the mind refuses to permit any positive thought of hope to enter; the purpose of this shadow is to avoid disappointment. By adapting a defense strategy of never having any expectation or thought of something good, it will never have to feel its heart sink into sadness because it will place itself there willingly and so have control over its annihilation.

Joseph Stalin had this Mercury shadow placement and was one of the most destructive rulers in history. He sadly fell victim to this doomsday parasite, engaging in incorrect thinking and decision-making. Though seen as a hero to some, it is hard to ignore the millions who died in the Ukrainian famine, also known as the Holodomor famine, under the apocalyptic projections of this leader's mind. Stalin could not permit any other way of thinking or flexibility, even when people kept dying in the hundreds of thousands, he clung to his paranoia. However, given what Stalin went through in his upbringing, beaten and abandoned by an alcoholic father, it is hard to project blame. He was jailed repeatedly for organizing illegal strikes and eventually exiled to a remote village near the Arctic Circle; all these hardships in his early life deeply contributed to his holding this shadow. It is important to gain perspective of this Mercury placement with the Cancer shadow that we may not make the same errors when placed in the same shoes. Sometimes it seems like there is only one option, one destiny, when really there are lots of choices and decisions to make; you just have to open your mind.

Example in Nature

More recently, a 2014 hippo attack in the same country left 12 children and an adult dead, according to AFP. The hippo flipped a boat transporting the group across a river en route to school, though the AFP report did not clarify whether the students drowned or were mauled, either by a single hippo or by a pod. "Ultimately it was 12 students, including seven girls and five boys, who died after the attack," Minister of Secondary Education Aichatou Oumani told AFP at the time. . . . He told AFP that locals like Fall continue to endure the wrath of violent hippos because the river is their only source of income. "They are evil monsters who attack us night and day," he told AFP. "Because of them, we haven't been fishing. There aren't any more fish at the market." But killing hippos is not an option, AFP reports, because they're a protected species in Senegal.

— Peter Holley, "'They Are Evil Monsters That Attack Us Night and Day': Senegal's Terrifying Killer Hippo Problem," Washington Post, May 30, 2016

♌

Leo Mercury Shadow

Mind Games

Birth Mercury: Aquarius ♒
Parasite: Pride

Natal Mercury in Aquarius gives a gift of an overactive mind; Leo in Mercury's shadow creates delusions of grandeur and mistakes the hive mind for the idea it generated itself. This shadow causes the imagination of Mercury in Aquarius to turn upon the ego itself. We all like to imagine who we are; we all see ourselves in a certain way. Here the mind creates an ego and identity that is heroic and a leader. This shadow can create problems when the ego becomes more than it is in reality, thus causing a hard confrontation with failure or when others do not support the image of the self that the mind shadow of Mercury in Leo has created.

Because Aquarius is already nonconformist and Leo focuses on the self, the danger of the Mercury shadow in Leo is that the self separates from others and attempts to go it alone. This will limit the amazing ability of Mercury in Aquarius to serve the community and do something for the greater good. The positive dipole of mind here is pushing to serve all of humanity, and the shadow is pulling the mind to serve the ego, the self and the self's image. The holder here must take real action, not imaginary, to put its intellect into the service of others and lead by action, not by talking. The shadow mind here will separate from popular opinion, but the native of this placement needs others for it to accomplish her mission. There must be careful limits on how much is taken and how much is given.

The Leo Mercury shadow demands that the individual find courage in being herself and battle her nature that seeks to give to others. The center is found between self and other not necessarily through compromise, but by sharing in an open space in a progressive fashion. This will take no small amount of labor to bridge the unique independent thoughts of the Mercury Leo shadow with others who do not think in the same way. The remedy for this shadow is communication and careful articulation of self-expression. Take your time; do not release your thoughts to others until they are well formulated and established. The task for those with the Mercury Leo shadow is to carefully build and substantiate the ideas they retrieve from their imagination.

Thomas Edison gained a controversial reputation in his lifetime, partly due to the lengths he was willing to go in order to obtain a patent. I was not present and have no judgment, but tales of Edison hiring Nikola Tesla to create patents and then refusing payment seem to be holding this shadow.* Ultimately, this forced Tesla to strike out on his own (to his betterment), but these patents were only the beginning. According to most sources, Edison chose patents that were slightly incomplete and then improved upon them to secure the end result and

*Albinko Hasic, "Why Scientists, not Investors, Should Decide the Future of Technology," *The Washington Post*, December 2, 2019.

credit for the patent—examples include the light bulb; the battery, which was probably from Alessandro Volta; and the phonograph, probably from Edouard Leon Scott.* Some controversial claims even state that Edison may have murdered the original inventor of the motion picture, Louis Le Prince, in order to claim the patent.† True, his hard work secured the end result, but some critics complain that he opportunistically preyed upon failed patents and then solved them. Regardless, this portrays the shadow of seeking a way to earn the collective's support without making something all your own.

Example in Nature

> *Piracy, or "kleptoparasitism" to use the technical term, is quite common in the animal world, occurring in everything from mollusks to mammals and 197 species of birds (representing 33 families). The slender-winged frigatebirds of tropical seas are so adept that an entire pirate ship has become embedded in their name. Benjamin Franklin cited the Bald Eagle's habit of stealing fish as a reason not to use it as the national symbol of the United States. . . . To scientists, kleptoparasitism is a curious, genre-bending kind of behavior. It's not foraging; it's not predation; and it's not even parasitism in the bloodsucking, leechlike way we typically think of it. When kleptoparasites rob a "host" of its energy, they do it before the poor animal has even ingested it.*
>
> — Hugh Powell, "Winged Pirates: Kleptoparasitism as a Lifestyle," The Cornell Lab, All about Birds, October 15, 2009

*Brooke Berger, "Many Minds Produced the Light That Illuminated America," *U.S. News and World Report*, March 21, 2013; Isidor Buchmann, "BU-101: When Was the Battery Invented?" Battery University website, last updated February 22, 2022; National Park Service, U.S. Department of the Interior, "Origins of the Sound Recording: The Inventors," July 17, 2017.

†Oliver-James Campbell, "Was Thomas Edison Guilty of Murder?," *The Spectator*, April 16, 2022.

♍ Virgo Mercury Shadow

Paralysis by Analysis

Birth Mercury: Pisces ♓
Parasite: The critic

The shadow Mercury in Virgo is very good at seeing what is wrong with something. The only problem is, Pisces Mercury natives sometimes see things they don't like about themselves and project those things onto others. A tendency to fixate on what's wrong in order to solve it or fix it takes over this mind parasite. There is a fixation on fixing problems. Obviously, it is beneficial to be able to solve problems, but people aren't problems to be solved. Your Mercury shadow may cause you to become obsessively attached to an individual you see needs fixing, when really you just had some failing or imperfection of your own that you won't accept and so seek to shame another to get the monkey off your own back and hand it to someone else. All people should take heed: if you have the tendency to offer unsolicited advice to people, or point out what is wrong with them, this is a toxic behavior and you would do well to turn that eye upon yourself. If someone asks you, offer a nonjudgmental perspective as an observer; do not impose your system of values upon another.

The danger of the shadow Mercury in Virgo is an inability to accept anything as complete. An undue need for perfection through perception will cause a relentless pursuit of improvement that can prevent completion and accomplishment. In the Bible, God accepted the world as it was and rested, viewing the project of creation as complete, and this has some wisdom in it for those who have difficulty releasing the grasp on what they have been placed in charge of. Although this gives a gift and an ability to do things well, you could miss the forest for the trees, and all the birth placement of Mercury in Pisces really wants is to bring something to an end and release the mind from thinking. Work hard at transmuting this shadow to permit yourself to rest and bring things to completion, even if they aren't quite done.

Musician Kurt Cobain had this Mercury shadow, and it may have contributed to his feeling that he needed to bring something to an end, after the parasite would not release his obsession with fixing things or with things left undone. The balance is needed here between making and ending, and if we are unable to bring things to an end, equilibrium steps in. We can see in many of the works Cobain created a feeling of incompleteness. In lyrics to his songs such as "Milk It," inferences to parasites and suicide are present. Although I don't like to read into art and see it as expression rather than prophecy, we can see that his mind was holding on to thought-forms that he needed to express.

To transmute this Mercury shadow, permit yourself to rest and not always to grow and achieve. Accept and celebrate your accomplishments and feel satisfied with them, even if they are not perfect. The end can come if you accept things and fulfill rather than finish. If you see someone holding this shadow, encourage him to celebrate his works even if he feels incomplete and remind him we are all works in progress. The only thing finished is death itself; till then we get to keep growing, and what a gift that is.

Example in Nature

"When we think about smart animals, we usually think about dolphins, crows, primates," said Marcelo Araya-Salas. . . . "But it's everywhere. Every animal is going to gain some clear advantage from learning about their environment. As behavioral ecologists, we are starting to unveil this other side of animal behavior.

"There was one male who got all the trials right; he never missed the rewarding feeder," Araya-Salas said. "And there was a male that did no better than you would expect by chance. So there was the whole range of performance on display." . . .

The researchers also noted that males with better spatial memory also sang more consistent songs. It's thought this ability is attractive to females, because it means the singer sounds less like an inexperienced youngster and more like a veteran survivor. . . .

"We always think we are the smart species—we are the ones with game-changing intelligence." Araya-Salas said. "But it's a matter of degree, and we are more similar to the other animals than we think."

— Hugh Powell, "Spatial Memory Allows Hummingbirds to Rule the Roost," Cornell Chronicle, February 8, 2018

♎

Libra Mercury Shadow

Judgy, the Judge

Birth Mercury: Aries ♈
Parasite: I think therefore I am

Mercury shadow in Libra comes with those who have a natal Mercury in Aries. The birth Mercury in Aries creates an individual with a mind that is stubborn, headstrong but decisive and gifted with the ability to execute his or her thoughts, an executive placement usually showing someone in a commander position. But in a twist of fate, the shadow Mercury in Libra ensures the natal Mercury in Aries will not be able to make a choice without others' approval. The shadow placement forces you to take into account the opinions of others when leading the team, even though you can make your own decisions very well. There is a limit placed here by the shadow parasite, pushing the mind to consider others, though this is not its nature.

The danger of this shadow placement is judgment and judgmental thinking. The mind parasite here tends to observe and decide things, as a judge might in a court, but perhaps may be doing this rashly, without gathering all the data. A real judge maintains integrity by seriously considering and weighing all the sides of the story before forming a conclusion; a false judge will leap over the truth, over reality, to promote his own bias or opinion before he has heard the whole story. There are two sides to every story, and the shadow placement here is making the mind see the miles walked in the other person's shoes, as uncomfortable as this may seem. Take heed all who read and understand that when someone judges you, there will be an urgency to tell your side; if you deny anyone her right to have her own version of the story, you absolutely are not fit to judge.

Since it is usually forced through the shadow, it takes quite a while to understand what is happening, so those with the Mercury shadow Libra will usually justify their judgments in self-defense (an Aries tendency) before being able to reconcile them peacefully. To transmute this shadow, spend time considering and listening to all sides of a story before arriving at your decision. The way out of selfish thinking is to include the other while figuring out if your thought is true beyond yourself. Even if you are very smart, two heads are better than one.

This is the Mercury placement of Rene Descartes, who equated identity with thinking and thinking with being, though few of his thoughts actually had anything to do with him personally. Here the mental focus is so driven to the individual, in a selfish way, that it will cause destruction in the warlike fashion of Aries. Descartes shifted thinking dramatically away from nature and spirituality to cold rationalism and decision-making in a toxic fashion that has left a long legacy. However, it is clear that Descartes was feeling the Libra shadow here because he decided to be fair: he needed to know if his thoughts were true in comparison with the greater collective consensus and how he could measure and test that. Descartes had so much trouble trying to discern the best way to make a decision and figure out what was true that he methodically developed a system of thought experiments that eventually were honed into the scientific method, a huge contribution and progeny of his engagement with this shadow. There were many flaws in his system, and it discounted many things other than mind and thoughts itself, which perhaps could have been avoided if he had included some other people in his thinking instead of his overwhelming self-focus.

Example in Nature

Certain personality traits (e.g. anxiousness, fearfulness), are known to affect the cognitive processing of environmental stimuli, such as the judgement of ambiguous stimuli (judgement bias). Our aim was to assess if personality traits are predictive of a more or less "pessimistic" or "optimistic" judgement bias in the domestic dog. . . . Linear Mixed Model analyses revealed that dogs scoring higher on sociability, excitability and non-social-fear had shorter response latencies to bowls in an ambiguous location, indicating a more "optimistic" bias. In contrast, dogs scoring higher on separation-related-behaviour and dog-directed-fear/aggression traits were more likely to judge an ambiguous stimulus as leading to a negative outcome, indicating a more "pessimistic" bias.

— Shanis Barnard et al., "Personality Traits Affecting Judgement Bias Task Performance in Dogs (*Canis familiaris*)," *Scientific Reports* 8, no. 6660 (April 2018)

♏

Scorpio Mercury Shadow

Muddy Waters

Birth Mercury: Taurus ♉
Parasite: Obsessive compulsion

With a Mercury shadow in Scorpio, the mind enters fully into Earth and the delight of the senses. When the metal mercury joins together with minerals in Earth, it binds to them deeply, forming compounds such as cinnabar, which was an important ingredient in the alchemical work of the ancient Chinese Taoists. There is a tendency for the mind to be repulsed from Earth, to want to leave and seek enlightenment, but in this shadow of Scorpio, the mind is bound to root deeper in order to find its escape.

The danger of this shadow Mercury parasite comes in the form of manipulation. When we want to try to alter Earth's reality and dissociate from it into the imagination rather than going through the body, the mind will create distortions upon reality to make it what it wants it to be, kicking the holder of this shadow into ungrounded delusion. To master this shadow, the native will be required to enter into delusional thinking before returning to its grounding—with fingers crossed in hopes that return comes through epiphany rather than physical crisis. In this Mercury shadow, the mind is uncomfortably and vulnerably welded to its Earth form, the body. This is the ultimate ideal of the tantric yogi who seeks to bring the body with it into enlightenment and raise up the most embarrassing filthy aspects of the bodily functions into a sacred and holy space. Often Mercury shadow in Scorpio will seek to alter the body through substances and feeling good through sensual pleasures, which range from the simple, such as the scent of a rose or fine wine, to the extreme, such as pain and danger.

I was given a synchronistic communication from spirit regarding the lotus flower growing from the mud, and this is the best metaphor for this shadow. This is the ace of pentacles card in the tarot, and avant-garde filmmaker and therapist Alejandro Jodorowsky speaks of it as well in his work on the tarot. The mind is much like the lotus flower that blossoms so beautifully out of the water but would never achieve this spectacle if it was not rooted below in the filthy mud. The ace of pentacles card is the gift of the Earth, the gift of the body, our roots in the mud from which our mind can grow. The lowest places of our existence can be the location where the most beautiful flowers grow. Without the swamps that birth the lotus, there is no fertility, no ecosystem, no lotus mind. The benefit of overcoming this shadow is to ascend as the lotus into the many-splendored beingness of Earth-based sentience in all its beauty. All you have to do is rise out of the temptations of hedonism. Piece of cake, right?

The shadow Mercury in Scorpio can also place an undue focus on survival to the point of paranoia. Suspicion and doubt of the other's integrity arises due to the Scorpio ability to see what lies beneath the surface. The birth Mercury in Taurus seeks security and comfort, and the shadow of this comes into a survival state of fear if any comfort or security is taken away and a state of terror ensues that will seek comfort wherever it can as a result to cope. Maynard James Keenan, the lead singer of the band Tool, has this Mercury shadow. Certainly, as a musician, the mind shadow here can feel, sense, and hear, perhaps more acutely than others, and the physical perceptions play a huge role in its cognition. The sensuality and approach of the physical is evident in much of Keenan's work and the message of many of his songs, which exhibit a depth of understanding of the predicament of this parasite, and working through the body, through the senses, through the pleasurable, to achieve a higher vantage point of understanding.

Example in Nature

> *The eyes, the skin, the tongue, ears, and nostrils—all are gates where our body receives the nourishment of otherness. This landscape of shadowed voices, these feathered bodies and antlers and tumbling streams—these breathing shapes are our family, the beings with whom we are engaged, with whom we struggle and suffer and celebrate. . . . All could speak, articulating in gesture and whistle and sigh a shifting web of meanings that we felt on our skin or inhaled through our nostrils or focused with our listening ears, and to which we replied—whether with sounds, or through movements, or minute shifts of mood. The color of sky, the rush of waves—every aspect of the earthly sensuous could draw us into a relationship fed with curiosity and spiced with danger. . . . We still need that which is other than ourselves and our own creations. . . . We need to know the textures, the rhythms and tastes of the bodily world, and to distinguish readily between such tastes and those of our own invention. Direct sensuous reality, in all its more-than-human mystery, remains the sole solid touchstone for an experiential world.*
>
> — David Abram, *The Spell of the Sensuous* (New York: Vintage Books, 1996), 9

♐

Sagittarius Mercury Shadow

The Exaggerator

Birth Mercury: Gemini ♊
Parasite: Pinocchio

Deception is an art form and certainly has its place. In mythology, the god Mercury is a thief and liar, using cleverness and intelligence to forge his way through the world. Some with this placement like to think that if it isn't an outright lie it isn't as bad, so they permit themselves to tell fibs. The Mercury shadow in Sagittarius is the tale of the big fish.

> *Lies, my dear boy, can easily be recognized. There are two kinds of them: those with short legs, and those with long noses. Your kind have long noses.*
>
> Carlo Collodi, *Pinocchio*

With this Mercury shadow you are prone to ungrounded thinking that overreaches and extends past anything possible. This is the mind that envisions the building of a skyscraper who doesn't have enough money to buy a cup of coffee, ignoring completely pragmatics to go beyond all boundaries of space and time. The risk here is a separation of mind and body: you may get too big for your own britches. Hyperbole thoughts blown out of proportion into exaggeration cause distrust from people who get wise to this shadow Mercury.

The sense of wonder for the Mercury shadow in Sagittarius takes over everything to the point of madness. You can't just make things up forever; the mind is useless if it is ungrounded completely. It is a gift and benefit to have a sense of wonder and an ability to tell tales, but nobody likes the boy who cried wolf.

L. Frank Baum had this placement. The benefit of his enormous sense of wonder is well established in his novels of the land of Oz. Few can dispute the benefits of his limitless expansion, even predicting scientific inventions that were yet to come. L. Frank Baum could envision a lot of things but create none of them except in writing. However, the shadow side of his madness was shown in his severe racism toward Native Americans, even gossiping poorly about Sitting Bull and getting swept up in a kind of righteous madness seeking to defeat the Native Americans as heathens and enemies. His imagination got the better of him, seeing enemies in others and constructing a narrative surrounding it. We can make things up in our imagination, but once we project our imagination onto other living breathing people, it is toxic, dangerous, and genocidal. Baum was a member of the Theosophical Society and did draw greatly from its principles and concepts in his writings, so some of those ideas were not his own but rather extrapolated from the spiritual teachings of theosophy.

Place a limit on how long you will let your nose grow. Be cautious not to point this Mercury shadow at anyone and be responsible for separating fact from fiction in your communications.

Example in Nature

> *When in a tight spot, animals "lie" to their own kind to get what they want, a University of Rochester biologist has found. In work described in the current issue of the* Journal of Theoretical Biology, *Eldridge Adams shows that within a single species, it is possible for some members to deceive others. By proving that the weaker are able to deceive the stronger to survive, Adams' findings runs counter to a common belief by biologists that communication within a species must always be reliable and honest. "We've shown that the communication is not always reliable, and that in theory, you shouldn't expect it to be," says Adams, who began the work as a graduate student at the University of California at Berkeley.*
>
> — Tom Rickey, "Do Animals 'Lie'? Yes, Even to Their Own Kind, Biologist Says," University of Rochester, September 25, 1995

♑

Capricorn Mercury Shadow

The Catcher in the Rye

Birth Mercury: Cancer ♋
Parasite: Cynicism

Shadow Mercury in Capricorn results from birth Mercury in Cancer, which bases thoughts on feelings and emotions. The shadow here develops from a need to compensate this mental tendency by repressing irrational thoughts and covering them with logic and material-based considerations. The holder of this shadow does a disservice to the keen intuitions of his natal Mercury and shames himself into not trusting his instincts. The mind game that's played here is self-doubt magnified against instinctual knowledge.

The mind parasite in this placement posits that everything is fake and a game. The concept that we are living in a simulation or a game isn't new; though it has lately gained popularity, it can be found in ancient Vedic and Buddhist texts, among others. Viewing everything cynically from this perspective creates a shadow disdain for life and a disrespect for the life we are given and even for loved ones, which can justify abusive behavior to others. To transmute this shadow, the holder needs to stay in a place of humility and play, rather than feeling there is no point in bothering with life because it's all a fake game. Watching the bias toward negating the value of life is needed here.

John Nash, the celebrated mathematician, had this placement of the mind parasite and suffered from mental illness, as well as being mentally gifted and a visionary. Nash, in keeping with this mind parasite, made advances in game theory, geometry, and partial differential equations during his twenties, but in 1959, at age thirty-one, he was diagnosed with schizophrenia, which he gradually recovered from, over the next ten years. For Nash, his mental illness was a change "from scientific rationality of thinking into delusional thinking," and he recovered, according to him, by intellectually rejecting his "delusionally influenced" thinking. Nash outwardly derided irrational knowledge and fought within himself between cold logic and instinct, as is evidenced by this Mercury shadow. The natal Mercury placement in Cancer makes the thinking instinctual and rooted in emotion, but the Capricorn shadow seeks to superimpose logical and material-based thinking over it, creating an internal struggle and division between these two states of mind.

In order to transmute this mind shadow, there must be a marriage between rational and irrational. There must be a space in which both minds can live and work together, for it is there we find the best answers to any equation, equally balanced and the sum of a whole rather than the parts. Sometimes a game is just to play and have fun, not a logical strategy to solve.

Example in Nature

The animal kingdom is full of frolicking, frisking, gamboling and romping critters. . . .

All sorts of animals play for all sorts of reasons. A fawn frolics in the meadow to become more agile. A kitten chases string so that one day it can chase a mouse. An octopus plays with a plastic bottle or Legos to entertain itself.

New Zealand keas, which are large parrots, seem to play just to irritate humans. Keas are native to the high mountains and spend their days making snowballs and doing aerial acrobatics for no reason scientists can discern. But it's when humans arrive that the real fun starts. Keas have been known to rip apart boots, tents and even car parts while campers sleep. I've seen them drop branches and rocks on tourists' vehicles just to watch them thump or break a windshield.

"They're thinking in very sophisticated ways, all this destructive behavior and cheekiness is coming from a place of intelligence," said Alex Taylor, Ph.D., an associate psychology professor at Auckland University.

— Erik Vance, "Where the Wild Things Play," *New York Times*, July 21, 2020

♒

Aquarius Mercury Shadow

The Spy

Birth Mercury: Leo ♌
Parasite: Hearing voices

Mercury shadow in Aquarius comes from the shade of the sun itself, Leo. The birth Mercury in Leo is very self-focused, trying to create an ego identity and a persona to hide behind. The shadow here forces the ego to be in service to the community, whether it likes it or not.

Under this Mercury shadow, the native may be forced to see the thoughts of others or see how her thoughts enter into others, which may not always be what she had in mind, or she may lose her self-identity and her claim to intellectual fame in the process. It is easy to simply tell someone to lose his ego identity, but this is something our subconscious will fight as if it is death itself, so it takes a large amount of fortitude and internal release to actually annihilate a created ego identity. Often the shadow Mercury in Aquarius will challenge the native to allow others to steal his thoughts or ideas, while receiving no credit at all himself for his role and his identity in his own thoughts; the thoughts and ideas are willingly given away, without a signature attached, to accomplish a greater good. In this way, an entire group or corporation could appropriate the native's creation, something unique to him.

The challenge here for healing is for the individual to offer up in sacrifice some of his creativity to serve the community or group. What is your offering to humanity with no claim to fame? Keep something internal, for yourself alone, that belongs only to you, so that you have something secret and special; doing this will nurse the wounds caused by lack of recognition. Spirit sees all you do and grants the validation that is worth more than the passing fancies of a crowd or audience.

Mata Hari, who had this Mercury shadow, was undoubtedly a genius with a morphable identity. Her Mercury shadow conjuncts her sun Mars and Uranus, making her unique indeed. This conjunction forced her to place her ego in service for the greater good, but whether her service was as a spy or a scapegoat remains mysterious. Natal Leo is forced into the Aquarius shadow. She paid the ultimate price and was executed by a firing squad for espionage when the mask of her false identity slipped and her true identity was revealed. Still, who she really was remains veiled, and it seems history may have misrepresented her. Perhaps there is more to be discovered in her true ego form, which she might have kept secret from everyone except herself.

Example in Nature

Two scenes, seemingly disjointed: the John le Carré shadows against the bright midway lights of county-fair Americana. But wars make strange bedfellows, and in one of the most curious, if little-known, stories of the cold war, the people involved in making poultry dance or getting cows to play bingo were also involved in training animals, under government contract, for defense and intelligence work. The same methods that lay behind Priscilla the Fastidious Pig or the Educated Hen informed projects such as training ravens to deposit and retrieve objects, pigeons to warn of enemy ambushes, or even cats to eavesdrop on human conversations. . . . The use of animals in military intelligence dates back to ancient Greece, but the work that this trio undertook in the 1960s promised an entirely new level of sophistication, as if James Bond's Q had met Marlin Perkins.

— Tom Vanderbilt, "The CIA's Most Highly-Trained Spies Weren't Even Human," *Smithsonian Magazine*, October 2013

♓

Pisces Mercury Shadow

Maybe

Birth Mercury: Virgo ♍
Parasite: Uncertainty

Uncertainty can be crippling for the mind and the mental sphere. Concern over making mistakes and making wrong choices can lead to making no choices at all, which does not work well for living in the world. The shadow Mercury in Pisces comes to the birth Mercury in Virgo holder. Mercury in Virgo is logical and articulate and seeks patterns. Shadow Mercury in Pisces will constantly destroy all knowledge, like Shiva destroying all that is known in his path. Pisces energy likes things to be mysterious, unknown and fluid. Virgo wants to know exactly what it is dealing with before it makes a decision, to avoid errors. The mind holding this birth placement may short-circuit when the uncertainty of Pisces prevents Virgo from firmly making a choice.

Mercury shadow in Pisces will refuse boundaries and seek oblivion. There can be a danger here of seeking relief from the never-ending mental gift of Mercury in Virgo, which creates a mind that never stops thinking, causing stress to the nervous system. Remedies from thinking can be substance related, so it's important for the native to seek out coping mechanisms to achieve oblivion from thinking that are not destructive. Immersion in sound baths or hot baths, for example, will prevent the Pisces shadow from overwhelming this birth Mercury Virgo. Providing space to stop thinking for a while will appease the shadow Mercury in Pisces, which seeks to end all thoughts. Individuals with the Pisces Mercury shadow tend to gravitate toward institutions that have structure so they can avoid making any decisions. When decisions are made for them, they can avoid the worst aspects of feeling lost under this Mercury shadow.

Amy Winehouse had this Mercury shadow, which may have contributed to her seeking substances and her codependency to avoid responsible decision-making. Seeking of oblivion from pain rather than clear-cut decision-making can be seen in some of the life scenarios of this talented chanteuse. We are more prone to come under the influence of the poor decisions of others when we remain paralyzed and unable to move.

Example in Nature

In philosophy, there is a concept called Buridan's ass. Buridan's ass is a hypothetical donkey that is equally hungry and thirsty, which is standing precisely midway between a bale of hay and a bucket of water. One assumes that the donkey would have ordinarily decided whether to choose between the hay or the water, based on whether it was more hungry or more thirsty, and if it was equally so, it would choose between the hay and the water, based on which of the two was closer. Given these assumptions, the donkey is now unable to make any rational decision about choosing hay or water, and therefore will stay rooted to the spot and die of both hunger and thirst.

— Thejaswi Udupa, "Don't Donkey with Decisions," *Hindu* (Chennai, India), October 29, 2018

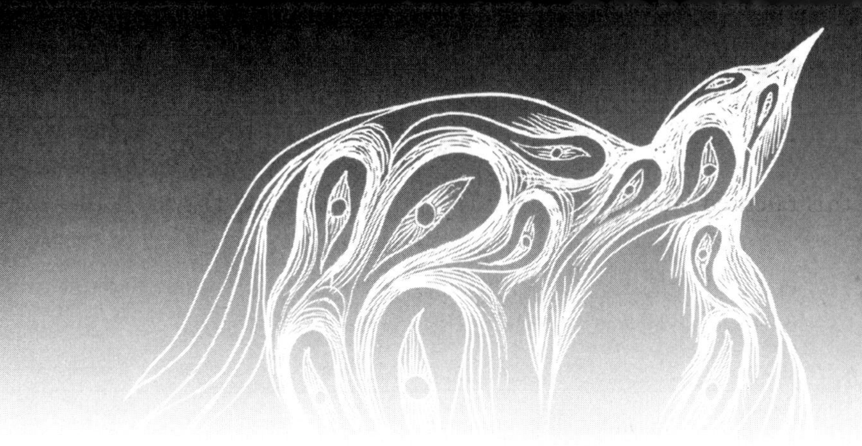

Venus Shadows

Tainted Love

> *The general harmony, of which Eros is the main instrument, Ficino does not place as large a framework as al Kindi. Only Giordano Bruno restores things to their true complexity in his vision of a universe in which each individual and even object is connected to all others by invisible erotic links. The expression* vinculum vinculorum amor est *is substituted for an analogous expression that we can ascribe to al Kindi; the bond of bonds is the ray . . . from living rays colored by passions, by their very existence prompting sympathy or antipathy, love or hate.*
>
> Ioan P. Couliano, *Eros and Magic in the Renaissance*

It has been said that opposites attract. When dealing with oppositional shadows, it is easy to see the relationship between love and shadow casting. Often the object of our attraction becomes an unwitting holder of our shadow projections. Venus rotates in the opposite direction to nearly all the other planets in the solar system: if you were on Venus, the sun would rise in the west and set in the east. Venus is the

ruler of attraction, and her contrary motion fascinates us and attracts our gaze. Uranus also rotates east to west, with its axis almost parallel to its orbit, and is rightfully the rebel who marches to the beat of its own drum.

Venus represents how we express desire, affection, and love, which can take many forms and many shadows. We may be attracted to things we identify as ourselves, or as the opposite of ourselves, but it is usually a combination of both. If we are hiding in our own shadow and do not like ourselves, we will substitute the object of our affection for ourselves and make it a receptacle of our pain. The ancient Greeks openly acknowledged homosexuality, an attraction of like gender rather than oppositional gender, and many Indigenous peoples have also articulated the many forms of love and their nuances in terms of acknowledging the complexities of attraction, so none of the following descriptions are gender related; rather they consider the psychology of affection. In this chapter we will be examining the shadow shapes that can accompany our beloved, in all forms regardless of gender and regardless of whether we love or hate them. The enemy and hating someone is also, after all, a form of intimacy and passion on equal and opposite footing to the lover; they both dwell in our hearts. A repulsive thought, but take a look and you will find that your lover and your nemesis both occupy your heart space. The roles are dynamic and change often the longer we stay with the lover. The interplay of Mars and Venus, nemesis and lover, are closer than we think. It's a thin line between love and hate.

How Venus is placed in the ring of our birth chart shows how we attract things to ourselves and what we are attracted to. Attraction does not only play an important part in our personal lives here on Earth; it's also a palpable universal force and is as real as gravity. Certain things will attract you and you will orbit around them; other things you could care less about; and still other things will completely repulse you. Observing and becoming aware and knowledgeable of your attraction-repulsion dynamics will help you to navigate your relationships.

Our need for love is a root instinct and is present from womb to tomb. People arrive with in-born love patterns, archetypally driven, and then additionally acquire and develop patterns over the course of their existence, beginning with their parents and continuing through their lives.

An aspect of Venus and the nature of desire is phantasmagoria: it is impossible to ignore the role that fantasy plays in love. We generate the most illusion when we are at the height of our adulation of the other. The nature of Venus will have a tendency to play on the imagination through desire. We look through the rose-colored glasses of what we want, which colors what is in front of us, in classic shadow projection style. It is vitally important in our romantic relationships that we become aware of our projections for the sake of ourself and the other. Stay present; see the person in front of you. Who are you, and who is the other? If role-playing or fantasy is involved, do so consciously and with consent so that everything remains above board, and you avoid the shadow realms.

Venus affects animals as well. Other life-forms engage in many different forms of mating behavior, of friendships and enmity. By observing and relating to nature, we can learn much; we can see how some ways of showing love can be very toxic and abusive. A predator loves to consume its prey, this too is a kind of love, a kind of intimacy. Pleasure and desire can take horrific forms. By comparing sometimes horrific and completely unacceptable human behavior to examples in nature, please note I am not justifying or excusing this behavior but rather using nature as a mirror to help us to gain understanding and to create strategies to recognize and deal with toxic behavior. Seeing the terror we do to one another as flukes or unusual is not helpful, especially when these behaviors aren't rare at all and happen all over nature. We need to recognize the wide prevalence of these behaviors so that we can learn how to manage them.

♈

Aries Venus Shadow

Love Is a Battlefield

Birth Venus: Libra ♎
Desires: Victory

In mythology, when Venus paired with Mars she did so by cheating on her husband, Vulcan. The couple remained together after Vulcan punished the pair by shaming them in front of an audience. Venus had many affairs, and even children, with other lovers, and she kept seeing Mars. So the shaming didn't seem to heal the shadow—and perhaps Mars, also known as Aries, had the last laugh after all. Someone with Venus shadow in Aries tends to focus on the love triangle, wanting both objects of affection to fight for her, or at least to receive affection from both. Triangulation is a key tactic of narcissists and egotists to guarantee they have a constant stream of affection from multiple sources.

The shadow Venus in Aries will need to battle for what he loves, and he will expect everyone else to do so as well. Often holders of this shadow will engage in court battles, the justice scale of Libra, and bitter divorces and accuse their lovers of not fighting hard enough for them. They may be terribly disappointed at the other for not engaging in warrior-level fighting to earn their affections and seek someone else willing to fight. This Venus shadow must learn the hard way that he won't get what he wants by fighting and must think of all the parties involved lest he lose the support of the other from being one sided and leaving the other out. The best way to transmute this Venus shadow is to be inclusive and accepting of others rather than keeping them as personal conquests.

Native American activist Leonard Peltier has this Venus shadow placement and was persecuted as a martyr due to his involvement in the group known as the American Indian Movement. Working at the Pine Ridge Indian Reservation in South Dakota, he was there for the controversial shootout in 1975. He was arrested, persecuted as a suspect, and villainized as an individual. Peltier was a warrior of love who was fighting for his passion, which was the protection of the civil rights of Native Americans. Peltier was unjustifiably held personally accountable by the American government for actions arguably intertwined with much larger groups, namely the FBI and the American Indian Movement. He was convicted and incarcerated for the shootings of two FBI officers, despite inconsistencies with evidence and witnesses. He briefly escaped from prison for three days in 1979 but was apprehended and further punished. His court battles and fight for justice continue to this day. With self-love and love of his culture, Peltier is still fighting the larger political fight of advocating for his own rights, his desire undeterred. If the reader is interested, please google ways you might be able to assist his fight. The natal Venus in Libra here means love battles that formed under the shadow Venus in Aries make it to the courts and involve the justice system sooner or later.

Example in Nature

> *In the mating ritual, rams use the size of their bodies and horns as a symbol of status. Nevertheless, females usually accept more males. This could lead to clashes between a dominant male and his subordinates. When this happens, rams headbutt to fight off other males and gain mating access to a particular ewe. These are generally epic combats that can last for over 25 hours. Because of the intense competition for females, rams generally don't mate until they are at least seven years old. Generally, younger males only mate if the dominant ram in their herd is killed or if they are strong enough to fight off the leader.*
>
> — James Ball, "Why Do Rams Headbutt?,"
> Wildlife Boss, August 1, 2022

♉

Taurus Venus Shadow

The Stalker

Birth Venus: Scorpio ♏
Desires: A bird in the hand

Shadow Venus in Taurus wants to control the object of affection in a deep, Scorpio way. The phenomenon of stalking doesn't receive enough attention in the general media, in my personal opinion. I have had a large number of stalkers over the course of my life and known of women who were murdered by exes stalking them. This is a serious form of love shadow, not to be taken lightly. I have a lot of respect for victims' rights activist Lenora Claire for her work in calling attention to this dangerous shadow form. I was first stalked at age fifteen, and many more stalkers followed. On my high school letterman jacket, a stalker saw the name of my high school and my first and last names, and then found my address, sending me perverse letters in the mail with drawings of men with vaginas for their mouths, their eyes surrounded by ants.

The birth Venus in Scorpio needs to feel a connection with its love that lasts forever and is a kind of loyalty akin to a widow who never remarried. The shadow form of this deep love in Taurus takes on a material literalness that causes the Venus in Taurus shadow to seek to never part from its affectionate object in other, more sketchy ways that are possessive.

These days, most folks engage in stalking through the internet, which makes it more accessible, easier to do comfortably and anonymously. It is another thing entirely, however, for someone to follow another in his car or spy on the victim in her home. Someone with Taurus Venus shadow may feel entitled to engage in this kind of boundary crossing because of his devotion to the object of desire and his investment in possession. Under shadow Venus in Taurus, the native becomes possessed with an obsession to track his "belongings" and makes sure they do not escape the boundaries of his territory.

Ted Bundy had this Venus placement. Bundy stalked his victims and enjoyed spying on people in general, in a peeping Tom fashion.

He burglarized as well and was generally good at sneaking around, unknown in the dark. He stalked his prey under the cover of night and took many victims this way. Under this shadow placement, Bundy expressed his devotion beyond death through necrophilia. He kept his victim's severed heads as mementos and, in his severe need to possess his victims completely, ate parts of their bodies.

Transmutation of this shadow Venus will require a discipline to not permit the mind to become obsessively focused on the object of affection. Resistance to permitting yourself to trespass the boundaries of others by focusing upon them is the best way to diffuse this shadow tendency. Self-focus and self-love can greatly assist and dissipate the need to track or get all up in someone else's life; that is really none of your business. Stay in your own lane and invite your crushes to hang out, rather than following their movements.

Example in Nature

When approaching prey, a stalking predator should consider trade-offs between the probabilities of early detection (by the prey, before the strike), spontaneous departure (of prey, before the strike), prey escape (following the strike) and interference (by rivals or predators). In this study we tested the response of a jumping spider, Plexippus paykulli *to a background with two different camouflaging properties, and two different prey types (maggots versus adult house flies). Spiders jumped towards adult house flies from greater distances on a non-camouflaging background, but background colour had no effect on jumping distance when the prey were maggots. Spiders stalking both prey types approached more slowly when camouflaged. Our experiments suggest that jumping spiders may be responding to changes in the trade-off relationships between the probabilities of early detection, spontaneous departure, escape and interference.*

— Allon Bear and Oren Hasson, "The Predatory Response of a Stalking Spider, *Plexippus paykulli*, to Camouflage and Prey Type," *Animal Behaviour* 54, no. 4 (October 1997): 993–98

♊

Gemini Venus Shadow

The Grass Is Always Greener

Birth Venus: Sagittarius ♐
Desires: Flattery

A free spirit seems like a blessing, but there is a shadow side to this open-minded friend, namely, the openness. The shadow Venus in Gemini tends to engage in excessive socializing. This shadow can take the form of the people collector who keeps roaming and making new connections, never settling down, always restless. Often these Venus shadows can have several spouses and might do better in polyamorous arrangements rather than trying to squeeze into a more traditional monogamous relationship.

Individuals with this shadow Venus placement want to share their love and need to attract and interact with as many people as possible. The location of this birth Venus in Sagittarius is quite close to the black hole at the galactic center, the force that the entire galaxy is circling around, so it has a strong attractive pull. Here a community or an entire nation will rotate around this shadow Venus. It could be a political leader, or it could be a charming individual who an entire town or village knows and likes. This is not a problem at all, unless you seek intimacy with this individual and are prone to jealousy. The danger of the social butterfly of this Venus shadow is that true intimacy and a one-on-one connection becomes practically impossible, and these individuals suffer in their most personal relationships, finding themselves surrounded by many fair-weather friends, rather than one or two solid and trustworthy people.

The nature of shadow Venus in Gemini is like a herd of antelope traversing the plains; they never stay still for long. The expanded attractive force of birth Venus in Sagittarius will attract danger as well as love; stalkers, opportunists, and thieves tend to find and take advantage of these open-hearted individuals, so they need to learn extreme discretion, to tell friend from foe, because the gravity of their generosity will attract both. A magnet can attract precious metals but it also attracts knives. David Bowie had this Venus shadow and certainly was a free spirit who deeply loved, and the world loved him. Like most celebrities he also had stalkers, one of which was a person who dressed in a pink bunny suit. Bowie pursued different types of relationships and expanded the norms rather than adjusting himself to fit society. One of the keys to transmuting this shadow is to learn to discern flattery in self and others. When someone is flattering you or offering flakey promises, you need to pay attention to those red flags and have compassion but learn a way to strategically deal with this person. Encountering an occasional bad apple may lead you to close your heart, but learn strategies, rather than withdraw and atrophy, and keep your love flowing.

Example in Nature

During a two-week breeding season, brown antechinus, mouse-like marsupials, begin a mating frenzy. In this promiscuous society, females mate with several partners, each copulation lasting from 5 to 14 hours, before producing offspring. Turns out, by sleeping around, the female increases the chances of her eggs being fertilized by a healthy father and in turn producing fit offspring. After such exhausting sex, before the babies are born, the male antechinus drop dead.

— Live Science staff, "Top 10 Swingers of the Animal Kingdom," Live Science, February 24, 2011

♋

Cancer Venus Shadow

Our Lady of Sorrows

Birth Venus: Capricorn ♑
Desires: Adulation

The number of smoldering celebrities with natal Venus in Capricorn is actually pretty mind blowing. This might be one of the most powerful oppositional shadows for attraction. The ability to manipulate erotic attraction is the superpower of this shadow Venus. Often, because of the influence of Capricorn, this manipulation is used for work and money or to fulfill needs. The shadow Venus in Cancer can feel all emotions, and it knows how others feel through subconscious empathy. Since the natal Venus in Capricorn is the most charged with sensuality, often this Venus shadow placement is literally the sexiest. Attractive sexual force in the shadow form of Cancer draws upon the instincts. Instincts are something that no one quite understands: the effect of a scent, a look, a gesture can have such a powerful effect on an unconscious level that it exceeds almost anything else in the universe. When the qualities and power of attraction are understood and tweaked in just the right manner, the Venus shadow here is powerful indeed in its ability to gain what it desires. Worldly and earthly power follows the person who attracts through instinct. Love is often won irrationally and is deeply felt within the bodies of those drawn to these individuals. Be aware of the dangers of using emotion to get a desired outcome or to get needs met, which can amount to blackmail and can be laden with negative consequences.

Brad Pitt has this Venus shadow, and the force of his attraction need hardly be stated—nor the fact that this shadow has certainly caused some ups and downs for him romantically. Brad Pitt was literally accused of blackmail by Courtney Love, but it's hard to discern celebrity gossip over all.

The powerful forces of attraction that this Venus shadow draws on, which include sensuality combined with deep emotions and instinct, requires that holders of this shadow use it with care and consideration for others and their feelings. Often this shadow will attract individuals who have not gotten much attention in their lives and who lack these powers of attraction and so they may be jealous of this Venus shadow. Those bitten by the green-eyed monster often surround this Venus shadow. If you hold this shadow, you can transmute this behavior by understanding where it is arising from. Transmutation of this shadow needs emotional sincerity. You may be tempted to be dramatic to win attention from the other, but remain aware of your own feelings and what you love lest you get lost in your performance.

Example in Nature

The evolution of altruism (helping a recipient at personal cost) often involves conflicts of interest. Recipients frequently prefer greater altruism than actors are prepared to provide. Coercion by recipients normally involves limiting an actor's options. . . . Forty years ago, Amotz Zahavi suggested that nesting birds may be "blackmailed" into increased parental care if offspring threaten to harm themselves (and therefore jeopardize the direct fitness of their parents). In a simple kin selection model, we expand blackmail to indirect fitness and highlight that blackmail can occur between any kin to drive reproductive division of labor. In principle, a recipient may place its own fitness at risk (brinkmanship), imposing sanctions on a relative's indirect fitness if the relative fails to cooperate.

— Patrick Kennedy and Andrew N. Radford,
"Kin Blackmail as a Coercive Route to Altruism,"
American Naturalist 197, no. 2 (February 2021)

♌

Leo Venus Shadow

Crimes of Passion

Birth Venus: Aquarius ♒
Desires: Peak experience

This is the lover who will dissociate and enter into weird imaginary territories, which he views as creative and romantic. The shadow Venus in Leo is idealized projections. A large amount of artistic fantasy projection will be present with this Venus shadow. On the surface this might sound like a whirlwind romance, but individuals with this shadow tend to idealize the object of their attraction and when that person deviates from qualities erroneously placed on them, violent outbursts, blame, and shame ensue. Seeing things differently than how they are will play tricks on the individual experiencing it. The desire shadow of Venus in Leo will tend to make-believe that things are not as they are. Much will be brushed under the rug, or under the ground, as the case may be.

Leo shadows in general tend to have big blind spots to their negative behaviors due to personal pride and a strong will to see the self as a hero and helper, doing service. Service to fellow humans is the need of the Aquarius energy present in the birth placement of this Venus. When we look into the etymology of the word *romance* itself, it was originally used to refer to bard-like songs or poems telling the story of the hero. The Leo shadow tends to be the most focused on romance and seeing the self ideally, as a hero to a community.

The serial killer John Wayne Gacy carried this Venus shadow (as did Richard Ramirez), which was evident in the way the majority of his victims looked; upon inspection, they were really idealized versions of himself. The projections involved in his complete indulgence of this shadow arguably created an alternate reality in the mind of this holder of the Venus in Leo shadow. Gacy hid the bodies within his home, which shows a kind of ownership, more than shame; he kept them close and created some kind of lasting connection to the deceased targets of his affections.

Murdering the object of affection is not unique to human beings; some arthropods engage in this behavior, such as praying mantises and black widow spiders. To understand this behavior, it is important to see the shadow operating, lest you fall victim to it. Although we certainly do not need to dwell upon it, acknowledging it and raising awareness can go a long way. To transmute this shadow, a deep root into reality is needed. If you own this shadow and you tend to veer off into flights of fancy, do your best to keep them grounded and resist this urge, or channel it into creative pursuits where it may benefit you and feed others rather than leading you into total illusion and phantasmagoria. Romance is not as nourishing as care, compassion, and sincerity. I would choose a helping hand over a bouquet of flowers any day. Keep it real.

Example in Nature

There are over 300 species of octopuses. . . . Of these, a handful—including the giant pacific octopus—have been known to brutally murder and eat each other after sex. In 2014, researchers described an instance in which a female octopus had sex with a male for 15 minutes, and then effectively strangled him with three of her tentacles by blocking his gills. But octopuses aren't the only ones who kill their sex partners. Female praying mantises often kill their mates, especially if they're hungry, and within certain species of spiders, the males will actually offer themselves as a meal for their newly impregnated partners.

— Katherine Ellen Foley, "Some Animals Kill Each Other after Sex Because Their Distinction between Hungry and Flirty Is Blurred," Quartz, February 14, 2017

♍

Virgo Venus Shadow

The Browbeater

Birth Venus: Pisces ♓
Desires: Resentment

Those with shadow Venus in Virgo will seek to attract someone upon whom they can project their resentments, someone they can blame and chastise for their frustrations. The shame of falling short haunts the natal Venus in Pisces, who often experiences frigidity or impotence. These failings are blamed upon the partner, who becomes the holder of the shame. Many scholars have cited resentment as the number one cause for the dissolution of many marriages and relationships. Once resentment sinks in, there is often no going back as the heart becomes hardened. Those with natal Venus in Pisces seek the death of love so that they may know it in totality, which means feelings of grief. Subconsciously, the Venus in Virgo shadow is trying to destroy the things the individual has attracted, as a kind of vetting or test. The shadow Venus in Virgo will attempt to perfect the love object through incessant correction and meticulous analysis. The person with shadow Venus in Virgo may speak poorly of all her exes and never find the perfect mate and so make herself a kind of love martyr or victim of love.

Leopold von Sacher-Masoch, the author of *Venus in Furs*, had this

Venus shadow placement, and his book intimately details how harsh criticism and demeaning words can emasculate and lead to impotence and a total lack of desire. Here the desire shadow seeks to destroy itself, not through violence but through disappointment.

The antidote to this shadow is to come into a kind of unconditional love, which is what birth Venus in Pisces is really looking for: a love that knows no boundaries and accepts everything. If you can't love the one you're with then leave that person alone; they didn't ask you to fix them. Go in search of your ideal and start with yourself. Often this Venus shadow will attract objects of affection that are imperfect, to force the native to open their heart and drop all rules, regulations, and conditions.

Example in Nature

Beverstock, who works at Domino's Pizza, said: "I decided to go to the safari park with my mom and dad to take some pictures of the lions. . . .

"We drove around a little bit and I noticed these female lionesses surrounding a male. All of a sudden they just pounced.

"They were biting at his back legs and his neck and pinning him to the ground, it looked really vicious and you can see in his eyes he thought he was going to die. . . .

"There could be any number of reasons why they were attacking him. It could be that they thought he was too old to be their leader or it could have been over food.

"He could have tried it on with one of the females, who knows, but they looked angry and pounced as if they are going in for the kill. . . .

"You could see car windows going up and almost hear doors locking as it happened, it was just really intense to watch and listen to the roars."

— Ed Chatterton, "Pack of Lionesses Stage Coup against King of the Pride," *New York Post,* September 7, 2018

♎

Libra Venus Shadow

Tit for Tat

Birth Venus: Aries ♈
Desires: Keeping score

The shadow Venus in Libra is more interested in the fight itself than in the actual person it is fighting with. Those with shadow Venus in Libra will engage others in a debate, but passive aggressively. This is a love for arguing, for the melee that ensues when two forces meet each other. Much like the thrill of the chase, the shadow Venus in Libra is the thrill of the verbal fight. Those with birth Venus in Aries want to win the day and emerge the victor, and so their shadow Venus actually picks fights so that they can put themselves on top.

Libra rules legal pursuits for a reason, the love of banter. This Venus shadow loves to engage with a battle of the tongues, and natives can make very good kissers once they stop arguing. Because the shadow Venus attracts, if you have this placement, you may attract an arguer and find yourself involved in a love pattern of court cases rather than romantic getaways. The danger of this Venus shadow is that you, in your primal quest to argue and banter, may lose the point of interacting with someone, which is to communicate and make connections. You may expend too much energy "counting rods," that is, keeping score of who did what and when and how often and keeping a laundry list of every slight to prove a point. This can be extremely exhausting for both you and your partner. We all have a need to make things fair, but try and be mindful about not overdoing it. To transmute this shadow Venus, make sure you state boundaries and preferences beforehand; that way you have a clear setup, with good boundaries, and can later state your case and avoid bickering.

Floyd Mayweather Jr. has this Venus shadow and as a professional boxer was a literal fighter, expertly using this shadow to his advantage in hashing it out in the ring. Unfortunately, he spent quite a bit of time in court fighting outside the ring with his love interests as his shadow got the better of him on several occasions in domestic violence incidents and allegations. It is vitally important wherever aggressive planets are involved that we work on these shadows and create strict boundaries to avoid indulging in violence that harms others and our mates. Practice good boundaries and coping mechanisms for yourself and keep your fighting in the right places.

Example in Nature

> *Male Grevy's zebras chase lactating females for up to one-third of a mile at a time, making it harder to attend to foals. Male spotted hyenas rush at females with ears cocked forward, trying to sniff or bite them. Female Trinidadian guppies often endure one mating attempt per minute involving high-speed chases. Male grey seals try to mount lactating mothers, reducing time they can spend nursing and therefore threatening the health of their young. . . .*
>
> *Scientists are piecing together the genetics of sexual coercion. Males in Gombe assert themselves, in part, by symbolic violence: charging and chasing females and puffing up their fur to look bigger. They also resort to actual violence like biting and kicking prospective mates. "Life is not easy for a female chimpanzee," says Joseph Feldblum, an anthropologist at the University of Michigan.*
>
> — Barry Yeoman, "Power Play," *National Wildlife*, October–November 2018

♏

Scorpio Venus Shadow

The Vendetta

Birth Venus: Taurus ♉
Desires: Possession

The holder of shadow Venus in Scorpio is obsessed with getting revenge against the lover who has wronged them. Here the affectionate nature is bent on payback. An individual with the natal Venus in Taurus seeks security, trust, and stability. If the partner leaves or abandons them, the Venus shadow will quickly step up to make sure the partner regrets it for the rest of their days. The threat of losing a secure relationship can rouse hellfire. Anyone who has ever felt the sting of love lost can relate, but here the shadow tendency amplifies this natural reaction and needs to be addressed to prevent fallout.

Those with Venus shadow in Scorpio often attract partners who themselves seek security and who will use these natives for their own purposes. Though being in this relationship makes the natal Venus in Taurus feel safe, it crumbles eventually. Invariably in these types of relationships, the individual with lesser means departs, due to lack of control of finances or other security resources, which causes the Venus shadow to rear its head. For the most part, the individual with Venus shadow in Scorpio will seek vengeance because the ego needs to punish the traitor, but on a deeper level, the shadow Venus wants the partner to pay for the perceived crime, literally financially. Taking shared resources, such as a house, or demanding alimony or other forms of retribution, are common with this placement. Often the punishment is greater than the crime and goes into excess in an attempt to dominate the partner.

Transmutation requires having better boundaries and vetting the love object, ensuring they can be trusted before entering into a relationship. Avoiding codependent relationships based solely on needs can do a lot to avoid this shadow battle. To transmute the shadow Venus in Scorpio will require forgiveness and understanding the other's actions so that the individual stops making it a personal vendetta, simply releases things, and moves on to a better, more sincere connection where there is real trust.

Amber Heard and Johnny Depp both have natal Venus in Taurus, so they hold this Venus shadow. Is it any shocker they both went after each other's money in court, in classic shadow Venus in Scorpio fashion? This was a war of the roses, each seeking revenge and payback from the other. Seeking justice for crimes committed, regardless of which side was at fault or guilty of the abuse, could have been done in ways that didn't entail money grabs. Most likely, they each abused the other, though it's hard to tell. If they were to look at the relationship closely in hindsight, they might see that they could have been attracted to each other on a spiritual level, in an effort to transmute this Venus shadow for the collective.

Example in Nature

Typically, ocean hermit crabs use empty snail shells that are abundant throughout as shelter and egg deposits. On land however, the only empty snail shells available are the few that happen to wash ashore. Pushed by scarcity, the terrestrial hermit crab adapted . . . [they] hollow out and remodel their shells, sometimes doubling the internal volume.

[T]he hermit crab still winds up in trouble since sooner or later it will outgrow its shell. In order to survive, the hermit crabs developed a sort of sacrificial social gathering. Thus, as three or more crabs gather around, others flock by the dozens as well, eager to trade up. Curiously, they first line up in a sort of conga line, smallest to largest by the shell, each holding on to the crab next to him. As they trade shells, most of the time the largest of the group gets more than he bargained for when he first joined, as he gets wrenched from its [sic] shell.

— Tibi Puiu, "Hermit Crabs Socialize in Order to Back Stab Their Neighbor and Steal Their 'Homes,'" ZME Science, October 29, 2012

♐

Sagittarius Venus Shadow

The Frenemy

Birth Venus: Gemini ♊
Desires: Easy come, easy go

Those with shadow Venus in Sagittarius need to make friends and need to be free. This is the shadow of the friend zone. The holder of this Venus shadow feels much more comfortable having a rotating circle of friends rather than a solid commitment and monogamy. Ideally, they could share some responsibilities with the object of their affection, to help shoulder the workload, but they are like a rolling stone and tend to move on before too long.

The difficulty with this shadow is an inability to master commitment. It could be that they don't need to root down, but when they find themselves in need and all they have are fair-weather friends, they start to wish they had formed deeper relationships. This Venus shadow has a tendency to make evasive maneuvers and is very avoidant, refusing to be pinned down but also avoiding confrontations.

If you have this Venus shadow, it will affect many areas of your life until you master it by forging relationships that suit your nature and finding others with similar natures to prevent resentment. Having open communication to ensure everyone is on the same page works wonders, so the best tactic for becoming comfortable with this shadow is to accept it and communicate your needs to others. Fly free and go forth in adventure. Communication takes the forefront with this Venus shadow, but you must be cautious not to kiss and tell. Gossip about the individuals you have had relations with haunt this Venus shadow and can create drama problems of varying sizes and consequences, so be aware of the impact of words and avoid spreading tales of your adventures. Be respectful of those who have shared the fruits of their bodies with you.

Singer-songwriter and sex symbol George Michael had this Venus shadow and suffered from quite a bit of gossip surrounding his love affairs and promiscuity, becoming the target of tabloid sensationalism for his sexual activities. Michael died from heart disease, but some of his friends believe he died from a broken heart that never healed after he lost his true love. Perhaps his heart was able to stretch to the full size of his Sagittarius Venus shadow, and he exceeded bounds most can only imagine.

Example in Nature

Honey Bee Queens Reign Supreme: In hives, females rule. Early in a queen's life, she makes several mating flights and can mate with anywhere from one to more than 40 drones. When a queen flies by, the males mob her, deposit their sperm, and then subsequently die. While the drones may not appreciate this lethal affair, the worker bees in the colony prefer more promiscuous queen bees. In fact, the number of partners a honey bee queen has influences how attractive the queen is to the several thousand worker bees in the hive and how long her reign is likely to be. Promiscuity may also improve colony disease resistance by boosting the genetic diversity of her offspring. The queen stores and uses the sperm of all these males throughout her lifetime so she can focus on her most important job of laying eggs.

— PBS staff, "Real Swingers of the Animal Kingdom," *Nature*, PBS, March 12, 2010

♑ Capricorn Venus Shadow

Coldhearted

Birth Venus: Cancer ♋
Desires: Sadistic

Shadow Venus in Capricorn is coldly calculating in its expressions of love and affection. Because this shadow is severely sensual, it will tend toward the dark side of the senses. Due to the protective nature of birth Venus in Cancer, individuals with this placement will seek to vicariously absorb the sensual feelings from a distance rather than through direct engagement, to keep themselves safe. They prefer to empathetically pick up feelings that others are feeling rather than go through the pain or pleasure of feeling themselves. This is someone who likes to watch, not engage. The instincts of attraction and the nature of Venus are heightened here to a hedonistic level, and nothing is too far-fetched for exploring what can be felt through desire. Base desires are elevated to the extreme just to see what can be sensed and how. It's not unusual for these individuals to experiment with celibacy as another way to push the limits of their desire as far as possible. The boundaries of pleasure without gratification or pleasure itself seem to be the paradox of this Venus shadow. Individuals with this placement routinely engage in manipulation to test the other's love, and the things this shadow Venus attracts to it are made to work for it. This can often be a placement for voluntary sex workers due to their high tolerance and ability to expand and extend their sensations.

The danger of shadow Venus in Capricorn is a lack of feeling, which seems strange due to the birth placement of Venus in Cancer, who feels more than most. Paradoxically, the feelings are so strong and run so deep they can go into overdrive and become numb. It's like giving the stimulant Ritalin to someone who is overly stimulated, which paradoxically calms the individual down. The shadow Venus in Capricorn is a comfortably numb phase of overfeeling and pushing past the limits of pain and pleasure entirely.

The Marquis de Sade had this Venus shadow, and for those familiar with his writings and escapades, need I say more? Marquis de Sade, among many other activities, was a proponent of free brothels funded by the state in order to decrease crime. Most of his works were written while he was in prison or asylums, which took up around thirty-two years of his life. Napoleon himself ordered one of his imprisonments, after being given one of his novels, *Juliette*, and pronouncing it "abominable" and "depraved." Too bad Napoleon would be called similar names and also imprisoned eventually, showing the fine line between the judge and the judged.

Example in Nature

On the Venn diagram of strange animal mating behaviors—from lobster golden showers to garter-snake orgies—duck sex is on the border between cartoonish and sadistic. . . . Forced copulations are "pervasively common in many species of ducks," writes Prum. These are socially organized "gang rapes" that are "violent, ugly, dangerous and even deadly" and even sometimes end in the death of the female. This represents a "selfish male evolutionary strategy that is at odds with the evolutionary

> *interests of its female victims and possibly with the evolutionary interests of the entire species," Prum writes. To spread their seed, these ducks are upsetting the natural order of selection.*
>
> — Susannah Cahalan, "The Horrible Thing You Never Knew about Ducks," *New York Post,* May 6, 2017

♒

Aquarius Venus Shadow

The Child

Birth Venus: Leo ♌
Desires: Avoidant

Those with birth Venus in Leo have no trouble loving themselves, it's others that present a problem. The Aquarius Venus shadow causes these natives to subconsciously project their parents onto their relationships. If you have told someone that he or she reminds you of your father or mother, you may need to clear this shadow. If someone else tells you that you are just like his father or mother, shadow behavior and illusion is gripping that person's awareness and he is projecting it onto you. No one is like your mother or your father: this is a red flag that the individual needs to clear this shadow out of his influence field.

Their shadow comes into full force when they are involved with other people, rather than when they are single. Rarely do these individuals need or seek love from others. The Aquarius Venus shadow sees no need for that; they have plenty of love to give all around. If you have this placement, you may have difficulty with boundaries and have different needs in a relationship than those who seek and are satisfied with monogamy. Do not feel like you need to conform, as the Aquarius shadow will only rebel if confined, like a teenager against a parent. Free expression, self-love, and acceptance shall help you come into mastery of this position in the heavens. Don't be shy to see your nature and to have mature discussions early in a relationship about your wants and needs. This will avoid drama and allow the other to see you for who you are, rather than as an idealized projection based on their own needs. Leo needs to individuate, and Aquarius needs others, so the role of parenting and community show up in this shadow to ensure individuation includes history and ancestors.

This is the Venus placement of Mary, the mother of Jesus, according to some scholars who have placed her approximate birth date. Obviously, the story of Mary is laden with this Venus shadow in so many ways. She is forced to give birth through spiritual impregnation and then made to engage in a community that eventually murders her son, but her own powerful love brings on the Pentecost, thanks to the birth placement of Venus in Leo. Her childlike innocence shines through it all, according to the tale. Mary is indeed free from the mother and father archetypes as she is clear of the lineage of the original sin of Adam and Eve as a result of the immaculate conception.

Example in Nature

> *[P]arental effects are an important concept in biology and have wide-reaching ecological and evolutionary implications. . . .*
>
> *Parents may adjust the personality of their offspring to improve the phenotype–environment correspondence. Alternatively, when the environment is highly unpredictable, parents may hedge their bets and actively diversify the personality of their offspring thereby ensuring at least some of their offspring will be a good fit. In either scenario, parental effects may be an important mechanism to generate and maintain behavioral variation and therefore may have substantial evolutionary implications. . . . Successful modeling of animal personality may have to account for parental effects, and the explicit development of personality theory with parental effects in mind would be a fruitful area for future work.*
>
> — Adam R. Reddon, "Parental Effects on Animal Personality," *Behavioral Ecology* 23, no. 2 (March–April 2012): 242–45

♓
Pisces Venus Shadow

The Porn Star

Birth Venus: Virgo ♍
Desires: Martyrdom

One of the many patterns I discovered while reading charts for clients was that an awful lot of porn stars and sex workers have planets in Virgo, the virgin, and these planets are often in the twelfth house, which is ruled by Pisces. In my experiences, this combination of planets in Virgo but in a house ruled by Pisces produces qualities similar to the shadow Venus in Pisces with birth Venus Virgo. I am certainly not implying that porn stars are shadowy, in fact they are more overt and uninhibited than most human beings, being straightforward and not concealed about their sexuality. Rather the shadow implies that those with this placement are inclined to sacrifice the body and their sexuality for others or to use them for a vocation. To me, most of the folks in sex work I have met were more like nurses and caregivers. They were providing a service, much like changing a bed pan, and not something shameful. There is an air of sacrifice and unconditionality to this shadow Venus.

The danger of this Venus shadow is that so much is given that the self and personal desire are lost. Those with natal Venus in Virgo will know exactly how they want something to be but will often give this up to please the other, so to transmute this shadow placement, natives must take care to include the personal desire nature in their pursuits. Otherwise, there is potential for substance abuse to numb the self's desires that are unmet.

Annie Sprinkle, American sexologist, performance artist, and former sex worker, has this placement in her chart. Her Venus in Virgo is in the twelfth house, and so she very much has this Pisces shadow. This places the shadow Venus with a very strong subconscious influence over others. This is the dream realm, the world of fantasy and the institutionalization of a fantasy. We can see that Sprinkle definitely lived up to this Venus shadow placement, becoming a porn star after meeting and becoming the mistress of Gerard Damiano, the director of the movie *Deep Throat*, the 1972 groundbreaking pornographic film. She owned this shadow by coming into her power by claiming her desire for herself while serving the community, as only the Virgo nature can, and survived Venus's ego death.

The ability to place the body into service (even if the service is just making the individual a living) is a transcendent form of using the force of attraction. Venus in Virgo seeks to be pure, and the shadow Venus in Pisces seeks for it to expand itself past ideals into wider territories.

Example in Nature

> *In a bizarre twist on who's coming to dinner, a desert spider mother goes to the extreme to get her kids off to a great start. . . . After being serenaded by the male with delicate vibrations on her web, the soon-to-be-dessert spider mom clutches her sac of fertilized eggs in a cocooned silk ball near her mouth. While the mom is protecting her encased sphere of soon-to-be baby spiders, she continues to eat a nutritious menu of various insects. Then when the spiderlings are ready to hatch, the mom helps them escape their wrapping and begins regurgitating the pre-eaten food. The thing is, this also triggers a waterfall of digestive enzymes, which pour into the mother's system and slowly liquefy her from the inside. This goes on for about two weeks, and all the while she is protecting and feeding her young, until she dies and they eat the rest of her before striking out on their own.*
>
> — Jennifer L. Verdolin, *Raised by Animals: The Surprising New Science of Animal Family Dynamics* (New York: Experiment, 2017)

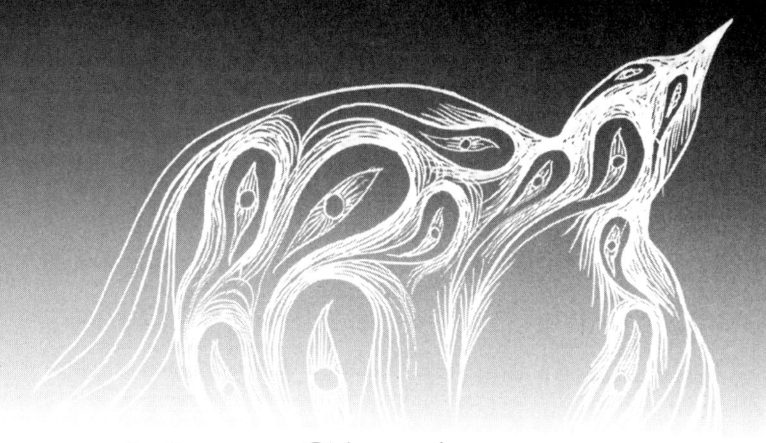

Mars Shadows

By Any Means Necessary

One must not let oneself be misled: they say "Judge not!" but they send to Hell everything that stands in their way.

FRIEDRICH NIETZSCHE, *THE ANTI-CHRIST*

HUMAN BEINGS HAVE IMPRESSIVELY CONTINUED TO STRIVE, again and again overcoming obstacles. As the old song goes, what makes an ant think it can move a rubber tree plant? Its high hopes, which fuel its ambition, its drive to succeed. The passion behind this irrational superpower comes from Mars. There is simply no way that humans would have gotten where we are today without Mars forcing us, lighting fires under our heels, keeping us going despite impossible odds that threaten doom and failure. Mars is our source of ambition. Ambition never gets tired, never sleeps. Ambition is what will get you to the top of that mountain. Without it you will never even consider an ascent.

At its best, ambition has forced human progress beyond even our wildest imagination. At its worst, ambition will cause someone to shove others down the mountain to ensure a victory. This is one shadow aspect of Mars. Because of this potential connection between victory and force, it's important that we keep track of our ambitions, encourage

them, and view them in a positive light to prevent cut-throat aggression, which can dismantle our greatest efforts. Shadow Mars is a powerful force and, rather than being subverted, deserves veneration and identification so that it can receive its due. It is also helpful to investigate the Mars shadow in case we do not have enough ambition—another shadow aspect. A healthy ambition is equivalent to a healthy libido and passion. If we have a shadow Mars that is deficient, we can work to build it up so that we don't stagnate and fail in our pursuits. If it is in excess we can raise awareness of this to avoid destroying self and others in the process of progress. Shadow Mars can cause us to become like Icarus, flying too high to the sun and descending in a fiery mess—but that, too, is nonetheless inspirational.

To master the shadow Mars means that we are able to hold and wield the power of our own ambition on greater levels to serve humanity as a whole rather than simply a single individual. The greatness of humanity was built one person at a time; the heights we reach are upon the shoulders of others. Humanity itself is the ambition that presses us onward. We have come here only through the libido of our ancestors. The seemingly pointless striving of the libido instinct has in fact landed you here to begin with, so honor this shadow. To leave the ancestors out is not only disrespectful but untruthful. The force of the shadow Mars will compel us to achieve regardless of our own will; mastering this force provides the individual with a will to power greater than the individual could achieve on their own.

Most people associate Mars, the planet and the god, with war and fighting without realizing why this is so. Why was it that the god Mars fought most of the battles in mythology? It was for his territory and to protect the source of his libido, namely Venus. Understanding what lies at the root of conflict is crucial for humanity. The main reason for wars of all kinds is because a nation (or a person) is trying to ensure that its libido will be able to accomplish its ambition, whatever that may be. If you really want to find something that is secretly controlling your actions and decisions, look no further than into your own pants.

> *I was taught to strive not because there were any guarantees of success but because the act of striving is in itself the only way to keep faith with life.*
>
> Madeleine Albright,
> *Madam Secretary: A Memoir*

♈

Aries Mars Shadow

Spy versus Spy

Birth Mars: Libra ♎
Ambition: The unclaimed victory

Those born with Libra in Mars will avoid war and fights at all costs; their ambition is aimed at balance and fairness. Mars in Libra is focused on a just outcome for all. Hating conflict, they will circumvent, strategize, and circle around any battle they may face. Mars is said to be in its detriment in Libra, which makes its shadow exalted or powerful in this placement. This desire to avoid open combat creates a shadow Mars that is a master at subterfuge. Here the shadow's motivation is to achieve the target of the libido without declaring itself. This shadow placement is understandable for organizations like the CIA and the NSA, who give themselves permission to use sneaky means to achieve their ends.

Though the Libra birth Mars will not confront another directly, a person with the shadow Mars in Aries will win what he needs behind the other's back. Bill Clinton was born with this Mars shadow. His birth Mars in Libra granted him the ability to dissolve many conflicts through diplomacy, but his shadow ruined him in a secret affair, where his Aries ego needed a secret victorious conquest. Some sources claim former president Clinton had involvement with the CIA in his early years at Oxford, and obviously any president will be well versed in the game of secrets and spying. Arguably, they would need to be adept at the art of deception. Being spied upon is also a form this shadow takes, and someone in a high profile such as Clinton should have expected to be spied upon on all fronts.

Individuals with shadow Mars Aries fight to win, to be the best, while their birth Libra Mars attempts not to do so, wants to be a peacemaker. These natives achieve great heights because they will not let themselves rest; Aries energy presses on, no matter the cost. The key to mastery of this shadow Mars is not to self-destruct in the process of climbing the mountain. If you must use shady ways to get to the finish line, make sure you can still walk afterward. The worst part of this shadow Mars is that even if you do play your cards right, you could still end up attracting spies to you.

Do not permit your shadow Mars in Aries to sneak behind your back, avoiding admitting your own need for victory. Secret victories shall rule and expose you unless you announce them for all to see and hear. Fight your wars in front of everyone, not behind their backs, and then you can reclaim whatever any spy tries to blackmail you with.

Example in Nature

In both the male-dominant capuchins and the female-dominant ring-tailed lemurs, the alpha subject in the majority of the study groups was significantly more vigilant than other group members were. In white-faced capuchins, the alpha male mates more often than subordinate males do; therefore, the greater degree of vigilance exhibited by the alpha male may correspond to the protection of his reproductive investment. In ring-tailed lemurs, there can be more than one matriline in a group. Thus, the greater amount of vigilance behavior exhibited by the alpha female may be related to protection of her matriline.

— Lisa Gould et al., "Why Be Vigilant? The Case of the Alpha Animal," *International Journal of Primatology* 18 (June 1997): 401–14

♉

Taurus Mars Shadow

The Bully

Birth Mars: Scorpio ♏
Ambition: Achieve security and possess protection

This is the bully who will steal your lunch money. For most bullies, please understand, they usually engage in this behavior because their parents can't give them lunch or the money to buy it. So they must take it from you to survive. Most bullies were bullied somewhere, which isn't an excuse for the behavior; it is the birth of this shadow. Here Mars wants to possess things and seeks to secure its earthly well-being, and so it sneaks up and takes it. The shadow Mars in Taurus will often take more than it needs to make sure that it has enough and is never in detriment.

Some keys to dealing with this shadow placement are to fast, to purge, and to learn to live with less. Taking time to purge and to confront the need to possess things and people will help temper this placement. Here the libido in the Taurus shadow will often cause those with this placement to become jealous or possessive of their mates and of other people around them. This can cause a lot of problems when the shadow Mars here becomes territorial over others and displays aggression. The bully aggressively acquires resources because he lacks them and so lashes out. Understand that the holders of this shadow behave in this way because they feel their basic survival is threatened. The libido becomes a thief if its security feels threatened, but more like a burglar who sneaks around in the middle of the night rather than overtly.

The libido of this Mars shadow, which seeks to secure possessions, reveals the universal truth that true ownership is an illusion. Securing resources does not mean they belong to you. A tie made and maintained through aggression and jealousy is insincere and easily severed. Can't buy me love, as the saying goes. The hard root work of the Mars in Scorpio birth placement is to form a bond based in trust and love, which will beat out the false security that this shadow tricks the native into thinking they actually have. Nothing can replace the true trust of a bond of love. This is the former Soviet Union, and the current Russia, forcing its way into sovereign countries and co-opting them, coercing them into becoming part of the USSR. These bonds based in fear, not love and trust, were inherently unstable. This shadow is the United States taking land from Native Americans and France taking resources from Africa, not just the child bully down the street.

When you set free the people or things you love and let them freely choose what they want, a stronger bond is established; this is a safer and more reliable bond than trying to control them by keeping them locked in a basement so that they won't escape. To overcome this challenging libido shadow, release what does not want to remain with you to make space for those who choose to be with you and are bound to you with true ties of love, which are unbreakable.

Example in Nature

> *Intense competition among males can also be observed . . . where males congregate and display communally to attract females. . . . Males arrive early in the breeding season and, through highly ritualized combat behaviors, compete for and establish their territories. Males . . . have evolved elaborate ornaments such as horns, antlers, and vocalizations that they use in intermale competition to attract females and to influence female choice. Females move through the arena (lek) in which males are displaying and mate with one or more males based on the quality of their leks (and resources within it) or on the relative qualities of the males . . . females exploit widely dispersed resources such as grasses (ungulates) and fruit (bats). At high female density, males of the Uganda kob form leks and display to females, but they defend harems (resource-based territories) at low density when defense is presumably economically feasible.*
>
> — Kimberly S. Orrell and Thomas H. Kunz, "Energy Costs of Reproduction," *Encyclopedia of Energy* (2004): 423–42

♊ Gemini Mars Shadow

Loudmouth

Birth Mars: Sagittarius ♐
Ambition: Shouting for all to hear

The libido in the shadow of Gemini seeks to place its voice in the collective. We can see this done in writing, spoken word, singing, politicians, public speakers, and other art forms. One way or another, this Mars wants to be heard. The birth Mars in Sagittarius is the philosopher's libido, usually taking the form of a religious leader, a spiritual warrior, or a sainted martyr. Here, the focus is more on getting the word out, in talking the talk rather than walking the walk. The danger of this shadow Mars is that words may be said that have no meaning. There is a need with this shadow placement to make sure what you say has integrity and truth, then you will be able to achieve the true nature of Mars in Sagittarius, which is deeply connected to higher truths. The Mars libido in Gemini's shadow can both perpetuate and fall victim to gossip, rumors, and slander. Displaying caution toward plagiarism and liable are of the utmost importance for this Mars to avoid, lest it thwarts its own deepest desires.

Oscar Wilde had this Mars shadow. Wilde used his voice in many ways, as a writer, a social critic, and a supporter of gay rights. He spoke up unabashedly no matter what the consequences. Wilde fell victim to gossip and slander regarding his sexual practices and was put on trial for gross indecency, which is considered one of the first celebrity trials. However, King James also suffered from inappropriate judgments on homosexuality and arguably shares celebrity trial status. Wilde was jailed, which many believe had ill effects on his health, and he eventually died of an ear infection, though there is some controversy over whether it was syphilis.

> *There is only one thing in life worse than being talked about, and that is not being talked about.*
>
> Oscar Wilde

The key to dealing with this Mars libido shadow is in minding your words. It is important to be authentic in speech and say what your heart needs to hear; however, some words could benefit from being careful and strategic. Understanding the times and what surrounds you could assist you to go the distance rather than the instant gratification of shooting arrows with the tongue.

Example in Nature

In 2011, two researchers at the University of Washington, each wearing an identical "dangerous" mask, trapped, banded and released seven to 15 crows at five different sites near Seattle. To determine the impact of the captures on the crow population, observations were made over the next five years about the birds' behavior by people walking a designated route that included one of the trapping sites. These observers either wore a so-called neutral mask or one of the dangerous masks worn during the initial trapping events. Within the first two weeks after trapping, an average of 26 percent of the crows encountered scolded the person wearing the dangerous mask. Around 15 months later, that figure was 30.4 percent. Three years later, with no action towards the crows since, the number of scolding crows had grown to 66 percent. Obviously, the crows were "talking" to each other about the humans, passing on the knowledge of the threat between peers and down through generations.

— Candice Gaukel Andrews, "Crows Are as Intelligent as a Seven-Year-Old Child," Natural Habitat Adventures, October 23, 2018

♋ Cancer Mars Shadow

The Ghost of the Alpha

Birth Mars: Capricorn ♑
Ambition: The once and future king

Mars shadow in Cancer emphasizes heightened instincts, and the natural need to survive and propagate comes to the forefront. The natal Mars in Capricorn focuses on ambition, but the Mars in Cancer shadow will force it to form a legacy that lasts on Earth for generations to come.

This is a ghost of nature that focuses on getting the species to persist over time. The need here is instinctual, an archetypal need for success that transcends the individual. I'll say that again: success here isn't a desire; it's a need. Individuals with this placement will beg, borrow, or steal and destroy everything in their path to succeed. When the true force of instinct is revealed, it is to be the one who survives over all else, making your mark upon the world so that you shall be forever known and immortal. This Mars shadow seeks immortality. One way to overcome death is through succeeding and carrying on your name through your children; this is the focus of this Mars shadow.

The individual achieving success is hidden within the shadow so the difficulty of this placement is that it often eludes him until he is able to transmute it. To do this, the natal placement of Mars in Capricorn must focus on what he loves rather than his achievements. By gaining emotional satisfaction and fulfillment, he will achieve success, not the other way around.

Albert Einstein had this Mars shadow and notoriously burned through all his loved ones in order to achieve his ambitions. Claims of plagiarism from his wife, who studied with Nikola Tesla, were vindicated when Einstein directed all the funds he won from his Nobel Prize to her. He made controversial racist remarks about Asians and lost nearly everyone in his life, except his sister Maja, which showed he could have used a bit more balance in his focus on ambition. He was so intent on ensuring the legacy of his relativity theories that he attacked and set about disproving quantum physics because it contradicted some of his findings.

Example in Nature

> *Finding a mate can be exhausting—so much that some animals die after finally meeting that special someone. . . .*
>
> *[W]e took a closer look at the reproductive strategy called semelparity, or suicidal reproduction, in which animals concentrate all their reproductive energies into one bout of mating before death. The poster child for this phenomenon is the male antechinus, a tiny, short-lived Australian mammal. The critter goes on a mad mating spree (sometimes as long as 14 hours), after which it suffers a fatal immune system breakdown and dies a ragged wreck. You could call it a parental sacrifice: Antechinus males die knowing they'd spread their sperm far and wide. "The trade-off is that semelparous species produce more offspring," says Jeyaraney Kathirithamby, an entomologist at Oxford University.*
>
> — Liz Langley, "5 Animals That Mate Themselves to Death," *National Geographic,* February 25, 2017

♌

Leo Mars Shadow

Your Lord and Savior

Birth Mars: Aquarius ♒
Ambition: Let me lead you

The shadow Mars in Leo wants to be your hero, whether you like it or not. Here the libido will be the hero of the story, no matter what. People with this shadow placement can serve the community, but they can also fall into total delusion and denial, refusing to see themselves as anything other than saviors. The birth Mars in Aquarius wants to serve the community, but its shadow wants to save the community and be remembered for its deeds forever. The native of this birth Mars placement is extremely uncomfortable with this shadow libido and ironically will more often than not force the shadow into the role of the villain. This shadow placement that is trying so hard to be the hero will make itself the villain through its bad behavior. Infamy rather than fame tends to dominate when this shadow takes over.

Although it might sound romantic to have a knight (or gender/s of your preference) in shining armor show up and save you, which is exactly what the libido shadow in Leo wants and desires more than anything, what this really creates is a codependent relationship. This is not to say we don't need each other and need help; it's good to receive assistance, and it feels good to rescue people. Those with this shadow may, however, assist people in such a way that they ensure recipients remain subordinate and dependent rather than viewing them as equals.

This shadow can take the form of moral grandstanding or virtue signaling, which has become problematic in the age of social media and is a perfect example of this shadow Mars. The desire to do good and be virtuous is laudable, but the key to this shadow is not to use it to support a perception of your ego identity; that's all.

Elon Musk has this libido placement and certainly does much for humanity. He stepped in to assist the Michigan clean water crisis, for example, acting heroic indeed. Maybe including and supporting others in the hero role could help balance the scales and transmute this shadow. In February 2022, Musk made a charitable donation of nearly $6 billion; initially, the recipient was a mystery, but it was soon revealed that all the money went to his own charity, the Musk Foundation.

Example in Nature

Dolphins tried to "push" an Australian surfer to shore while he was being stalked by a 20-foot shark. Bill Ballard was surfing at Wallagoot Beach, on the New South Wales coast, on September 25 when he noticed that the dolphins—which were feeding on a swarm of salmon in the area—began acting differently than usual, The Courier *reported. Ballard had encountered dolphins in the area before, so he was well versed in their usual behavior. "It's hard to describe, but they kept coming up to the surface to look at me and also began swimming back and forward, coming closer and trying to push me towards the shore," he told the Australian newspaper. Shortly afterward, an aircraft—which had been watching the dolphins' feeding frenzy from above—swooped down to warn him that a 20-foot shark was lurking in the waters nearby,* The Courier *reported. As the two passengers hung out of the low-flying aircraft, they screamed at Ballard, "Shark, shark!" and pointed at a large shadow of something swimming nearby.*

— Robyn White, "Dolphins Tried to 'Push' Surfer Being Stalked by 20-Foot Shark to Shore," *Newsweek*, October 4, 2022

♍

Virgo Mars Shadow

The Perfectionist

Birth Mars: Pisces ♓
Ambition: Immaculate conception

The libido in the Virgo shadow seeks a kind of unattainable perfection; its will is bent toward it. There is a high degree of self-consciousness focused on performance that enters with this shadow placement. The libido judges and criticizes its own ability to execute and folds over on itself, often leaving it in a state of falling short of the target. The birth Pisces Mars is ambiguous and unfocused; it's fluid and seeks expansion and flow. The Virgo shadow treats this inability to articulate an end as a shameful failure rather than an expanded horizon.

Mars in Pisces has no boundaries and respects no one's boundaries, in empathetic fashion, and so the shadow of Mars placed in Virgo seeks a place to cross the finish line in rebellion and creates boundaries. The critique of failure is heightened for this libido, and often it will cast this shadow on others that it feels are not hitting the mark or are up to par. This can be a beneficial superpower when placed in the position of a coach or teacher, but can turn detrimental when unsolicited or self-destructive.

Vincent van Gogh held this Mars shadow and died thinking his work was a failure. The role of imperfection or incompletion played a large part in his psychology, according to works regarding his personal feelings. Often his criticisms turned destructive as van Gogh sought something that could match the boundlessness and fluidity of his Pisces ideal. His self-doubts plagued him in his endeavors, and we are all grateful for the fruits of his struggles with this Mars shadow that is never satisfied with itself. The cause of his death remains controversial, though most believe it was suicide.

Example in Nature

Many animal species die after they reproduce. But in octopus mothers, this decline is particularly alarming: In most species, as an octopus mother's eggs get close to hatching, she stops eating. She then leaves her protective huddle over her brood and becomes bent on self-destruction. She might beat herself against a rock, tear at her own skin, even eat pieces of her own arms. Now, researchers have discovered the chemicals that seem to control this fatal frenzy. After an octopus lays eggs, she undergoes changes in the production and use of cholesterol in her body, which in turn increases her production of steroid hormones—a biochemical shift that will doom her. Some of the changes may hint at processes that explain longevity in invertebrates more generally, said Z. Yan Wang, an assistant professor of psychology and biology at the University of Washington.

— Stephanie Pappas, "Octopuses Torture and Eat Themselves after Mating. Science Finally Knows Why," Live Science, May 18, 2022

♎

Libra Mars Shadow

Partner in Crime

Birth Mars: Aries ♈
Ambition: Ride or die

An individual with this libido wants to join forces with another who agrees with her aims and ambitions and unite together against a common enemy. Even though the birth Mars in Aries seeks to put the self forward, the individual realizes the only way she can do this is by joining or mating with another. The impulse to team up need not be gender specific, and this urge is implicit in the individual's realization that if she wants to put herself forward, she needs another. The Libra Mars shadow ensures that those with birth Mars in Aries are not seeking just for themselves.

The very real danger of this Mars shadow is that natives feel they do not need to seek consent from others to form a partnership, at least in the shadow mind of those holding this libido. The combination of birth Mars Aries with shadow Libra, which influences justice and reciprocity, of this shadow means theses natives will be involved in court cases that involve others who seek justice because the holders of this placement disregarded them. If they are unable to raise their conscious awareness and change their behavior, the shadow will force them to consider others through legal consequences in court. This shadow will also pull others in to participate in its schemes or ideas by finding someone open to its influence or charm and gaining a follower.

Cristiano Ronaldo, a Portuguese soccer player, has this Mars shadow. As an athlete who is part of a team, Ronaldo must consider others, and as someone under the public spotlight, he must consider accountability. Ronaldo has a family and is married to Georgina Rodriguez who has stuck with him through the difficulties of both fame and court cases. A woman accused Ronaldo of raping her. The judge dismissed the case, because the plaintiff's lawyer was found to have engaged in misconduct, and ordered the lawyer to pay Ronaldo over three hundred thousand dollars. This situation ended well for Ronaldo but illustrates how this Mars shadow can end up in court against another. In 2005, two other women accused Ronaldo of rape. There is no way to tell if the accusations were accurate, but the nature of this reflects the Mars shadow. Even if Ronaldo was only on the receiving end of the accusation, the court ordeal and forced partnership in an unhealthy fashion mirror this shadow.

Ronaldo is the person who holds the title of the most followers on social media, and in ego fashion, holds Mars in Aries birth placement, the libido of the ego. He has certainly won the ego game, at least in terms of numbers. Hopefully, no matter what the truth is, due to the amount of people watching, this Mars shadow will gain awareness and we can learn how trying to force people to be your partner is not the correct way to go about things. It could be that after getting so much attention, false accusations and libel are brought to this libido shadow, but there is still a forced relationship here, through the courts requiring engagement.

To transmute this Mars shadow, make sure all your partners are willing and serve more than just your own wants and needs, which will be evident through consent and friendship, trust and commitment, not forced participation.

Example in Nature

Wolves form monogamous breeding pairs and remain together for the duration of their life. Together, the pair will maintain a territory, search for prey, and, above all, remain loyal to one another and their family unit. It seems only natural that wolves should symbolize strong, loving relationships.

— "Wildly Romantic Wolves Symbolize Love and Loyalty,"
Wolf Conservation Center, February 14, 2020

♏

Scorpio Mars Shadow

Creeping Death

Birth Mars: Taurus ♉
Ambition: Stealth bomber

This shadow placement of Mars is a secretive destroyer of obstacles that stand in the way of its libido's pursuits. The libido in this placement enjoys sabotaging people behind the scenes but does not need to take credit for its subterfuge. This is a fascinating placement because natives do not need to make announcements or take credit for throwing someone under the bus. That they have accomplished what they need to do is good enough for holders of this shadow; no one else needs to know. They have neither guilt nor shame because for them the simple fact that someone is threatening their desire is justification enough; others' pain is nothing more than a casualty of war. All is fair in love and war, after all.

The libido is then free to pursue its desires having removed all obstacles. The obvious danger of this shadow placement is that when the holder views an individual as standing in the way of his goals, he will act secretly against this person, which could take the form of a smear campaign or keying his rival's car. His efforts could take many forms, such as purposely redirecting his competition away from his competitor's goal, thereby creating quite a karmic debt for himself in the process.

Bram Stoker, author of *Dracula*, has this birth placement. Stoker was focused on hiding his sexual orientation. There are many reasons for his subterfuge, such as the death of his friend and possible lover Oscar Wilde, who was heavily persecuted in court for his homosexuality. Besides Wilde, Stoker was linked to several homosexual men, though never publicly, among them poet Walt Whitman and a man named Peter Doyle, with whom he had a decades-long relationship. He hid his proclivities and did get married. Jealousy is a main theme in his classic work *Dracula*, and he perhaps vicariously indulged this emotion in his writing through his characters, though secretly, rather than in the light of day.

Transmutation for this shadow libido will happen when we do things outright and in plain sight. We can feel liberated if we express our needs and actively seek success rather than stewing over what other people are doing. We don't need to hide anything; we can just be ourselves. Often society presents obstacles to being honest, such as unfair laws and social condemnation, which forces the individual to go undercover. If that is your situation, finding a creative outlet can be very helpful to process the emotions that arise as a result.

Example in Nature

> *It is unclear how a pursuit can be effective when the prey is faster than a non-cryptic predator. . . . [W]e considered the strategy of red lionfish as they pursued a faster prey fish under laboratory conditions. Despite swimming about half as fast as* C. viridis, *lionfish succeeded in capturing prey in 61% of our experiments. This successful pursuit behaviour was defined by three critical characteristics. First, lionfish targeted* C. viridis *with pure pursuit by adjusting their heading towards the prey's position and not the anticipated point of interception. Second, lionfish pursued prey with uninterrupted motion. . . . Such periods allowed lionfish to close the distance to a prey and initiate a suction-feeding strike at a relatively close distance. . . . Finally, lionfish exhibited a high rate of strike success, capturing prey in 74% of all strikes. These characteristics comprise a behaviour that we call the "persistent-predation strategy," which may be exhibited by a diversity of predators with relatively slow locomotion.*
>
> — Ashley N. Peterson and Matthew J. McHenry, "The Persistent-Predation Strategy of the Red Lionfish (*Pterois volitans*)," *Proceedings of the Royal Society of Biological Sciences* 289, no. 1980 (August 3, 2022)

♐
Sagittarius Mars Shadow

The Influencer

Birth Mars: Gemini ♊
Ambition: Ruler of the world (or internet)

This shadow Mars placement will carry the native to greatness, but at a cost. The combination of Sagittarius shadow and Mars creates an energy that is ever expanding and seeks to expand even further. This ambitious libido is positioned to be a global conqueror and usually achieves that goal. But expanding into a global influence can't be maintained for long. The problem with expanding past the container is that the container breaks. There is a reason why people form communities in the areas that they live. Once things get too far from home, they can no longer relate to the day-to-day situation. Anyone who has ever tried to lead even a small group of people can see that things fall apart the further from the center you go; this is a sad fact of gravity.

> *The Tower of Babel is one of those mythological narratives that, in the words of the 4th-century philosopher Sallustius, "never happened, but always are." Man in his arrogance always strives against his own nature and circumstances to bring together the different nations of the world and establish an order that can facilitate some lofty ideal and he always fails. Just as Nimrod's tower fell, so did Alexander's, Cyrus's, Attila's, and Napoleon's. This sort of geopolitical project—even when buttressed by the best reasons and most noble goals—never succeeds.*
>
> Michael Shindler

Ambitions of global dominance can be achieved under a unifier. Finding that unifier can be difficult, though, unless one is well versed in the archetypes. When you know the common denominators and needs of people, you can form a campaign of unity that plays upon this and succeed. The Sagittarius Mars shadow can find an overriding philosophy that unites many people, such as a slogan, a symbol, or a common grievance or goal. The true gift of the Mars libido shadow of Sagittarius is that these natives can find a common philosophy that appeals to the most people and can then form their rulership and realize their ambition. Going big is the gift of this shadow.

The person with natal Mars in Gemini is very good at speaking and a gifted communicator, with an ability to express through media. However, this ability tends to be undermined by the shadow in Sagittarius, which forces the Gemini Mars to endure gossip and rumor. Gossip—people talking about the things being talked about—destroys that common philosophy, and a potential unifier or leader crumbles under the weight of defamatory words. Expansion with no end will bring any libido to its knees, and no one can keep going forever. To deal with this libido shadow, know your limits, keep things within a manageable range, and feel content with a series of small goals and achievements spread across many places, as natal Gemini Mars would truly enjoy the diversity.

Alexander the Great had this shadow libido, which propelled him to be one of the most famous world conquerors of history. Credited with being one of the best speakers of all time, we can see how he exemplified the qualities of Mars in Gemini. His influence spread widely and rapidly, but he passed away early, at age thirty-two, and his Macedonian Empire soon crumbled thereafter. He was believed to have died from typhoid fever, but modern research from the NIH actually indicates West Nile Virus, obtained in his travels, causing encephalitis. Becoming too big too quickly is a sure recipe for disaster and perhaps his brain became too large for its skull in a strange karmic occurrence? How interesting that Alexander the Great could have been taken out by something so small as a mosquito.

To get a hold of this shadow libido, we must become aware of how we are influencing others and not simply increasing our circle of influence. A few deep connections count far more than thousands of superficial ones, and social media has made it all too easy for many folks to reach a global audience and exert a global influence. Pause and contemplate how you want to influence people. What is your message and philosophy, and who does it serve? Even influencers need to be mindful of what is influencing them, lest they lead their flock astray.

Example in Nature

Caribou, from numerous populations, were found to have the longest existing migrations in the world, with the round-trip distances exceeding 745 miles (1,200 km). Despite exhibiting the longest migrations in the world, a few species moved more than caribou in a year. Gray wolves and khulan (Mongolian wild ass) all moved more than caribou when considering their entire annual GPS track. A gray wolf from Mongolia captured the title of top terrestrial mover, having traveled 4,503 miles (7,247 km) in a year. To put this into perspective, it would be similar to you walking from Washington, DC to Los Angeles . . . and back . . . in a year.

— Kyle Joly, "Confirmed! Caribou Have the Longest Land Migration in the World," National Park Service, November 12, 2019

♑

Capricorn Mars Shadow

Ambition Monster

Birth Mars: Cancer ♋
Ambition: Ride the high

The person with libido in the shadow of Capricorn wants others to love her and wants to solicit an emotional response; she wants you to feel and wants to watch you feel it. The natal Mars in Cancer is usually focused on ambition and success, and the oppositional shadow of Capricorn focuses the libido on the sensations and feelings that are generated from that success. One might say that the whole reason for achieving and succeeding is to have that feeling of fulfillment that usually accompanies success, the fullness of being and satisfaction of potential realized. The individual with the Capricorn shadow wants to feel this through both herself and others. More than a feeling of celebration, it becomes a feeling of completing a goal. Completion brings peace.

The danger of this shadow placement is that the native is not so much chasing a goal as he is chasing a feeling, a never-ending summer. He becomes a kind of ambition monster who doesn't really have a goal or purpose but is only chasing. When the libido is focused on this type of shadow, the danger of excess and loss of focus overwhelms the person and keeps him seeking instant gratification, unrelated to his true purpose, and so he never achieves his goal. This is the hare who takes a nap before completing his journey and so loses the race to the tortoise.

Sir Edmund Hillary had this Mars shadow. It seems remarkable that he received so much attention when the Sherpa who accompanied him up Everest, Tenzing Norgay, is known by few. Hillary dedicated most of his time after his ascent to assisting the Nepalese people with charity and development in their communities. He kept on thrill seeking after achieving Everest: treks to the North and South Poles, including one with Neil Armstrong. This made him not only the highest climber but also the only person to reach both poles, among many other achievements—fitting for this Mars shadow.

Example in Nature

Last summer, scientists reported finding the world's highest-dwelling mammal, a yellow-rumped leaf-eared mouse, which was seen scampering among the upper reaches of Llullaillaco, the world's highest historically active volcano, straddling Argentina and Chile. It's incredible that anything could live that high, at 20,340 feet—there is no vegetation, and seemingly nothing to eat. Here, at the edge of the Atacama Desert, there is little rain, and temperatures sometimes plunge below minus 75 degrees Fahrenheit. "It's hard to overstate how hostile an environment it is," says Jay Storz, a biologist at the University of Nebraska, Lincoln, and a National

Geographic Explorer. Intrigued by the discovery, Storz organized an expedition to the volcano in February specifically to search for rodents. And rodents he found.

— Douglas Main, "Mouse Found Atop a 22,000-Foot Volcano, Breaking World Record," *National Geographic*, March 23, 2020

♒

Aquarius Mars Shadow

The Cuckold

Birth Mars: Leo ♌
Ambition: The watcher

Mars in Leo wants to be onstage; in fact most folk I know with this placement are performers. So in typical shadow fashion, the Aquarius shadow of this libido expresses itself by sitting in the audience and watching the show. These natives will oscillate between taking center stage and watching others perform and fulfill their dreams. This shadow will force the holder to watch what he wants to do until the day he finds the courage to simply stand up and do it himself and stop watching. Porn addiction can be an issue for this shadow Mars, or only engaging in sexual role-play with professionals, seeking strictly sexual relationships free from ties of any kind, thus precluding intimacy.

Some people prefer an impersonal, indirect expression of the libido. The courtship and confrontations involved in sexual intimacy aren't for everyone and can become exhausting, not to mention the dangers involved from sexually transmitted diseases or unwanted pregnancy. Seeking self-protection through noninteraction can hardly be judged when we consider all the risks involved with sexual interactions. Aquarius could be said to represent free love and unique expression, needing to experiment, remain fluid in sexual and gender identifications; this placement rebels against sexual norms. From this shadow we find release from sexual oppression so it serves for the sexually creative libido. The danger of this libido is natives can dehumanize sexuality, or find mates who do not share their view points.

Consent and communication are needed for this type of libido to steer clear from the expectations and assumptions of others and from unnecessary shadow projections that others may visit upon these free-spirited natives.

Fyodor Dostoevsky had this Mars libido shadow and sought to express much of it through his writing. He also sought the company of prostitutes to avoid intimacy with others. Although we are all grateful for his visionary works, he certainly represents this placement's tendency to dissociate sexuality and jump into an experimental free-for-all, where he would play out his needs and have others watch or vicariously read of his exploits.

Example in Nature

The name "tongue-eating louse," as horrifying as it sounds, barely begins to do Cymothoa exigua *justice. This marine parasite isn't satisfied with consuming the tongue of its host—it actually replaces it. And that's after a sex change during the process. Let's back up. First, a cadre of juvenile lice will infiltrate the gills of a hapless fish and mature into males. Upon reaching adult size, at least one will transform into a female, ostensibly to even out the sexes. The newly minted lady louse will then wriggle up the fish's throat, anchor herself to her host's tongue, and slowly begin to drain the organ of its blood. The poor fish's tongue withers into a useless nub, leaving the mouth vacant for the louse itself to physically take its place, helping its host move food around its mouth and grind big morsels down to size. During its off hours, the bug contentedly feeds, relaxes and bumps uglies with the gill-dwelling males.*

— Katherine J. Wu and Rachael Lallensack,
"Fourteen Fun Facts about Love and Sex in the
Animal Kingdom," *Smithsonian Magazine*, February 14, 2020

♓

Pisces Mars Shadow

The Debaser

Birth Mars: Virgo ♍
Ambition: Surviving shame

The libido placed in the shadow of Pisces is difficult because Mars wants action and Pisces craves oblivion and stillness. This is a recipe for shadow opposition if ever there was one. The birth Mars in Virgo seeks perfection in performance; the Mars shadow in Pisces is impotent through incompleteness. Pisces sees no end, and Virgo wants completion and judges incompletion, so where is the compromise? As things unravel, or success inches away, there is an inability to bring things to completion. A good way to transmute this shadow placement is in tantric sexuality. The need to complete can be sublimated through tantra, which purposefully extends things, never seeking gratification. When the purpose becomes no purpose, or the activity is an end in itself, this seeming failure of Mars and the inability to realize ambition has less of an impact and becomes more of a learning experience.

Because the shadow Mars in Pisces usually fails to finish, the Mars position in Virgo has a tendency to enjoy humiliating or being humiliated. The act of failing becomes the focus of this libido, and the holder of this placement may deal with failure by shaming others. There is a tendency to rub another's nose in failure, so to speak; in this way the native vicariously seeks to sublimate his own failures through the shadow of humiliation. The natal Mars in Virgo wants things to be perfect, wants to be successful, so under the shadow, the native enjoys watching others get humiliated and will often engage in shaming behavior. Sometimes these individuals shame themselves, sometimes they project shame onto others, and sometimes they place themselves in situations where others can shame them. The danger of this shadow placement is abuse to self and others, and it needs to be addressed and expressed creatively rather than subconsciously. The best creative expression of this is S&M or bondage, where humiliation can be explored safely and consensually with compassion and understanding and not expressed destructively in the shadow realm.

Charles Manson had this shadow libido, which he obviously manifested by violently shaming others for their transgressions, scapegoating them for his own agenda since he himself did not reach his perceived ideal of perfection. Anyone who tries to arbitrarily punish someone with violence due to their own ideals is clearly operating in some kind of shadow projection. Perhaps if he had had a proper outlet for his feelings of shame for himself, he could have avoided projecting blame onto others. There is quite a lot of data about Manson, obviously, along with the deeper conspiracies. The book *CHAOS: Charles Manson, the CIA, and the Secret History of the Sixties* by Tom O'Neill suggests to me that this shadow can involve some deeper scapegoating, reaching beyond Manson as an individual.*

Example in Nature

> *Hauser (2000b) observed what could be labeled embarrassment in a male rhesus monkey. After copulating, the male strutted away and accidentally fell into a ditch. He stood up and quickly looked around. After sensing that no other monkeys saw him tumble, he marched off, back high, head and tail up, as if nothing had happened. Once again, comparative research in neurobiology, endocrinology, and behavior is needed to learn more about the subjective nature of embarrassment.*
>
> — Marc Bekoff, "Animal Emotions: Exploring Passionate Natures," *BioScience* 50, no. 10 (October 2000)

*Thanks to my friend Jodi Wille for telling me about this book.

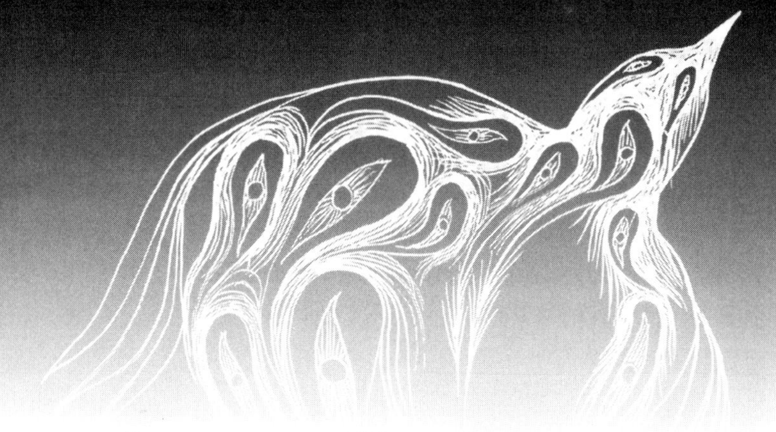

Jupiter Shadows

Overreaching Indulgence

Some of the gods encouraged Jupiter's anger, shouting their approval of his words, while others consented silently. They were all saddened though at this destruction of the human species, and questioned what the future of the world would be free of humanity. Who would honour their altars with incense? Did he mean to surrender the world to the ravages of wild creatures? In answer the king of the gods calmed their anxiety, the rest would be his concern, and he promised them a people different from the first, of a marvellous creation. Now he was ready to hurl his lightning-bolts at the whole world but feared that the sacred heavens might burst into flame from the fires below, and burn to the furthest pole: and he remembered that a time was fated to come when sea and land, and the untouched courts of the skies would ignite, and the troubled mass of the world be besieged by fire. So he set aside the weapons the Cyclopes forged, and resolved on a different punishment, to send down rain from the whole sky and drown humanity beneath the waves.

OVID, *METAMORPHOSIS*

Nothing can keep growing forever; every bubble must burst. Jupiter doesn't like pesky limits and boundaries and enjoys bursting people's bubbles. Jupiter has the energy of Shiva, the supreme god who creates, destroys, and transforms. Jupiter is the arrow that never stops, never stills, and knows no bounds. Jupiter has a positive energy and generates optimism. The planet Jupiter itself is said to produce more energy than it takes from the sun, a seemingly impossible feat, pronouncing its own source of independent energy. But there's a flip side to every coin: Jupiter shadows seek to have it all, to go into excess, to party large and force growth where it perceives stagnation. The Saturn shadow wants to be the only one, while the Jupiter shadow wants to be everyone and everything.

Never-ending growth in individual life-forms and of species is destructive. Examples are cancer or an invasive species that overwhelms an ecosystem. The Jupiter shadow is the storm that never ends, much like the perpetual lightning eye on the planet itself. It is the fire that burns everything, unrelentingly. We all need some amount of Jupiter shadow to keep us seeking growth. Similar to the Mars libido shadow, the Jupiter shadow will push forward, and without it, we stagnate or are underachievers who cannot attain fulfillment or be productive. If humanity was without Jupiter's ominous expansion, humans might still be living in caves, too afraid to emerge and explore. Jupiter will keep us reaching, keep us going into outer space, keep us exploring the depths of the sea—not for the ego or the self, like the Mars shadow, but for the sake of the adventure itself, to feel expanded, to be large, to go big.

Sometimes simply amassing growth is a success strategy that nature uses. Sheer numbers and expansion can ensure survival, so this is the natural defensive action in Jupiter's shade. A colony of ants will last longer than a single one. Size matters, much as we wish it didn't. When a corporation becomes global, it is less likely to fail, until, that is, it becomes too big for its britches and overextends itself. People or entities seeking to rule the world often spread themselves too thin, and the Jupiter shadow, seeking ever-expansive territories, fails or falters when it can't contain its own boundaries.

♈

Aries Jupiter Shadow

Full of Myself

Birth Jupiter: Libra ♎
Limit Advised: Restrict self-justifications

The indulgence of this Jupiter shadow is in its own ego. In olden times it was said of the rooster that he was so full of himself, he thought the sun rose because it heard the rooster's call. We call people cocky because they think the sun rises and sets just for them. Here the ego has expanded past its own reality in a way that becomes exaggerated and unsustainable. The predicament of Jupiter in Aries's shadow is a personality that overwhelms much of its thinking and causes it to lose sight of others and its grip on reciprocity. Carl Jung had Jupiter in Libra natally so had this Jupiter shadow. We can see how he used it to look into the concept of the ego itself and expand it far beyond the work of his teacher Sigmund Freud. Certainly this shadow placement literally forced the ego into everyone's consciousness through the works of Jung and expanded it far beyond anyone's understanding previously. Unable to look away from the fascination of the ego itself as an entity, it became the focus of much of Jung's work as he strove to understand it, while carrying no small amount of it himself.

The danger of this ego shadow placement is that the individual will not take into account the ideas of others and will fall in love with a personal ability to think and comprehend things. This becomes an ego bias that makes the individual think they are right no matter what, and then creates difficulty to a partner due to resistance to letting anyone else in. The individual will fight to preserve a personal opinion in the face of others who are offering alternate views. Others can benefit from this individual, who will share unique ideas and thoughts, which may differ from others, but it can become a bit self-masturbatory after a certain point.

To transmute this shadow you need to have discussions with others and not feel threatened or feel the need to hold to your self's concepts of what ego is. For example, in this book, maybe you have different ideas about what the ego is and how I discuss it or present it through the signs. Perhaps you disagree? If I were to hold tightly to my own concepts at the exclusion of yours, I would be holding this shadow because concepts of ego in astrology are much larger than my own ideas, which have their limits. It would be foolish of me to think otherwise. Jung dealt with the ego concepts he held through myth and history, concepts that hardly belonged to him and that deserve equal merit and praise.*

Example in Nature

The symbolism of the fighting rooster that expresses a fierce independence is easily observed in text and art of early America and the nineteenth-century South. Journalist James Agee reminded us in 1934 that "the eagle was chosen to symbolize the U.S. by only two votes over the cock." . . .

The Confederacy placed images of the rooster on its currency. . . .

Creative spirits have used the cockfight for symbolism in poems, paintings, and short stories. . . .

In America institutionalized opposition to cock-fighting, and other forms of alleged animal abuse, can be dated to 1866. . . .

The American Humane Association came into being a decade later, and these two organizations have led their fight against cockfighting and more into the late twentieth century. Significantly, women—not men—have been the backbone of the opposition. Women constitute the core of activism and continue to generate the critical attack. One historian noted, "Were the support of the women of America suddenly withdrawn, the large majority of societies for the prevention of cruelty to children and animals would cease to exist." Another historian reported the complaint of a pit-sport enthusiast in 1979:

"The Ladies League came in, and when the women control you, that's it."

— Lynn Morrow, "History They Don't Teach You: A Tradition of Cockfighting," *White River Valley Historical Quarterly* 35, no. 2 (Fall 1995)

*I must say that I disagree with Jung's personal shadows of potentially abusing his clients and students to the point of controversial accusations of rape, specifically from Sabina Spielrein.

♉

Taurus Jupiter Shadow

The World Is Your Oyster

Birth Jupiter: Scorpio ♏
Limit Advised: Be part of an ecosystem

The Jupiter shadow in Taurus causes indulgence and lack of restraint toward Earth, her resources and territory. There are many things that contribute to the fall of empires. One is expansion into too great a territory. Another is lack of food and resources because the army is spread too thin, or overextends itself into places that don't have enough food to support it. Famines are real and continue to happen. Survival on Earth is real and deserves respect.

In this Jupiter shadow, it is taken for granted that the individual can take land and food wherever they want and suffer no consequences. The balance of nature and root needs from the natal position of Jupiter in Scorpio will teach you things, should you wander too far into the folly of this Jupiter shadow. Often the danger to the individual with this shadow is overindulgence in food and acquiring too much property, which the individual cannot manage. The corrupt landlord who turns into a slumlord and the corporation that abuses low-income communities are common with this placement. When these abuses become too egregious, society pushes back, demanding an increase in real estate laws that favor the tenant, with restrictions to prevent abuse.

This shadow is particularly offensive because the shadow holders believe all Earth belongs to them, and can be used as a territory as they wish, regardless of whoever else might be living there. The need to secure earthly resources overrides all else and is completely blown out of all proportion and often used purely for profit. The entity that owns the most real estate in the world is the British royal family, followed by the Roman Catholic Church. Showing up in other countries and claiming their land, taking it from the people while infiltrating their culture, is an excessive abuse of resources and ecosystems. The best way to transmute this shadow is to redistribute the wealth and return things that were stolen from people and cultures, and a large portion of what needs to be returned is the land itself and all the resources on and in it.

Example in Nature

For decades, elephants' invasion is known to be associated with severe environmental consequences leading to escalated depletion of environmental resources (plants, water, wildlife and soil). This paper examined the effects of elephants' activity on the environmental resources in Hong and Gombi Local Government areas of Adamawa State, considering the damage they usually cause. . . . Results showed that the extent of damage was highly significant for all the crops namely; mango, guava and orange while the types of damage done to plants, water, wildlife and soil . . . water pollution, soil erosion, scarring of smaller wild animals, enhanced desertification, emigration of wild animals, blockage of waterways and extinction of some less resistant plant species. Further investigation revealed that a large sum of money was lost due to elephants' activity on the horticultural crops such as mango, orange and guava.

— Michael Awi, "Elephant Invasion and Escalated Depletion of Environmental Resources in a Semi Arid Tropical Ecosystem," *Animal Research International* 4, no. 3 (2007): 758–61

♊

Gemini Jupiter Shadow

The Braggart

Birth Jupiter: Sagittarius ♐
Limit Advised: Shut up, sometimes

The shadow of Jupiter in Gemini is unmistakable. You won't be able to miss those under this shadow's influence because they refuse to stop talking. Just look for the open mouth if you are looking for this shadow form. Although freedom of speech is a wonderful thing, and open communication and the ability to speak freely are certainly virtuous and much needed, there comes a time to be quiet to keep the scales balanced. A mouth that always speaks cannot hear itself and cannot listen, and this can cause problems even if all the words spoken are great.

Overexpansion of the mouth will invariably lead to gossip and grandiose speech, including hyperbole, and with that follows a general loss of impact due to overuse. There can be a lot of words said but not much meaning with this shadow as well. Sagittarius Jupiter will go big and achieve big things, great things. Its shadow in Gemini will talk about them—a lot. There is a lot of wisdom in advice not to boast about achievements. It is important to spread the word on things, but overdoing it invites the negative shadows associated here. The practices of the Greek Stoics, who practiced temperance and living in accordance with nature, can balance and transmute this Jupiter shadow. Communicate specifically and succinctly rather than shooting for sheer volume.

Life coach Tony Robbins has this Jupiter shadow, and not to diminish his accomplishments, he has, perhaps, spoken too much and too freely and overshot the mark, exemplifying well the folly of this Jupiter shadow. To effectively transmute this placement, focus closely on which words are important and when. Also let other people speak about you and what you have done as well; this provides inspiration for others and gives them a chance to participate in your achievements rather than always speaking up on behalf of your own wisdom and glory. A truly wise person speaks more about the wisdom of others than their own and in this way comes into humility and the ability to measure the spoken words, thereby gaining more through fewer words.

Example in Nature

Sea lions produce sounds both above and below water. California sea lions are among the most vocal of all mammals. Vocalizations include barks, growls, and grunts. During the breeding season, male California sea lions bark incessantly when establishing territories; once established, the males bark only when maintaining and defending their territories. During periods of nonbreeding, submissive males become more vocal than dominant males. Females use a specific vocalization during the mother-pup recognition sequence. This occurs when a female returns to the rookery after feeding to locate her pup. The female emits a loud trumpeting vocalization, which elicits a bleating response from her pup. . . . Females become very aggressive immediately before and after giving birth. Their "threat vocals" progress from a bark to an intense squeal to a more forceful belch and finally to an irregular growl. Pups make a bleating mother-pup recognition call and a high-pitched alarm call.

— "Communication: Sound Production,"
SeaWorld Parks & Entertainment, seaworld.org

♋

Cancer Jupiter Shadow

Melodrama

Birth Jupiter: Capricorn ♑
Limit Advised: A little goes a long way

The birth Jupiter in Capricorn is restrained, just as in the myth, Saturn (ruler of Capricorn) seeks to suppress his son Jupiter. The toxic Saturn patriarch of Jupiter attempts to suppress Jupiter's big feelings until this placement finds boundless freedom in its Cancer shadow. In the Cancer shadow placement of Jupiter, the holders give themselves permission to unload all the feelings they have within, often with the assistance of a substance or alcohol, and may indulge in anger or misery that, though justified, seems disproportionate to the immediate situation. The important thing to realize is that people with this shadow placement are seeking and need to freely express emotions, which may not reflect reality and could be hyperbolized. Somewhere, emotional expression was minimized, and so the shadow acts to counteract or compensate for the restrictions and restraint natives have experienced by grandstanding and venting, taking their emotions out on others. It's someone angered by what happened at work, who goes home and kicks the dog.

The antidote is to learn to safely express anger and communicate directly with the people who dismiss and disregard your feelings. If someone else did not appreciate your ability to feel deeply, or you yourself failed to recognize your feelings, make sure you don't do the same thing to others. You probably haven't liked it when someone used emotions against you to get even, in a subconscious retaliation. The danger of this shadow placement is that the reaction is not equal to the offense, and the holder of it may seek to emotionally annihilate someone for the smallest perceived slight. If you have ever felt a toxic emotional residue left on you for seemingly no reason, it could very well be from someone holding this shadow placement and influence.

Drag queen and reality show host RuPaul Charles has this Jupiter shadow and was able to achieve mastery of it by using his tendency to be overly dramatic for entertainment. His ability to wrangle drama for aesthetics is where RuPaul found his stride, to the delight of us all.

Example in Nature

> *At first glance, the hagfish . . . looks very much like an eel. Naturalists can tell the two apart because hagfish, unlike other fish, lack backbones (and, also, jaws). . . .*
>
> *Hagfish produce slime the way humans produce opinions—readily, swiftly, defensively, and prodigiously. They slime when attacked or simply when stressed. On July 14, 2017, a truck full of hagfish overturned on an Oregon highway. The animals were destined for South Korea, where they are eaten as a delicacy, but instead, they were strewn across a stretch of Highway 101, covering the road (and at least one unfortunate car) in slime. Typically, a hagfish will release less than a teaspoon of gunk from the 100 or so slime glands that line its flanks. And in less than half a second, that little amount will expand by 10,000 times—enough to fill a sizable bucket. Reach in, and every move of your hand will drag the water with it.*
>
> — Ed Yong, "No One Is Prepared for Hagfish Slime," *Atlantic*, January 23, 2019

♌

Leo Jupiter Shadow

Toxic Optimism

Birth Jupiter: Aquarius ♒
Limit Advised: Negative energy needs to be seen

Being positive is important, and there is no doubt that having a good attitude can shift things for the better; however, under the shadow of Jupiter in Leo, positivity knows no boundaries and becomes toxic. Someone who ignores potential difficulties and dangers and charges ahead enthusiastically can cause more problems and, ironically, negativity than if he had been a cynical fuddy-duddy. For our own safety and survival, balance is needed in our enthusiasm. When we overblow or misrepresent positive results, this can cause real damage because we risk raising false hopes and false expectations among others, who then may be deeply disappointed or even have their lives ruined, if, for example, they put time, energy, and money into a project that failed. By stubbornly clinging to a positive attitude and denying potential negative consequences, we endanger others. Some things are not OK, and if you tell yourself they are when they are not, this doesn't serve. Be aware that when people tell you things are fine, when you know they are not and you are trying to alert them to danger, they may be falling under the toxic positivity shadow. Rather than being angry at their seeming gaslighting, you can assist them. Differentiate between someone trying to manipulate you and someone who is inappropriately or delusionally holding on to a positive outcome or attitude.

Marie Curie, the pioneering physicist and chemist, had this placement. She was so excited about her research and discoveries that she ignored the danger she was placing not only herself but also her husband, Pierre, in. In her enthusiastic drive toward discovery, she exposed herself and her husband to radiation—the very thing she researched successfully and tried so hard to prove—which landed them both in early graves. Even some of her notebooks, inscribed with her optimistic research notes, were so contaminated they are protectively sealed.

Example in Nature

Binge-drinking elephants, drunk on local hooch, have killed three people and destroyed 60 homes in a four-day rampage in east India.

Yesterday they were reported by local officials to be sleeping off hangovers as shocked communities tried to clear the wreckage left by the 70-strong herd in remote villages on the borders of the states of Orissa and West Bengal.

With a local festival approaching, villagers had stockpiled the fermented-rice based drink which is stored in earthenware vessels and, according to Bijay Kumar Panda, a local administrator, the elephants found and drank it.

They then staggered through the surrounding area and began "to fall asleep hither and thither, throwing life completely haywire."

— Jason Burke, "Elephants on Drunken Rampage Kill Three People," *Guardian* (Manchester, UK), December 3, 2010

♍

Virgo Jupiter Shadow

The Giving Tree Gone Bad

Birth Jupiter: Pisces ♓
Limit Advised: If you expect something back, don't give it

Guatama Buddha, also known as the Buddha, had this Jupiter shadow placement. Birth Jupiter in Pisces holds the Virgo shadow. His philosophies certainly spread throughout the globe, and one might say he is the most successful guru of all time, if we do not count messiahs.

Guatama Buddha traveled and sampled many different religious traditions, seeking practice after practice. His Jupiter located in Pisces required an ego death and a near total death of the body, as evidenced from statues depicting his emaciated form under the Bodhi tree. After his complete Pisces ego death, Buddha's Jupiter shadow in Virgo tried to articulate, regulate, and taxonomize his experience into a set of laws.

Birth Jupiter in Pisces can expand big enough to see spirit in a totality, beyond religions: the nature of Jupiter simply cannot contain this Piscean energy because it will burst forth from it. As the Virgo shadow of Jupiter crept in, analysis paralyzed liberation and shrank it back down to size.

There are many traps all around on the path to enlightenment. The danger of this Jupiter shadow is that the contraction that occurs after an ego death expansion can be so severe that it annihilates all the gains made. Think upon these words for a moment: If it is possible to expand past the ego, into a state of bliss and liberation, what is the next course of action? To decree a bunch of moral codes for others to follow, or to teach them to reach the same state of being? There is a vast difference between listening to the words of someone who has achieved ego death and actually having an ego death. This is a vital shadow to become aware of: avoid being deceived into accepting words from one who is enlightened versus becoming enlightened. If you are seeking enlightenment and you listen to words from the enlightened rather than doing the work yourself, you will be waylaid and benched, like a spectator watching a sports match.

This I learned from medicine man Kelvin deWolfe, DAOM, when we were talking about how Gautama the Buddha, despite all that he achieved, was a "bad dad" who abandoned his wife and son. According to most historical records, Gautama never returned to his family and had no concern that his abandoned kingdom underwent invasions where they could have been killed for all he knew. Even if he did return to his family post-enlightenment, the fact is that initially he completely abandoned them. The wife of Gautama was his first cousin, so there is also the shadow of incest—however, times were different then; his mother had also married a cousin.

Buddha eventually died from food poisoning, from eating either wild mushrooms or tainted meat. Do not let the words of the enlightened placate you; take action for yourself. Walk the path with your own two feet.

Example in Nature

Slow lorises—a small group of wide-eyed, nocturnal primates found in the forests of south and southeast Asia—might look adorable, but think twice before snuggling up to one. They may look harmless, but a slow loris can pack a gnarly bite laced with venom powerful enough to rot flesh. . . .

"If the killer bunnies on Monty Python were a real animal, they would be slow lorises—but they would be attacking each other."

A bite from a loris is no joke. They have glands underneath their armpits that ooze noxious oil, and when they lick those glands, their saliva combines with the oil to concoct the venom. It fills into their grooved canines, which then deliver a grisly bite strong enough to pierce through bone. The imbued venom causes the victim's flesh to rot away, and some lorises have even been seen with half their faces melted off, Nekaris tells the Times.

— Rasha Aridi, "The Cute-but-Deadly Slow Loris Reserves Its Flesh-Rotting Venom for Its Peers," *Smithsonian Magazine*, October 22, 2020

♎

Libra Jupiter Shadow

An Eye for an Eye

Birth Jupiter: Aries ♈
Limit Advised: Justice not justification

According to our known findings, the earliest written languages (aside from petroglyphs) were proto- or pre-Sumerian clay tablets from Iraq, most of which regarded economics, rules, regulations, and laws. Debatably, the earliest of these was the Kish tablet, though scholars cannot agree on what this tablet says. The Code of Hammurabi, inscribed on a stone around 1780 BCE, is one of the first known articulated codes of law written. In this code is the famous eye-for-an-eye demand for justice. Under the Libra Jupiter shadow, there is an overregulation and a preponderance of rules meant to protect, but that end up stifling everything due to severity or misunderstandings. The Libra shadow effect on Jupiter causes it to regulate itself to death.

Even death is regulated under this Jupiter shadow, which institutes regulations far beyond what is needed to keep society functioning. Bureaucratic red tape ties up everything, grinding everything to a halt; conflicts get dragged out in court, when a simple conversation might have sufficed. The natal Jupiter in Aries will want to fight, so it haggles and refuses to give or compromise, which births rule after rule. It eventually becomes impossible to get anything accomplished outside of court. This is not always beneficial as many things do not require such severe regulations, and many individuals will be unable to participate in the judicial system because they lack financial resources and so will never see justice.

Defensive behavior is natural; being overly defensive turns into aggression. We are all due justice, a balancing of the scales; that's fair. But when we seek to weight the scales, we can swing to an extreme, away from justice toward punishment for the sake of punishment. If we have a debtors' jail, for example, and we send someone to prison for nine years for not paying a sixty-dollar parking ticket, this is aggressive and damaging, overregulating to the point of harm. This shadow of understanding the difference between justice and punishment is a serious issue in our society. It is erroneous to assume strict punishments are the best solutions for decreasing crime. The old adage of throwing the baby out with the bathwater comes to mind here, where extreme laws take everyone out, including people who are still useful and wonderful but who made a small error or misstep. Understanding what it means to be human means there will be mistakes. The total value of a person's life is far greater than the errors committed, and it is not always in the interest of the greater good to enact devastating punishment toward those who commit crimes, especially if there is nuance present. Justice is a wonderful thing; we all have an innate need for it. However, when we strangle the freedom of everything with rules for our safety, there is no life present and misery prevails. Punishment and destruction are indulgences in Jupiter excess.

Example in Nature

Although positive reciprocity (reciprocal altruism) has been a focus of interest in evolutionary biology, negative reciprocity (retaliatory infliction of fitness reduction) has been largely ignored. In social animals, retaliatory aggression is common, individuals often punish other group members that infringe their interests, and punishment can cause subordinates to desist from behaviour likely to reduce the fitness of dominant animals. Punishing strategies are used to establish and maintain dominance relationships, to discourage parasites and cheats, to discipline offspring or prospective sexual partners and to maintain cooperative behaviour.

— T. H. Clutton-Brock and G. A. Parker, "Punishment in Animal Societies," *Nature* 373 (January 19, 1995): 209–16

♏

Scorpio Jupiter Shadow

Overkill

Birth Jupiter: Taurus ♉
Limit Advised: An ounce of prevention is worth a pound of cure

The Scorpio shadow of Jupiter will take its survival needs to the extreme and lose track of clear boundaries between self and other in the process. For this Jupiter shadow, safety lies in the extermination of a threat, rather than more rational ways of handling things. The holder of this shadow placement will protect resources and will overreact to a threat, triggering an inappropriate amount of force.

The best way to transmute this powerful and dangerous shadow is to win your security through sincerity, by vetting your trusted loved ones over time. If you are self-sufficient enough to include others not out of need but out of joy, you will be less likely to make power grabs and fight over resources. You do not need to live in fear of loss when you have your own self-respect and know that everything is free to come and go without your need to control it.

Julius Caesar was born with this Jupiter shadow, and in keeping with this shadow's influence to protect resources and challenge any threat, he directed his energies toward expanding his empire. Caesar was such a genius at protecting and defending his territories that he thought he could replace the democratic republic of Rome with his own ways of governance. This short-sighted move resulted in the senate rebelling and retaliating; fifty to sixty senators stabbed him twenty-three times, over and over again, way past any wound necessary to end his life, leaving a bloody mess of what had been Caesar on the portico steps of the Curia of Pompey.

Example in Nature

A chef killed a snake—but the snake had enough time to kill him back.

Chef Peng Fan, of Guangdong Province in China, cut off the head of a spitting cobra as he prepared to dice its body for a soup, the Daily Mail *reports.*

But 20 minutes later, as Peng was tossing the head in the trash, the head was still functioning. That's when the venomous creature bit the chef, who died before anti-venom could be provided. "We . . . could hear screams coming from the kitchen," says one restaurant guest.

The bite results in paralysis and asphyxiation, the Daily Mirror *notes. . . .*

Reptiles can usually function for up to an hour, even after being decapitated. "By the time a snake has lost its head, it's effectively dead as basic body functions have ceased, but there is still some reflexive action. It means snakes have the capability of biting and injecting venom even after the head has been severed."

— Matt Cantor, "Cobra's Severed Head Bites, Kills Chef," *USA Today*, August 26, 2014

♐

Sagittarius Jupiter Shadow

The Snake Charmer

Birth Jupiter: Gemini ♊
Limit Advised: There is a season, turn, turn, turn

Since the planet Jupiter rules Sagittarius, in this shadow we see the worst excesses of Jupiter's nature. These include too much food, drink, sex, and partying and boastful speech. There is a point where overreaching our limits hits the disaster zone, and it is here. Birth Jupiter in Gemini means natives will tend to live in social realms, and the placement also expands communication. It is easy to see how Jupiter in Gemini provides a perfect space for this shadow to enter and take over, if one is not mindful of the risk. The issue and confusion with the power of this shadow is that hedonism is a profound religious and spiritual practice that is effective and beneficial. Please understand, I am not anti-hedonistic and, as a Sagittarius, have had no small amount of research in this area. Too much of a good thing is still too much of a good thing.

The danger of this shadow is in overdoing hedonism to the detriment of the mind, body, and spirit. The limits to pay attention to are mind and body becoming ill. We can only socialize so much before we lose ourselves. Periods of rest are needed, not just for work but also for fun. This does not mean do not have fun. These shadow holders are gifted at having fun and being liked, which makes it all the more difficult to keep this shadow in check. To transmute this shadow, you need to go on periodic retreats to disconnect from others and tune into your body and mind, your feelings and ideas outside the influences of others and substances. If you cannot, you risk being consumed by your indulgences.

Charlie Sheen has this Jupiter shadow, and it has threatened to consume him more than a few times as he has struggled with substance abuse and even overdosed once. When we reach our limits it is important to pay heed to our heart's inability to function and to step back and see how we are affecting others, how our self-abuse can change into abusive behavior toward our loved ones.

Example in Nature

*Because they [the black swallower fish] swallow their prey whole, the food in their stomach sometimes doesn't have enough time to digest and actually starts decomposing within their stomach. If that's not gross enough, this dead decomposing animal in their stomach starts producing gas which forces the black swallower to the surface of the ocean, effectively killing them in the process. Back in 2007, a dead black swallower with a length of just 19 centimeters (7.5 inches) was found on the shores of Grand Cayman Island. Inside its stomach was an 86 centimeters (34 inches) long snake mackerel (*Gempylus serpens*) which had fallen victim to the predator. The swallower was eventually killed because of the gas which forced him up to the ocean surface, and the greed of wanting to eat a creature 4 times its own size!*

— Jody McCallum, "12 Incredible Black Swallower Facts," Animal Stratosphere, December 4, 2020

♑
Capricorn Jupiter Shadow
The Sore Loser

Birth Jupiter: Cancer ♋
Limit Advised: Ethics are always available

Jupiter is very uncomfortable in a Capricorn shadow because of the presence and influence of Saturn, who tried to eat Jupiter as a baby. Capricorn is restrictive and repressed, while Jupiter seeks to expand, making things bigger, and push everything out further. What we see with this shadow is an excess of control. The birth Jupiter in Cancer has big feelings, big emotions, and powerful instincts; the shadow side of this is a fear of feeling grief and loss, due to the enormity and depth of emotion. The Jupiter shadow in this placement will make sure it wins, and so it becomes an entity that ensures victory, even if that means cheating. This is the CEO that fudges the books to claim success that isn't there. Corporations set themselves up to draw from bigger resources than a single individual can provide, placing the ego in a position to go bigger and further, even generationally, through a brand of corporate success that serves more than just one person. They are willing to pay fines and penalties for crimes they feel they need to commit to put themselves ahead of the game. Lack of morals and ethics tend to accompany this Jupiter shadow because excess and indulgence are so key to success that the means do not matter as long as the end is reached.

George W. Bush has this Jupiter shadow. Bush controversially won the presidential election against Al Gore. He lost the popular vote, which resulted in the common perception that he won the presidency by cheating, by inappropriately securing the electoral votes he needed. After the Florida Supreme Court ordered a statewide recount of that state's votes, the Bush campaign asked the U.S. Supreme Court to stay the state supreme court's decision and halt the recount. The Supreme Court voted to halt the recount and allow the certification of the vote, enabling Bush to win Florida's electoral votes and the presidency. Some accused the Supreme Court of being unduly swayed by the Bush campaign. It's hard to say what the truth is; either way, this situation was definitely under the influence of this shadow.

Example in Nature

Without any orders or direction, individuals from the rank and file instinctively stretch across the opening, clinging to one another as their comrades-in-arms swarm across their bodies. But this is no force of superhumans. These are army ants of the species Eciton hamatum*, which form "living" bridges across breaks and gaps in the forest floor that allow their famously large raiding swarms to travel efficiently. . . . The ants exhibit a level of collective intelligence that could provide new insights into animal behavior and even help in the development of intuitive robots that can cooperate as a group, the researchers said. Ants of* E. hamatum *automatically form living bridges without any oversight from a "lead" ant, the researchers report. . . . The ants will create a path over an open space up to the point* *when too many workers are being diverted from collecting food and prey. "There's no single ant overseeing the decision, they're making that calculation as a colony," Lutz said.*

— Morgan Kelly, "Ants Build 'Living' Bridges with Their Bodies, Speak Volumes about Group Intelligence," Princeton University, November 30, 2015

♒

Aquarius Jupiter Shadow

Infinity Is Too Small

Birth Jupiter: Leo ♌
Limit Advised: Even aliens need friends

The Aquarius Jupiter shadow longs for alien experiences and is an outer space explorer. Jupiter meets the imagination in this shadow placement, which can be a beautiful thing, but also gets ungrounded quickly. This shadow placement will send the holder so far past previously established boundaries that it is literally inconceivable. The advantage of this is the discovery of new thoughts, new ideas, and revolutionary inventions. The darkness and unknown of outer space itself is the shadow-forming substance with this placement, and we can only stare into the abyss for so long before we start to float off into it, isolating from the rest of humanity, becoming an alien.

Occasionally tripping out or mind wandering is wonderful to experience, but if we don't journey back down into the soles of our shoes we might miss out on life. Basic joys and pleasures become disconnected, and our senses become deranged, pushing us further into the imaginative realms. I love expanding my consciousness through meditation techniques and exploring consciousness, but I have to be home by six to cook dinner for my kids, and I'm grateful for this.

To get an idea of what Jupiter in Aquarius looks like when it isn't in shadow, Virgin Galactic's first crewed space flight occurred in July 2021 with Jupiter in Aquarius, which was also the placement when the *Challenger* disaster occurred in 1986. It will be interesting to witness the shadow when it comes to us in 2026; we should see individuals striving for space expansion in unprecedented ways. Because the birth Jupiter will be in Leo under this shadow, it is important for the individual to be able to seek community when going exploring, to touch down and be with other people and family and not wander too far. I might recommend giving a listen to the song "100 Tampons" by Marcia Belsky to get a humorous look at how even NASA scientists can be wildly ungrounded, letting their imagination get the better of them from time to time.

Example in Nature

> *Tardigrades are one of the most fascinating creatures on Earth—and the moon. In 2019, the Israeli spacecraft Beresheet crashed on the moon, spilling thousands of the dehydrated tardigrades that scientists loaded onto the lander (along with human DNA samples). The tardigrades were in "tun" form, a dormant state where they shrivel up into a ball, expel most of the water in their bodies, and lower their metabolism via cryptobiosis until they enter an environment better suited for sustaining life. They can exist like this for decades. They're also pretty hardy and can endure even the harshest environments, including subzero temperatures—and, you know, lunar crash landings.*
>
> — William Herkewitz and Daisy Hernandez, "7 Fascinating Facts about the Tardigrade, the Only Animal That Can Survive in Space," *Popular Mechanics*, October 21, 2022

♓

Pisces Jupiter Shadow

The Prophet

Birth Jupiter: Virgo ♍
Limit Advised: You can't control spirit

This is the cult leader or guru who destroys the egos of all their followers. The shadow of Jupiter in Pisces is the ego obliterator preaching infinite expansion. Here the Jupiter shadow presents promises of religion and heaven while leading an entire church and breaks down the power of the individual into a soupy Pisces mess, while the natal Jupiter in Virgo takes total control and guides and leads all their actions based on a set of rules and discipline. Mind control is usually a large part of this Jupiter shadow. The difficulty in discerning the difference between this Jupiter shadow and a healthy necessary component of spiritual advance, namely that of ego death, is that a holder of this Jupiter shadow will not only break the ego of another person but will also replace it with propaganda of the holder's choosing.

In nearly all spiritual traditions and physical disciplines, the ego is broken, like a horse that needs to be domesticated, but the signature of the Jupiter shadow in Pisces is that the individuals are then turned into zombies to be used for whatever purposes the prophetic mastermind wishes. Obviously, this creates many dangers and can last through generations if left unchecked. Millions of people can be victims of their Jupiter shadow, hiding within religion and spirituality. People willingly surrender their egos to the cause, thinking they are providing for their afterlife and becoming holy by being subservient and virtuous. All manner of abuses tend to follow this—sexual, physical, emotional, and spiritual.

> *The most dramatic instances of directed behavior change and "mind control" are not the consequence of exotic forms of influence, such as hypnosis, psychotropic drugs, or "brainwashing," but rather the systematic manipulation of the most mundane aspects of human nature over time in confining settings.*
>
> PHILIP G. ZIMBARDO, *THE LUCIFER EFFECT: UNDERSTANDING HOW GOOD PEOPLE TURN EVIL*

Sex offender Warren Jeffs, the prophet of the Fundamentalist Church of Jesus Christ of Latter-Day Saints, has this Jupiter shadow. Jeffs assumed full control of the church after his father's death and forced all his father's widows to marry him. He assigned wives to husbands, including marriages of men to underage girls, while he married girls as young as twelve. He was convicted of multiple counts of rape and sexual abuse and is serving a life sentence. Quite a few religions and cultures marry off young girls to men, so it certainly is not a practice unique to this church, but it is one that was abused by a charismatic guru holding a Pisces Jupiter shadow.

Example in Nature

Wasps are horrible, awful, pointless creatures, and we hate them. . . . But some of them are inexplicably worse than others: Enter the Glyptapanteles. These wasps are not content to sting and kill their prey (in this case, the gypsy moth caterpillar), but actually inject their eggs inside of the victim's body. So their victims aren't just killed and eaten, but are first impregnated via interspecies wasp-rape. And yes, did you even need to ask? Of course the wasp babies eat the caterpillars from inside.

And yet, still, the caterpillars do not die. . . . Some of the larva hatch and burrow out of the caterpillar's skin, sure, and that's horrible, but others stay behind . . . to take control of its brain. *The mind-controlling pupa inside manipulates the caterpillar into standing guard and protecting their vulnerable brethren outside, occasionally even forcing it to spin protective silk over them. So the caterpillar not only gets stung, raped and hollowed out, but also actually has to sit there and guard its attackers against all predators.*

— Luke Taylor, "The 5 Creepiest Ways Animals Have Mastered Mind Control," Cracked, August 24, 2011

Saturn Shadows

The Beast Master

Saturn is fallen, am I too to fall?
Am I to leave this haven of my rest,
This cradle of my glory, this soft clime,
This calm luxuriance of blissful light,
These crystalline pavilions, and pure fanes,
Of all my lucent empire? It is left
Deserted, void, nor any haunt of mine.
The blaze, the splendour, and the symmetry,
I cannot see—but darkness, death and darkness.
Even here, into my centre of repose,
The shady visions come to domineer,
Insult, and blind, and stifle up my pomp.—
Fall!—No, by Tellus and her briny robes!
Over the fiery frontier of my realms
I will advance a terrible right arm
Shall scare that infant thunderer, rebel Jove,
And bid old Saturn take his throne again.

John Keats, *Hyperion*

THE SHADOW OF SATURN IS PRETTY DARK, likely because Saturn is basically the grim reaper. The poets and musicians might have you believing the moon to be the culprit in our shady underpinnings or subconscious, but they know nothing of the cold Saturnine affairs that grip us all eventually. In the thousands of charts I've seen as an astrologer, if there is one thing I can attest to it is that the Saturn return is real. Saturn carries the scythe to reap the harvest of the grain once it has reached its fruition, which places Saturn in the grain gods category. Saturn sought to keep so much control and rulership in the world that he ate his own children in order to prevent anyone else from sharing in the glory. No king was born from himself; to come into existence, rulers are beholden to Earth and sky, to the Titans. Saturn contains the energy of the patriarchy, which, rather than being confined to "father," is the toxic expression of masculine energy. Masculine energy moves, protects, and binds; the shadow of masculinity controls, possesses, and imprisons. The quintessential error of patriarchs is to ignore how they came into being and to seek to control females, creating a make-believe world in which they can pretend they exist independently and owe no one anything. Ask any bank what it owes Earth for its existence, and suddenly it cannot find a number on the calculator.

Our shadow Saturn is the place where we have a deep need to put our mark on the physical world as ruler and king. If we have to, we will murder all other competition so that we can be the eternal pharaoh, forever and ever. Saturn must be the boss. What most human beings do not understand in their actions to rule and win, to put their name on something, is that it isn't even them that wants it; they are housing an archon who seeks domination, who uses them like a puppet. To be the single thing that stands above all things is a certain kind of energy, and it is Saturn who is influencing this shadow behavior. This energy peaks at Saturn returns at age twenty-seven to thirty and fifty-seven to sixty, like ticks on a clock. Julius Caesar and Alexander the Great housed the Saturn shadow in the extreme. Not only in humans, but also in nature we find this archetype expressed. The alpha male lion, for example, will eat the offspring of other males so that his genetic line prevails, and commonly kicks his own male children out of the pride to maintain his dominance. Polar and grizzly bears also exhibit this behavior. Countless adult males, including primates, banish male children or engage in infanticide as a breeding strategy: killing babies fathered by another male and impregnating the dead babies' mother. This natural, common behavior is a hierarchical shadow in the animal kingdom that also exists within our own biology, expressed to serve various purposes for survival and competition. Here we learn the deep need for dominance comes not from any part of our true self, but rather from a consequence of life within a natural system on planet Earth and verily some sort of cosmic entity that has crystallized into the being known as Saturn. Until we see it in this broader sense, we will never become its master and transmute this shadow.

All secrets are in Saturn.

PYTHAGORAS

Shadow Saturn serves to show us where we are not evolving, growing, or coming into our higher natures, where we are remaining trapped within our inner child. I believe we need to observe the lessons of the Saturn shadow as it plays a crucial role in our mastery of the Saturn return in our astrological natal chart roughly every thirty years. Mastery of the Saturn shadow is the most difficult and rarely achieved, so understand you are now entering the palace of rulership when you seek to step into these lands. Saturn is not for the faint of heart but rules your flesh regardless. The Saturn shadow is here to remind us of our biological antecedents and what we leave behind in legacy. For overcoming this influence, you will need time, humility, and patience and to release the desire to dominate. *Devotion* is the antidote to the Saturn shadow in Vedic astrology, which is the domain of Hanuman, the ardent devotee of Rama, and *bhakti* or devotional worship. Dig your heels into your commitment. Saturn is the ruler of karma, which is not punishment, but a cyclic consequence.

In the words of Helena Blavatsky,

> Some theosophists, in order to make Karma more comprehensible to the Western mind, as being better acquainted with the Greek than with Aryan philosophy, have made an attempt to translate it by *Nemesis*. . . . With the early Greeks, "from Homer to Herodotus, she was no goddess, but a *moral feeling* rather," says Decharme; the barrier to evil and immorality. He who transgresses it, commits a sacrilege in the eyes of the gods, and is pursued by Nemesis. But, with time, that "feeling" was deified, and its personification became an ever-fatal and punishing goddess. . . . "The inevitable"—represents Nemesis as the immutable effect of causes created by man himself. Nemesis, as the daughter of *Dike*, is the equitable goddess reserving her wrath for those alone who are maddened with pride, egoism, and impiety. . . . In short, while Nemesis is a mythological, exoteric goddess, or Power, personified and anthropomorphised in its various aspects, *Karma* is a highly philosophical truth, a most divine noble expression of the primitive intuition of man concerning Deity. It is a doctrine which explains the origin of Evil, and ennobles our conceptions of what divine immutable justice ought to be, instead of degrading the unknown and unknowable Deity by making it the whimsical cruel tyrant which we call providence.*

If we are forever in debt to our mother, Gaia, Earth for feeding us, the only way to set the scales back into balance is to feed others who are unable to do so themselves. The more you are able to feed, you become lord, the bread holder, the one who distributes the bread. This is the key to the story in the Bible of Jesus feeding the hungry with loaves of bread. He becomes their lord, by ruling his own Saturn shadow, which would otherwise have taken bread from them to ensure only he survived. Rulership is something that is earned through merit, not forced through domination; this is the lesson of the karma of Saturn. True leadership comes when power is shared with all, lest things circle back

*Helena Blavatsky, *The Synthesis of Science, Religion, and Philosophy*, volume 2 in *The Secret Doctrine* (London: Theosophical Society, 1888), 305.

around and those you took from seek revenge. We see Saturn's influence in all leaders who take everything to enrich their own empire. Karma is the master of the Saturn influence, and once you perceive and acknowledge how your actions will affect future generations and make choices for the good of the many, you are the lord of Saturn.

> *The tragic element in poetry is like Saturn in alchemy,—the Malevolent, the Destroyer of Nature; but without it no true Aurum Potabile, or Elixir of Life, can be made.*
>
> Henry Wadsworth Longfellow, *Prose Works*

♈

Aries Saturn Shadow

The One Who Would Be King

Birth Saturn: Libra ♎
Master Key: Unite all under spirit not under self

We need look no further for an explanation of the shadow Saturn in Aries than Genghis Khan. Genghis Khan was born with his Saturn in Libra, giving him an Aries Saturn shadow. This Aries Saturn shadow made sure his mark and his genes far surpassed any before or after him. Saturn shadow of Aries will use force, come hell or high water, to ensure that the individual remains supreme and singular over all others. It is no coincidence that with this placement, Genghis Khan is considered a "super Y" or one of the living men who fathered more children than any other man. Supreme ruler was a title he earned through exploits. Birth Saturn in Libra shows one who rules by law, and Genghis Khan was arguably one of the first rulers of many of the tribal nations he conquered to impose a set of just and consistent laws to help govern the people. True to his birth Saturn in Libra nature, law was an important aspect of his outwardly expressed identity.

Shadow Saturn in Aries will place forward the ego or individual as leader, rather than, say, a nation or all of humanity. The Aries in Saturn wants to be the one king, not part of a tribunal or a democracy but a singular executive over all. This shadow Saturn position is certainly advantageous in business models, such as competitive marketplaces, or for inventors, CEOs, or team leaders. People born under this Saturn shadow create huge enterprises, and you can be sure their name is on those companies, long after they die. Most likely a native of this placement will make sure his children inherit the enterprise, not so much to honor his children, but more to cement the family name, his name, in place long after he has left his body.

To master the shadow Saturn in Aries, it is vitally important that the lineage first of all be honored. Sacrifices to the matriarch are the best way to overcome this influence. Attempts to subvert what came before or what will come after shall have disastrous karmic effects for this individual, locking her in isolation, leaving her wondering what went wrong. The actor who receives the Oscar and thanks her mother first and foremost has conquered this influence. If you seek to be the parent while ignoring your own parents, you shall not travel far under this shadow and could create a nasty legacy in your stead. Many Native American and Indigenous people recommend a vision that can see seven generations past and seven generations forward; adapting this ability could be the smartest choice you make as a Saturn shadow Aries sign. Any time the father archetype becomes too strong, the oppositional antidote is simple: the mother. Mother work involves feeding people and other motherly nourishing activities.

So fret not if you have found yourself in this predicament; look no further than Mother Nature to expand your shadow into its true power by honoring what comes before and after you. The stark truth is that any one is only many. If you are seeking to dominate and rule, do not forget that you tread upon things created by a spirit larger than yourself, Earth. Honor and acknowledge this contribution to your very existence, and you shall find a firm footing in overcoming this shadow placement. When the shadow Saturn in Aries is mastered, the individual becomes a leader of humanity, providing service, protection, and justice for all. The destiny of this shadow is to lead by example and be remembered through service and justice not domination. Make the goal the omega, not the alpha, and victory is assured.

Example in Nature

On the hardscrabble lands of the American West, blood is spilled by the most innocent-looking of outlaws—the white-tailed prairie dog. These social rodents, native to Colorado, Wyoming, Utah, and Montana, ruthlessly bite and thrash Wyoming ground squirrels to death, leaving their bloody bodies to rot, a new study says. The killers' offspring then live longer, healthier lives—probably because their parents bumped off their competition for food. It's the first time that a herbivorous mammal has been seen killing competitors without eating them, suggesting that a plant-based diet doesn't preclude mammals from having a taste for bloodsport. In my 43 years of research, this is perhaps the most provocative, puzzling, and far-reaching discovery I've ever made.

— Michael Greshko, "Prairie Dogs Are Serial Killers That Murder Their Competition," *National Geographic*, March 22, 2016

♉

Taurus Saturn Shadow

Blood Sport

Birth Saturn: Scorpio ♏
Master Key: Blood brothers

The shadow Saturn in Taurus is the lord of blood. We all take our blood for granted, but it drives our lives with every beat of our hearts. It is important to realize the history of our blood, where it comes from and the role that nature plays in this vital fluid. The earliest known animals to have blood were arthropods, and they are in our lineage and make up our ancestors and grandmothers. We can only go by what has been discovered and understand there could be more hidden behind the fossils of Earth, but the earliest blood ancestor was found in the Chengjiang fossil site in southwest China, which is the oldest record of Cambrian fossils yet discovered. The arthropod *F. protensa* had evidence of blood and a circulatory system. It is important to look at the ones who came before and the giants whose shoulders we stand upon. Arthropods include myriapods, arachnids, crustaceans, and insects, such as bees.

> *Humans and honeybees share a common ancestor that has been estimated to have lived 600 million years ago. While our ancestors evolved into fish and then moved on land, the honeybee's ancestors evolved into crustacean-like ocean-dwelling animals, some of which moved ashore and became insects.*
>
> Carl Zimmer, "To Bee," *National Geographic*

The birth placement of shadow Saturn in Taurus is in Scorpio, and scorpions are arthropods who share this common ancestry of our blood brood. As disturbing as this might seem, it deserves a nice, hard look nonetheless. For those who enjoy watching violent movies and bloodshed from a safe distance, please consider the origins of blood and its nature. Arthropods have a hard shell that protects their blood and keeps it from spilling out. The body protects the blood, and the blood contains the immune system that protects the body: your blood fights. The immune system is where all our internal battles occur; scientifically, your defense mechanisms are the blood itself.

Taurus masters animal and plant life on Earth, and the invention of blood was an invaluable mastery of living on Earth. Earth elements are in blood, among them the metals iron, cadmium, chromium, manganese, copper, mercury, and zinc and sodium, the salt of Earth. Among blood types, the oldest seems to be a toss-up between type A and type O; the others being possible mutations of these two. But it's hard to say, and that's only what currently available data points to. Want to know the real root of all emotional defensiveness? Let me spell it out for you; B-L-O-O-D.

> *When my face is flushed with blood, it becomes red and obscene. It betrays at the same time, through morbid*

reflexes, a bloody erection and a demanding thirst for indecency and criminal debauchery.

GEORGES BATAILLE, *THE SOLAR ANUS*

Georges Bataille had this Saturn shadow. For those unfamiliar with him, he was an infamous author of obscenity, but more importantly he examined taboo and human nature in its shadow and instinctual forms. His examination of the role of instinct, blood, and guts show he was a shadow worker and was seeking to understand the physical role of his roots in a primordial visceral fashion.

Example in Nature

Moray eels, as well as many other eel-like fish of the order Aguilliformes, have toxic proteins in their blood. They are usually referred to as ichthyotoxins, which simply means "fish poisons." They are among the oldest toxic substances from marine critters known to mankind. Fishermen in general are aware of the fact that certain fishes have to be heated above 75°C (167°F) to destroy the toxins. Consequently, making moray eel sushi is not a good idea. Ichthyotoxin poisoning can lead to spasms and heavy breathing. These substances are also haemolytic and should not touch your eyes, mouth, or open wounds. Bleeding moray eels should be handled carefully.

— Marco Lichtenberger, "Moray Eels Bite—But Are They Poisonous?," *Tropical Fish Hobbyist,* September 2007

♊
Gemini Saturn Shadow

Propaganda

Birth Saturn: Sagittarius ♐
Master Key: Language is powerful

Controlling information becomes the keen pursuit of the shadow Saturn in Gemini. In its positive polarity, Sagittarius birth Saturn values education, religion, philosophy, and learning. The shadow form of these qualities in Gemini creates a manipulation of information, disinformation, and control of the press. This is the conspirator, the smear campaigner, the one who spreads a rumor for the purpose of controlling perceived enemies. It is one thing to shit-talk an acquaintance; it's another to start a propaganda campaign against a notable person, seeking his demise, or against an entire nation or race.

Here, words are blown out of proportion, with big talk used to control through Saturn's influence. Elimination of the competition is the goal of this shadow through control of the narrative. We are presented with many narratives in pop culture and media, but what grabs my attention the most is the single dominant narrative that excludes all others. Wherever we have a dominant narrative, we must look closely at the influences behind it and what data is allowed through the censorship bottleneck to reach the consciousness of the masses. Anyone disseminating propaganda to the masses will be unveiled as a hypocrite before too long, and people will only remember the propagandist, the representative ego in the forefront, and miss seeing the financial backers and Saturn energy that profited from the propaganda. Corporations need only dissociate from the scapegoated individual, and they can then shape-shift into something else to live another day and keep their narrative going.

The main transmutation of this Saturn shadow requires that those promoting a message, whether propaganda or a TV show, live up to the image they present, or they will face a public tar and feathering from the mob, who will call them out for their inconsistencies, even if individuals in the mob are themselves guilty of the same thing. Failing to live up to the propaganda we promulgate is a high crime indeed; if we are unable to walk our talk, propaganda catches up to us in terrible ways.

Che Guevara had this Saturn shadow, and his face became utilized in pop culture propaganda that continues to persist. As someone who was passionate about freeing Latin America from oppression from the United States and the West, my guess is that having his image reproduced and sold for profit on T-shirts might not have been what he had in mind. Teaming up with Fidel Castro, Che Guevara succeeded in his aim to free many people but then imposed a rather unpleasant rule in its place, which many have criticized, accusing that he certainly did not keep any of his propagandic promises.

The unsurprising antidote to this Saturn shadow is integrity, which means we say what we do and we do what we say, a simple formula that, it turns out, is difficult for humanity to uphold.

Example in Nature

> *Double crossing moths: A yucca moth deposits its eggs inside a yucca flower. Normally, moths pollinate the plants at the same time as they lay their eggs. Once hatched, the larvae feed on the product of pollination: yucca seeds.*
>
> — Gerry Allen, "Natural-Born Cheaters: A Look at Double-Dealing Animals," *Scientific American*, 2023

♋

Cancer Saturn Shadow

In the Name of the Lord

Birth Saturn: Capricorn ♑
Master Key: We do not own people

One of the deities who has been attributed to and syncretized with Saturn in pagan history is Ba'al. Though there is some scholarly disagreement on the origins of this deity, all agree that the word *Ba'al* means "lord," "owner," "master," or "husband." The ownership ascribed to Ba'al is that of possession, to be possessed or to own and possess something. The word *Ba'al* was also used as an honorific, affiliated with a last name, with the suggestion that you possess the name of your ancestors. Through the patrilineal line, determined by the father's last name, a father possesses his children, which is very Saturn indeed: the patriarch sees his offspring as a commodity to serve him. A name can be used to claim or establish a brand in business. In a world overtaken by branding of all kinds, we can see that this shadow rules many, even if they do not realize it. The king of the brand name is this Saturn shadow. Your name can own you, depending on who your ancestors are, and color everyone's approach to you, akin to the mark placed on Cain's arm. A brand is also something burned into cattle to claim ownership over their flesh.

This Saturn shadow is also the energy of usury, where the bank always wins and owns everything. Here we see huge amounts of interest added on to keep the borrower indebted to the lender; the borrower is so deeply in debt, so financially encumbered, he will never get free.

> *The indignation and rage of the small merchant against the monopolies was given eloquent expression by Luther in his pamphlet "On Trading and Usury," printed in 1524. "They have all commodities under their control and practice without concealment all the tricks that have been mentioned; they raise and lower prices as they please and oppress and ruin all the small merchants, as the pike the little fish in the water, just as though they were lords over God's creatures and free from all the laws of faith and love."*
>
> ERICH FROMM, *ESCAPE FROM FREEDOM*

This is the shadow Jesus was crucified for when he turned over the money changers' tables. Millions of people are currently owned by this shadow. Even death does not permit escape as liens and grabs by banks and Medicare will make sure the lender's investment pays off, even if that commodity is your body.

This Saturn shadow is used to justify keeping slaves, whether outright or economical. Humanity has held the shadow of slavery for all of known recorded history. If anyone reading this can contribute to an end of all forms of slavery, you will be recognized by none other than the heavens above for your labor in this persistent, horrific shadow form. It is important to see and study how slaves are also present in nature, to observe how animals take advantage of each other in this way as well, especially insects. Given the sheer number of insect species that participate in slavery, this Saturn shadow seems very attached to that life-form, and perhaps humans carry a memory of this and so feel the need to engage in slavery. Perhaps by gazing at our insect relatives, we can begin to transmute this shadow.

Example in Nature

> *The attack begins with a female wasp stinging and temporarily paralyzing one of the spiders. She then glues its [sic] eggs onto the incapacitated arachnid's abdomen and flies away. . . . After the eggs hatch, the parasites latch themselves onto the spider's outer body, feeding off the insect's blood. As time passes, the wasp larva also gains control over the spider's nervous system, transforming the insect into a zombie slave that will obey its orders. In this case, that entails the spider abandoning its daily routine and spending hours weaving a protective web—[o]ne that the wasp larvae can use when it is time to pupate. . . .*
>
> *[T]he crafty insects have figured out how to enslave the poor spiders and force them to do the job. . . . As soon as the resting web is complete, the larva molts, kills the spider, and gobbles it up. It then spins the silk-like web into a cocoon and hunkers down for the next ten days to complete its metamorphosis to a pesky wasp. The one thing that remains a mystery is what the wasps inject in the spider to trigger the cocoon building.*
>
> — Shariqua Ahmed, "The Crafty Wasps That Turn Spiders into Web-Weaving Zombie Slaves," Dogo News, September 24, 2015

♌

Leo Saturn Shadow

Deal with the Devil

Birth Saturn: Aquarius ♒
Master Key: Own your art

This Saturn shadow seeks to be the sun. Being the one light that draws and commands all others is the dream of this shadow and it will do its darndest to convince you to follow its light and not the sun. In this way, it functions as a mock sun.

> The planet Saturn was designated as Shamash or "sun" by the Assyro-Babylonian astrologers; and as far back as 1910 M. Jastrow (*Revue d'Assyriologie,* Vol. 70, p. 171) proposed "the idea that Saturn was a 'steady' or 'permanent' mock-sun—performing the same function of furnishing light at night that Samas performed during the day." . . . Furthermore, there is undeniable evidence that the concept of a "night-sun" as well as a "day-sun" existed in ancient Babylonian astrological thought.*

This is a usurpation of the creative light of the ego and a stealing of the Promethean flame. Since Prometheus stole the flame in the first place, maybe there is a deeper story, but it is the shadow form shown here, the false light. According to occult literature and ancient myths, Saturn used to emit a large amount of light, specifically a kind of violet UV light and X-rays. Immanuel Velikovsky, a psychoanalyst, even proposed that Earth was once a satellite of Saturn and wrote at length about this. He proposed many controversial ideas, which were widely debunked as pseudoscience, but provided fascinating suppositions nonetheless. We can perceive an ultraviolet aura from Saturn, and a Hubble photograph captured a strange hexagon-shaped vortex crowning the planet on its north pole.

The sun represents the solar and creative ego of the individual, and Saturn presenting as a double sun encourages people to fall under the illusion that they require a boss or leader to create or to earn income from their creations. This is the company that owns your art and refuses to allow the artist and creator to prosper in society so that the company can have workers that contribute to its visions alone.

---

*Lewis M. Greenberg and Warner B. Sizemore, "Saturn and Genesis," *Kronos* 1, no. 3 (Fall 1975): 46.

Be cautious about building your creative pyramid under a pyramid scheme, where you contractually sign over your creative energy to an overlord who is not necessary and will bleed you dry. This is the con man, and the birth Saturn in Aquarius adds to the clever inventive intelligence of those who seek out the intellectual properties of others to use for themselves, without honoring the creators. In order to transmute this Saturn shadow and avoid being manipulated, creators must not work for exposure and validation. Artists who work independently and accrue value unto themselves for their creative abilities threaten this shadow. Until that hurdle is cleared, rest assured many middlemen will swoop in and attempt to leech money from the work of independents, whether it comes in the form of excess taxation, fees to charge for products and goods, or business regulations. When we focus our attention on the intercessor who takes from the creator, we may incline toward conspiracy theories, thinking those in power are actively conspiring to take advantage of creative people. But maybe someone is simply offering an opportunity, or it's the free market system at work.

I am grateful to a friend who recommended the 1929 graphic novel *God's Man: A Novel in Woodcuts* by Lynd Ward. It wordlessly and adeptly tells the tale of an artist who signs away his soul for a magic paintbrush and fame. My friend was a Hollywood producer who tried to assist creatives to keep their own value rather than being parasitized. Be cautious signing contracts that give everything over to the contractor, who claims ownership in perpetuity of your work. All creators should get lawyers and advocates and redline contracts that greedily claim too much ownership.

Example in Nature

Female banded mongooses lead their groups into fights then try to mate with enemy males in the chaos of battle, new research has found. Meanwhile, males bear the costs of these fights—injuries and deaths are common.

The research team, led by the University of Cambridge and

the University of Exeter, say "exploitative leadership" of this kind, which is also seen in human warfare, leads to frequent and damaging conflicts.

"Female banded mongooses start fights between groups to gain genetic benefits from mating with outsiders, while the males within their group—and the group as a whole—pay the costs," said Professor Michael Cant.

He added: "A classic explanation for warfare in human societies is leadership by exploitative individuals who reap the benefits of conflict while avoiding the costs.

"In this study, we show that leadership of this kind can also explain the evolution of severe collective violence in certain animal societies."

The findings suggest that decoupling leaders from the costs of their choices amplifies the destructive nature of intergroup conflict. . . .

"The mortality costs involved are similar to those seen in a handful of the most warlike mammals, including lions, chimpanzees, and humans," [said Professor Rufus Johnstone].

— University of Cambridge, "Female Mongooses Start Violent Fights to Mate with Unrelated Males," November 10, 2020

♍

Virgo Saturn Shadow

The Saint

Birth Saturn: Pisces ♓
Master Key: I did it all for you

The Saturn shadow in Virgo presents itself as virtuous and deserving of your adulation and trust. In this way those under this Saturn shadow can be lords and leaders of large flocks of sheep who also want to be virtuous or at least want to be perceived that way through their connection to the saintly individual. There are real saints who die a martyred death, and then there are those who love to play the victim and blame you for their sacrifices, which you never asked them to do but which they claim they did for the greater good. This Saturn shadow claims to make sacrifices no one asked for, while avoiding acknowledging wrongs they may have committed. The shadow Saturn in Virgo wishes to be seen as the embodiment of purity that can do no wrong, even if they didn't earn the title. Someone under this shadow will forgive you for a crime he committed—and make quite a big show of his forgiveness.

The shadow Saturn in Virgo postures in this way not only on a personal level, but represents corporations and larger entities, presenting itself as the face that you want to attach to and feel sorry for and so forgive the larger entity for its epic-level insanity. The birth Saturn in Pisces seeks egoless expansion of an institution with spiritual considerations and seeks to achieve a high level of spiritual advancement for an entire entity, not just itself. Just because something is done on a large level does not mean it has been done for the greater good. Carefully choosing a representative to hide behind is a tactic that is chosen often in the human predicament. Say for example we hide our behavior behind an astrological identity; is this much different?

Pope Francis has this Saturn placement and is certainly in the role of representing a large religious organization in a saintly fashion, which has nothing to do with the ego identity of Francis, himself. This is an example of placing an individual ego, a kind face, to meet the masses, while a huge corporation carries out its objectives behind the scenes. Rather than the Vatican simply issuing many apologies through Francis, it could have offered recompense and resources to the victims of atrocities committed by Catholic priests, which would transmute this shadow Saturn. I place no blame on Francis either, as that would be a shadow behavior known as scapegoating.

Example in Nature

If the predator learns that a certain signal is associated with unattractive prey and thus avoids attacking individuals that carry that signal, then an undefended species that also carried this same signal would gain protection from predators. This is the

> *phenomenon of Batesian mimicry. In this case, there is asymmetry in the relationship between the two species with the same signal: the defended (or otherwise unattractive) one is called the model, and its signal is copied by another undefended species, the mimic. . . . Imperfect mimicry may be possible when the model is particularly unpleasant for predators, making the predators much less likely to experiment with something that just might be a model.*
>
> — Eben Goodale and Graeme D. Ruxton, "Antipredator Benefits from Heterospecifices," in ed. Jae Chun Choe, *Encyclopedia of Animal Behavior,* 2nd ed. (Cambridge, Mass.: Academic Press, 2019), 298–303

♎

Libra Saturn Shadow

Supreme Court

Birth Saturn: Aries ♈
Master Key: And justice for all

This shadow seeks to create a system of justice that serves itself. The birth Saturn in Aries will do what is right, for its ego. The shadow that is cast into Libra will entangle others in its self-justifications, rather than true justice. Because the shadow is actively distorting, the inspiration for the system of justice is actually hidden behind it. Rather than serving the greater good, justice here is tainted with self-serving vindication, vengeance, and retribution. Rather than being based in mercy, growth, and reciprocity, the rule of the shadow Saturn in Libra is to get even while undeservedly claiming to be the victim.

We see corruption of the court under this shadow, with bribes and corporate payoffs. Here, corporations and other entities abdicate their responsibilities because they have grown so large they can no longer be held accountable at the grassroots level. This is a total failure of the justice system, given the size of the corporations and of the judicial system itself and the number of individuals who suffer when there is a miscarriage of justice. The victims of this corruption are individuals and are far smaller than the Saturn-sized perpetrators, who include the systemic runners of the court—state courts, Supreme Court judges and politicians, international courts—none of whom will be personally affected. People whose lives are ruined by these corruptions are essentially casualties of war of the shadow Saturn in Libra. The natal Saturn Aries individual is completely swallowed whole by this shadow Saturn, and if you have some relationship to this placement, you very well may have been one of its victims or participated in an entity that engaged this energy at some level.

If you are a lawyer, you will be exposed to this shadow Saturn sooner or later, and the key in dealing with it will be to form groups, to seek others and team up. To face this dragon as an individual may seem romantic, but you will most certainly require resources, time, and patience to make any progress digesting this shadow. One of the hardest things about confronting this shadow is that whatever entity or system is causing the harm will cry out that it is the one deserving the pity. The purveyors of the crime will fall upon the mercy of the courts, begging to be forgiven while bribing them or lining their pockets. Meanwhile, none of the human beings affected are addressed or recompensed. Not only do they have to deal with the crime itself but they are additionally faced with stomaching the corruption and false display of crocodile tears. Saddam Hussein had this Saturn shadow placement and implemented capital punishment and ruled with an iron fist. In an interesting twist of fate, he was himself punished with the death sentence of execution that he had imposed upon so many others. Begging the courts for the mercy he refused others, he shed quite a few crocodile tears.

This Saturn shadow will crush the souls of those involved and make you want to give up altogether on the justice system should you be unfortunate enough to encounter it. Despite this there are individuals who dedicate their lives to confronting it and holding it accountable. Thank goodness there are whole institutions focused on remedying this shadow, and the suffering of some individuals have led to reforms. Any assistance we can make to transmute this Saturn shadow will benefit the many and keep justice clear of self-serving agendas.

Example in Nature

In mythology, tears of the crocodile are attributed to feigned sorrow. . . . This crocodilian remorse is considered insincere because the crocodile continues to gobble its prey. . . .

George Johnson examined these foundations most recently (Johnson 1927). After applying a mixture of onion and salt directly to the persistently dry eyes of four species, he concluded that "the popular notion of Crocodiles shedding tears is entirely a myth." . . .

*On 22 March 2006, we digitally filmed seven crocodilians—two common caimans (*Caiman crocodilus*), two Yacare caimans (*Caiman yacare*), and three American alligators (*Alligator mississippiensis*)—as they were fed. Other species within the order Crocodilia, such as crocodiles and gharials, were not examined. Five of the seven crocodilians developed moisture in their eyes, bubbles, or overflow bubbles within minutes before, during, or after eating.*

— D. Malcolm Shaner and Kent A. Vliet, "Crocodile Tears: *And thei eten hem wepynge,*" *BioScience* 57, no. 7 (July 2007): 615–17

♏

Scorpio Saturn Shadow

The Lord of the Flies

Birth Saturn: Taurus ♉
Master Key: Attack and defense are two different things

Territoriality grows into lordship and the need to defend the territory begets weapons and the military. The ultimate manifestation of this Saturn shadow is total control through martial law, which enables the holder of this Saturn shadow to exert complete ownership of its territories with threat of force. How can a lord have a territory if it cannot be protected and kept? The ancient purpose of royalty was to protect the inhabitants of its territories.

Ultimately, force must be used to be respected. If it isn't used, it becomes a mere bluff that can be easily challenged, as inconsequential as stepping over a literal line drawn in the sand. However, when that line is a nuclear weapon, one will think twice before trespassing. The birth Saturn in Taurus enables the native to possessively acquire land or possessions. If there is no defense for these, they can be taken by whomever comes along who has more might than the possessor. This is a sad fact of reality, and this shadow form of brutality has caused a huge amount of suffering but has also driven innovation. Human beings are maniacal at devising clever ways to keep others from their spoils, enabling and possibly driving some of our most developed technologies.

Ironically, arms to protect the land are produced using resources from the land one is trying to protect. Resources aren't infinite and so a limit will be reached and more resources will be needed to build arms to protect the territory, and so a nation, under this shadow Saturn in Scorpio, will trespass the boundaries of its enemy's territory and steal its enemy's resources to build more arms to protect its own resources from the enemy it is stealing from. If the nation's enemy does this to it—invading and stealing, perhaps in retribution—it will unleash its arms upon its enemy, completely missing the point and the origin of the whole fiasco. As we slide down the slippery slope of increased military force and stealing to support it, often from the enemy because that can be justified to self and others, we become the thing we are defending against in a samsara serpent circle.

Projecting weapons to the other's territory is a perfect manifested example of projecting the shadow. To harm a faraway enemy with projectiles safely launched from home turf, the damage unseen and not directly felt, geographically removes fault and blame, at least for the citizens of the home country; the shadow is literally projected, nay, launched upon the perceived enemy. There is something uniquely psychotic and shadow laden about distance in combat. The intimacy of hand-to-hand combat seems so much more sportsmanlike. The dirty trick of sending a bomb from miles away to annihilate a town is truly sociopathic. Destroying an entire city is madness of a kind only shadow could create. Stare deeply into the eyes of this and its implications; this shadow sign could be the heart of the abyss. Nuclear weapons were developed in 1939 with Saturn in Taurus, making them hold this shadow Saturn in Scorpio. The Manhattan Project began under its influence as well, harkening to the nature of this underbelly.

Example in Nature

> *Many insects are armed with venom, which they can inject into their enemies via a sting. The African ant* Crematogaster striatula *is no exception, but its arsenal has a disturbing twist—its venom goes airborne. The ant can raise its sting and release its toxins as an aerosol spray. Its targets are termites, whose nests it raids. Even without making any contact, the ants can induce seizures in the termites, eventually paralyzing them. All* Crematogaster *ants have a mobile sting. The sting sits on the ant's rear-end, which connects to its torso by a flexible stalk, so the ant can aim it in virtually any direction. . . .*
>
> *When it finds a termite, it raises its sting into the air, releasing chemicals that summon nearby nestmates. If the termite is a soldier, armed with powerful jaws, up to 15 ants can gather round. All of them stay a centimeter away from the termite, aiming their stings at it like fencers with swords outstretched.*
>
> — Ed Yong, "Look, No Hands: Ants Kill Termites with Airborne Chemical Weapons," *National Geographic*, December 15, 2011

♐

Sagittarius Saturn Shadow

Liability

Birth Saturn: Gemini ♊
Master Key: The pen is mightier than the sword

In the beginning was the word, so they say, and so we must watch what goes out of our mouths. Speech and written words are not to be discounted as they can hold lordship over individuals, and so when we write things we must be cautious about accusations and implications directed at individuals or groups because that has consequences. Perhaps some of the folks I use as examples in this book would say I need to also heed my own words, and so I must remain open to correction, criticism, and amendment in all the words I write and say because I could be incorrect, or my sources could be. My examples are meant to exemplify and unify, but I have shadows too, and some could find my examples insulting or untrue.

Gossip grows into liability as businesses and corporations are created in a transpersonal way that extends past speaking poorly of an individual and crosses the line of threatening the profits of a company. Phrases you could say nonchalantly about your neighbor down the street become fighting words if you affect someone's ability to earn income. Gossip becomes a threat to lucrative reputations at certain levels, so there are laws against libel that pertain to corporations, companies, and even countries. Holding people accountable for damaging speech is a positive thing, but you must be able to prove damage and threat. We can observe how countries war with each other over their reputations, which mirrors siblings fighting and insulting each other, trying to see who can make the other look like the biggest villain. Harsh words are quickly used against each other to justify gaining ground, only these words are called "libel" or "slander" instead of name-calling when they reach the Saturn-level proportions of corporations, nations, and larger groups who have lords and leaders protecting them.

Certain insults are harmless and normal. We all, at times, disapprove of each other and mention it in confidence to friends, or call each other out, but if we make up uncorroborated lies about people, we might find out the hard way that this is not permitted. Word gets around and come back to bite you. Alex Jones, the media figure, has this placement and has certainly been confronted with and faced consequences over his lies. Some words are hurtful; hate speech and targeted accusations, such as blood libel, which accused Jews of using the blood of non-Jewish children in rituals, can lead to dreadful consequences for all involved. To transmute this shadow, if someone complains to you about something you said, consider if it was true or fair and apologize for hurting her feelings if you were incorrect. A little attention can prevent escalation; try speaking to the individual first before you speak about her. Sometimes this is impossible, but consider erring on the side of caution.

Example in Nature

> *Roaring is an integral component of African lion* (Panthera leo) *ecology as it facilitates social cohesion and territorial defense. Despite the importance of roaring, there is a limited understanding of the configuration of this behavior in spatiotemporal dimensions. Here, we mapped the configuration of lion roaring at the home-range scale and quantified temporal signatures in roaring frequency. We tested whether spatiotemporal patterns of roaring vary with position within a lion dominance hierarchy using a dominance shift that occurred in a reintroduced group of lions. . . . While our findings were based on a limited sample, our study suggests that the spatial strategy and frequency of roaring varies in relation to social rank and patterns in space use of rival coalitions.*
>
> — Steven M. Gray et al., "Spatiotemporal Variation in African Lion Roaring in Relation to a Dominance Shift," *Journal of Mammalogy* 98, no. 4 (August 1, 2017): 1088–95

♑

Capricorn Saturn Shadow

The Sins of the Father

Birth Saturn: Cancer ♋
Master Key: Ancestors are a blessing and a curse

The worst aspects of Saturn are housed in this shadow placement. Fearful of losing his power, Saturn in mythology ate his children to keep them from replacing him. Instead of viewing them as blessings to continue his legacy, they were competition for his throne. Much like the brand indicated in the Saturn shadow in Cancer, here we see a larger legacy that demands protection, which could even have several entities and extend into a global empire that leaves out its children in favor of a larger empire. This cautionary tale appears again and again among humans, with many kings murdering family members, in a recapitulation of this shadow, and in nature we see species also exhibit this behavior.

Saturn in Cancer in the birth chart is an ancestor placement and connects to the instincts, combining them with ambition through the shadow of Capricorn. In this placement, the current generation gathers or inherits the gifts of the ancestors but uses them to acquire material goods. This is a shadow behavior because the ancestors have learned that ownership is an illusion and that in death all things are taken from you, so there is usually family drama that ends up dissolving the empires built by the greatest human beings simply due to inheritance demons. The role of family politics, inheritance, and betrayal fill the cup for this shadow form. Here success is built upon the family name, but along with this success come the ghosts of the past. This shadow is the classic story of the man who builds an empire, only to have his son inherit it and lose it within a short amount of time. Most folks are familiar with the saying "the sins of the father are to be laid upon the children," but here we see the sins of the offspring. Inheritance crime extends beyond money to strange familial entanglements.

Angelina Jolie has this Saturn shadow. Though abandoned by her actor father, Jon Voight, when she was a baby, she did not allow her father's abandonment to prevent her from becoming successful in the same field of acting. In addition, unlike her father, she has been generous with her six children, three of whom are adopted, which shows a total mastery of this shadow.

Example in Nature

A novel type of filial cannibalism has been reported in pipefishes, in which the eggs are absorbed through the male's brood-pouch epithelium. The present study explored the applicability of stable isotope analysis for the detection of paternal brood cannibalism in the seaweed pipefish Syngnathus schlegeli*. . . . This finding indicates that males occupy a higher trophic position than* *females only during the reproductive season, and it is probable that this difference is a result of paternal uptake of nutrients from embryos in the brood pouch.*

— Atsushi Sogabe et al., "Application of Stable Isotope Analysis for Detecting Filial Cannibalism," *Behavioural Processes* 140 (July 2017): 16–18

♒

Aquarius Saturn Shadow

The Secret Society

Birth Saturn: Leo ♌
Master Key: Do not let rebellion conceal mimicry

An individual with birth Saturn Leo wants to have a unique identity, but the Aquarius shadow will force him into a group. The shadow Saturn in Aquarius needs a group identity, but a unique one that no one else has. Being part of a unique and secret group serves this shadow Saturn best. To keep the group special, the Aquarius Saturn shadow will control not only who is accepted in the group but who gets to talk about it; this Saturn shadow wants to keep things close to the chest. Careful vetting of members and establishing a hierarchy are signatures of these groups, along with binding pledges of allegiance.

This mix of Aquarius and Leo creative energy means the group will form special narratives that are new or slightly different than other groups. Humanitarian justifications for the existence of the group will underlie it so that it feels virtuous and like it is serving the community in a heroic manner, but more importantly serving the group itself in the best way possible. Members in this secret group will swear to protect one another, value honor, and punish defectors or those who talk openly to nonmembers without permission from the leader.

Often these groups will form out of rebellion to a dogmatic community, such as a religion or a government, under the Uranus influence of Aquarius, who detests dogma. Most of the shadow Aquarius energy seeks to form its own club because it is tired of following the rules and dictates of a greater authority and seeks freedom to self-express. Of course, like all things in the universe, things circle back around, and these splinter groups often become like the authority they initially rebelled against, enforcing control in much the same way.

> *A defense strategy favored by many "spiritual" people is an elaborate form of denial, an assertion that the individual has "gone beyond" the shadow qualities of sexuality, anger, passion, desire, and self-interest. Many religions cater exclusively to this strategy. Priests, ministers, gurus, and "enlightened masters" who adopt a posture of transcendent superiority have great appeal to people with similar defense systems, who are able to escape their personal confrontations by identifying as members of an elite, "enlightened" group.*
>
> STARHAWK, *THE SPIRAL DANCE: A REBIRTH OF THE ANCIENT RELIGION OF THE GREAT GODDESS*

America was founded under the influence of this shadow Saturn. Freemasonry was an established fraternal order in Colonial America and several Founding Fathers were Freemasons, among them George Washington and Benjamin Franklin. Around this same time, Adam Weishaupt founded the Bavarian Illuminati in Germany in 1776. Secret societies who form to rebel against authoritative leaders and claim to be freedom lovers often become lords in their own right and use their power and influence to control others in much the same way they were once controlled.

Example in Nature

*The deep sea is vast, empty and dark—not an ideal place for animals to communicate via visual signals. Yet the Humboldt squid (*Dosidicus giga*), a social species that lives in groups of hundreds of individuals, can communicate visually at depths of 600 feet or more. Cephalopods including squid, octopus and cuttlefish are known for a stunning array of visual displays. These* *marine creatures possess pigment cells called chromatophores surrounded by muscles that expand and contract, allowing for a wide variety of colorful patterns. While researchers understood these abilities, a question remained regarding just how deep-sea cephalopods might make these displays visible in their dark, deep environment. . . .*

Lead author Burford found that the Humboldt squid's use of bioluminescence is unique.

— Hannah Knighton, "Deep-Sea Squids Glow to Communicate in the Dark," *Smithsonian Magazine,* April 6, 2020

♓

Pisces Saturn Shadow

The Antipope

Birth Saturn: Virgo ♍
Master Key: For thine is the glory, not mine

Pisces is ruled by Neptune, the planet that represents religion and spirituality. In the Pisces shadow we will see spiritual overtones and a need to expand into a greater state of being past the ego and past dogma. Saturn seeks control and dogma, and Virgo natal Saturn is focused on following the rules and regulations of religion, dominating and punishing severely those who don't obey. The shadow Saturn in Pisces will completely lose the point of religion and spirituality and become obsessed with the laws and rules surrounding it, divorcing spirit from the practice and engaging in discipline for discipline's sake. This is the nun in a Catholic school who hits her young students with a ruler to establish and maintain her power, not to educate—and certainly not to follow the teachings of Christ.

This Saturn shadow is a religious dictator, fueled by righteousness and the fires of hell to justify countless crimes. Often religious texts are taken out of context and bent to accommodate unnecessary punishments and used inappropriately to severely damage the followers and keep the leader in total control. The key to surpassing this shadow is to break free of rules, regulations, and dogma and have a spiritual experience outside those structures. There are regulations and then there is religion, which is the tie that binds people together through shared beliefs, not through punishment. Virgo is the virgin who is innocent and free of dogma and really just wants validation.

This is the Saturn birth placement of Lana Wachowski, the famous transgender director who, with her sister Lilly Wachowski, directed *The Matrix*, among other films. Wachowski did attend Catholic school as a child, which she rebelled against because of the strict dogmas forced upon her. It seems the institution of the Catholic Church projected this Saturn shadow on Wachowski, and she became its master by taking an oppositional stance, which took courage and heart.

Example in Nature

The elevated posture and folded front legs of the praying mantis might lead you to believe that this cunning predator is a seemingly benign, upstanding member of the insect kingdom—but don't be fooled . . . with a new study by zoologists finding that praying mantises have been documented killing birds and devouring their brains across the globe.

If that makes it sound like mantises have been infected by some kind of zombie contagion compelling them to hunt down and consume our feathery friends, don't worry—that hasn't happened. . . . The truth is this is just an amazing natural behaviour. . . .

Mantises infrequently prey upon small vertebrates—also including frogs, lizards, and snakes—in addition to their regular fare of arthropods, up until now scientists weren't clued in on how universal the bird buffet was.

— Peter Dockrill, "Praying Mantises Are Killing Birds and Devouring Their Brains All over the World," Science Alert, July 10, 2017

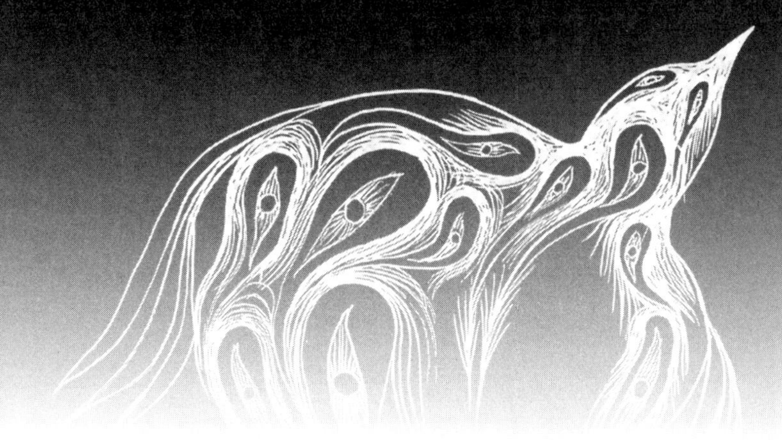

Uranus Shadows

Universal Revolutions

It is not light that we need, but fire; it is not the gentle shower, but thunder. We need the storm, the whirlwind, and the earthquake.

FREDERICK DOUGLASS, FIFTH OF JULY SPEECH, 1852

URANUS IS A GREEK PRIMORDIAL GOD, one of the Titans and the ruler of time and space. Many attribute time to Saturn (Cronus in Greek mythology), others to Uranus. Depending on which source you use, there is quite a bit of syncretization here. I would say that Uranus relates to time in the sense that things are cyclical, and so it relates closely to revolutions and revolutionary actions and ways of being. Though it has been said that there is nothing new under the sun, there is rebirth, renewal, new beginnings, and the start of new cycles. Uranus energy shows us where these revolutions are needed and how to reinvigorate tired systems and release what is no longer needed to serve the greatest good. Unique authenticity, a Uranus quality, is part of something new, something not seen or experienced before. The fact that the universe is so old but that something unexpected can happen is nothing less than a miracle.

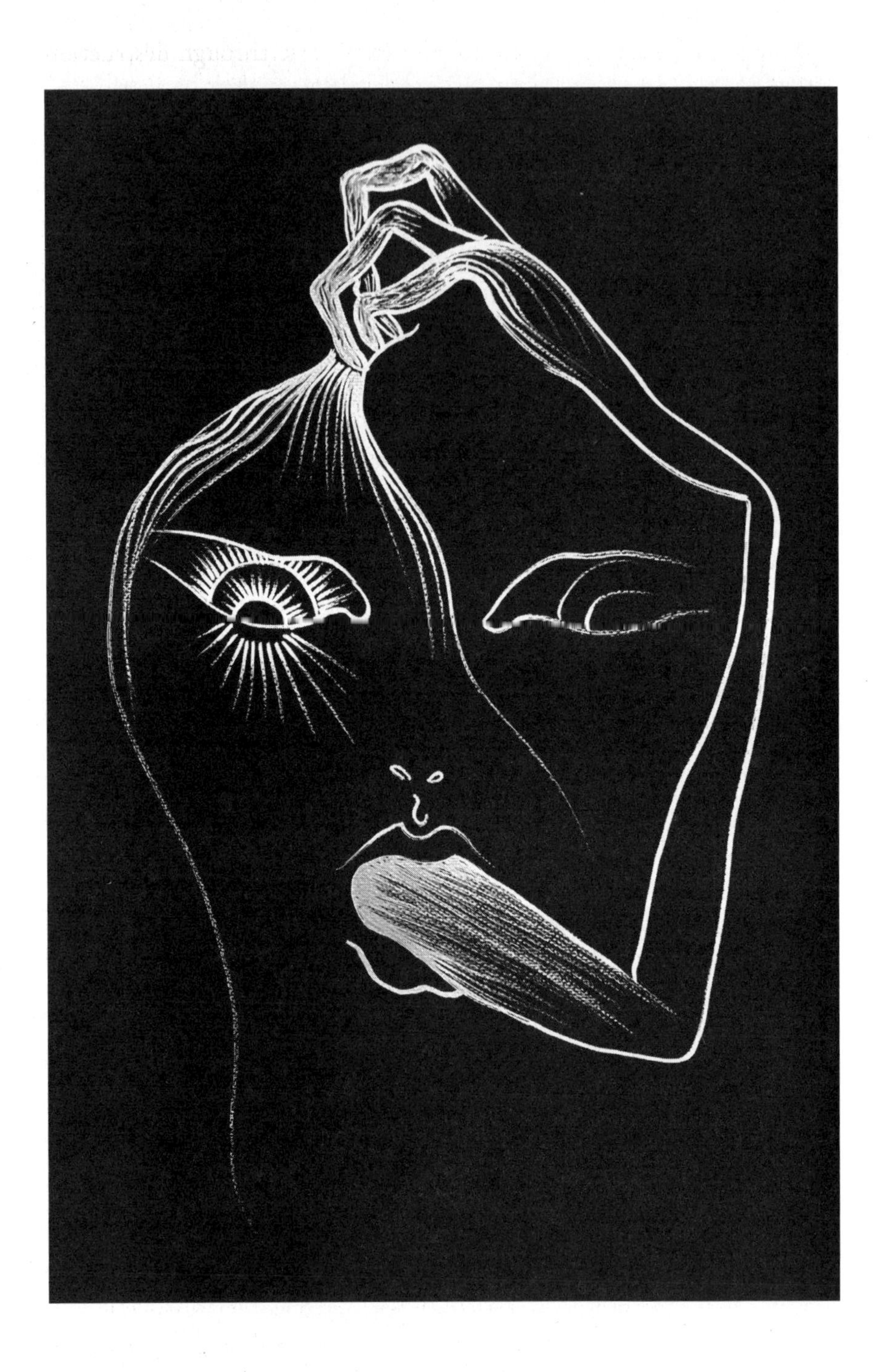

The shadow of Uranus is upset, disruptions, and explosions. Some new beginnings are unwanted because they come through destruction. The Uranus shadow is the forest fire that, in its aftermath, stimulates new growth or the revolution that changes a corrupt government. This shadow is the earthquake, the lightning strike, the storm that forces a renewal whether we want it or not. In the Greek myth of Uranus, from traditional sources, Cronus castrates Uranus, who is his father, so that he can take his place as ruler and ensure the power belongs to him and him alone. Little does Cronus know that when the severed phallus of Uranus falls into the sea, it sprouts forth in the form of Aphrodite (Venus) herself, resplendent and beautiful, bringing waves of love into the world and rejuvenating all she touches. Being reborn from violent trauma is not something that is easy or wanted, but it happens quite often in nature.

We hate and love the shadow of Uranus for its uncontrollable chaos. What would life be without the power of an unexpected obliteration that shakes us free from our doldrums? Well, it would be quite boring, no doubt. No one seeks the level of change Uranus brings, but we sure do grow from the Uranus shadow, on that you can rely.

Revolution is not a one-time event.

Audre Lorde, *Sister Outsider: Essays and Speeches*

♈

Aries Uranus Shadow

Grassroots

Birth Uranus: Libra ♎
Revolution: Systemic justice

Uranus in Aries shadow means birth placement is in Libra, the sign of justice and equality. We get a lot of upset in justice here in this shadow influence and the need to prove or validate the personal worth of the individual in the face of injustice. Here we are made to self-justify because we are not getting justice in the collective. The shadow in Aries forces individuals, through their persecution, to know and understand that they are just as deserving of worth and value as the collective. Constantly, the status quo pushes back against this, and periodically it falls on the shoulders of one warrior to stand up for self and others, endure persecution from society, and unite everyone in a bid to obtain justice. The need to group together and support one another, rather than approaching things in isolation, is highlighted in this shadow. Individuals working as a group rather than enduring persecution in isolation is the ideal here, as those in power attempt to keep the many divided and polarized. You may not be experiencing such persecution yourself, but you can still support the Uranus Aries shadow of those seeking justice and help them overcome persecution. Understand and see this shadow for what it is; rather than seeing individuals standing up for their personal rights as "criminals," identify where the system has failed them.

The danger with this shadow placement is that the individual will justify violence against those he believes have treated him unfairly. I am no one to judge this, and I am a self-defense advocate, personally; however, when taken to an extreme, this can quickly grow misguided. Witness none other than Adolf Hitler, who had this placement in his birth chart. But so did Tupac Shakur, who was a real victim of injustice on many levels, though some might argue he was slain righteously by those seeking retribution themselves. Who is right? Be cautious of being so justified in your campaign against injustice that you bring violence to others and yourself. In certain situations, where society is oppressive and has severely curtailed freedom, it may be impossible to avoid violence. Still, be self-aware and recognize your bias and find some friends.

Example in Nature

Fairness also seems to be a part of primate social life. Researchers Sarah Brosnan, Frans de Waal, and Hillary Schiff discovered what they call "inequity aversion" in capuchin monkeys, a highly social and cooperative species in which food sharing is common. These monkeys, especially females, carefully monitor equity and fair treatment among peers. Individuals who are shortchanged during a bartering transaction by being offered a less preferred treat refuse to cooperate with researchers. In a nutshell, the capuchins expect to be treated fairly.

— Marc Bekoff and Jessica Pierce, *Wild Justice: The Moral Lives of Animals* (Chicago: University of Chicago Press, 2009)

♉

Taurus Uranus Shadow

The Green Thumb

Birth Uranus: Scorpio ♏
Revolution: Agriculture

The birth placement of Uranus in Scorpio focuses on root needs, our connection to our ancestors and culture and the role of survival and food in humanity. Under the shadow of Uranus in Taurus, we witness revolutions in agriculture, in growing plants and producing food. But because this is a shadow, there are many ways these revolutions can be corrupted, necessitating reform. Although plant-based revolutions can take the form of increased production in agriculture and better distribution of food, they can also encompass the many kinds of drugs we get from plants. Under the Taurus shadow, we can see these forces corrupted into hoarding food, practicing unsustainable agricultural methods, or making illegitimate claims on territory. The farm crisis of the 1980s in America, as well as what led to the Ethiopian famine, were under this shadow and stand as perfect examples of what can occur when this shadow gets too big for its britches.

When the agricultural revolution values profit over produce, we see the bull of shadow Taurus take over, with greed superseding the providing of basic needs. This is a very important shadow for all to look upon now as currently Uranus is in Taurus, which is opposing this shadow. It may be hard to see so far into the future, but current issues appearing in agriculture throughout the world are setting the stage for the coming revolution in the next cycle of this Uranus shadow. For example, take a look into who has currently purchased all the farmland, consider what occurred with land values during the farm crisis of the late 1970s and early '80s under this influence, and, based on this information, attempt to extrapolate into the future. Booms in growing crops like coca leaves for cocaine and poppy plants for opium and heroin also occurred at the same time as the farm crisis, for example, which eventually developed into the crack epidemic. Obviously, there are many factors contributing to all of these issues, racism not being the least of them, but it is important to see the shape of this shadow on the land.

The current crisis for farmers in India and their protests should not be ignored. Shifts in agriculture and how we grow food are tied into earthly and planetary cycles, and we as a species should learn as much as we can from these cycles. The seeds we plant into the ground become the crops we reap, so please take a moment to cast a glance on this shadow form of Uranus.

Example in Nature

Let's take a look at the spotted bowerbird, a species studied in Queensland, Australia, where recent research discovered that the birds engage in gardening, of a sort. Male spotted bowerbirds build elaborate nests, or bowers, from twigs and decorate them with various objects to attract females. One decorative object much loved by females, and hence much sought by males, is the yellow-green, often purple-tinged berry of the potato bush—in fact, more berries on the bower means better mating success for the male. Males don't generally build bowers in areas where the berries grow in abundance, but by the time a bower is a year old, it usually has a few dozen potato bushes growing nearby, giving the male more opportunity to decorate with more berries. The males throw shriveled berries outside the bower, affecting the distribution of the potato bush. Not precisely agriculture as ants and humans may know it, but still a form of opportunistic gardening. It also is the first known example of the cultivation of a nonfood plant by a nonhuman species.

— Roger Di Silvestro, "Animals That Grow Gardens," National Wildlife Federation, January 5, 2016

♊

Gemini Uranus Shadow

The Hot Poop

Birth Uranus: Sagittarius ♐
Revolution: Data flow

Shadow Uranus in Gemini is a revolution in communication, empowering individuals to share data and information among themselves without relying on larger, more dominant forms of media. These are the zinesters, the independent media operators. They rebel against the larger media sources, which can form one-sided narratives that seem corrupted or fabricated. Those with natal Uranus in Sagittarius seek to get data to the masses in their own way, free of dogma. They are the independent publishers who vouch for freedom of public speech. Uranus traveled through this shadow in the late 1980s, when the first internet service provider companies were formed. New ways to share information through a network, rather than being dictated through a single source, were created at this time.

Technically, the internet, as it now exists, originally came from CERN, also called the European Organization for Nuclear Research. Tim Berners-Lee, a scientist working at CERN, invented the World Wide Web in 1989 to automate data sharing among scientists working at universities and institutes around the world (in order to serve the project). CERN is a perfect example of how the benefit of having access to data can become a shadow as those with resources seek to usurp and control the flow of information for their own use, rather than supporting the free use of data for one and all. This early information sharing happened under the influence of this Uranus shadow, though they did, in a transmutation of this shadow, release the technology to the public four years later in what we now know as the world wide web. CERN was able to rise above this shadow and release this tool for the greater good.

This time period also gave us cellular phones and a huge revolution in cellular communication devices. How fascinating that both the world wide web and cell phones became available under this Uranus shadow influence, at once providing increases in our ability to connect while simultaneously developing huge industries to charge the public for access to this ability.

The key to this Uranus shadow is to open source data and remove the power of individuals to sequester and manipulate this revolutionary force. This doesn't mean ignoring source citations; it means increasing access to information and being reasonable about access without exorbitant fees.

Example in Nature

Male elephant seals recognize their rivals by rhythmic patterns in their call, according to a study published Thursday in Current Biology. . . .

[M]ale seals battle to establish a pecking order, sometimes fighting to the death. The strongest control the female harem. . . .

"It is a high stakes environment," Caroline Casey, . . . a doctoral candidate in ecology and evolutionary biology . . . told the NewsHour. "We wanted to know what these animals are saying to each other—what information is embedded in these calls that the seals use to avoid a fight, and which components of the calls are important."

Casey had previously shown that elephant seals can identify the calls of their rivals. "Alpha" males sing out to warn low-ranking seals to stay away or fight. . . .

Upon hearing the original call, the lowly beta males retreated akin to what they do when avoiding a fight. But, when the beta males heard the call with a considerably modified rhythm, they took no notice, leading the researchers to conclude that the rhythm is key to recognition.

— Teresa Carey, "Elephant Seals Recognize Vocal Rhythms to Avoid Bullies," *PBS NewsHour*, July 20, 2017

♋

Cancer Uranus Shadow

The Beat Generation

Birth Uranus: Capricorn ♑
Revolution: Sensual expression

The shadow Uranus in Cancer wants to feel and will rebel against insensitivity and censorship of sensuality or when its emotional territory is threatened or suppressed. Staunch traditionalism that denies nuance and feeling, leaving no space for emotional expression, will not live through this Uranus shadow. The beatniks arose during this Uranus shadow and were viewed as perverts at the time. The Beats pushed for homosexuality to be more accepted, and through them, huge strides were made toward acknowledging gays and lesbians and achieving justice for them. But it came at the cost of censorship: Allen Ginsberg's poem *Howl* and William S. Burrough's novel *Naked Lunch* were subjected to prolonged obscenity trials. The Beats had to fight to express their depth of emotion and sensuality through this Uranus influence. Other heroes of this time were Lawrence Ferlinghetti, Jack Kerouac, Gregory Corso, Neal Cassady, Diane di Prima, and Audre Lorde.

The work of the Beats in this area paved the way for the hippies and the consciousness revolution of the sixties through expanding traditional versions of acceptable expressions of emotion and sexuality for the greater good. Some place the sexual revolution in the sixties, but I feel it really belongs to the brave Beat poets who came out with their sexuality and made massive headway toward the sexual revolution and formed their own rebellious totally Uranus revolution a decade earlier.

The energy of Cancer attempting to protect its vulnerability combined with the Capricorn hedonism probably caused an overreaction from the public against the free expression of this Uranus shadow placement. The key to this revolutionary shadow is to read the crowd and come into relationship rather than rebellion—allow the people to see you as one of them, not an enemy who poses a threat. Defensive tactics of the shadow in Cancer could prevent unity that really exists between us. This shadow Uranus rebels against repression but must temper itself to avoid the public rebelling against its rebellion with censorship.

Example in Nature

In 1910, a team of scientists set off on the Terra Nova Expedition to explore Antarctica. Among them was George Murray Levick, a zoologist and photographer who would be the first researcher to study the world's largest Adélie penguin colony. In his notebooks, he described their sexual behaviour, including sex between male birds. However, none of these notes would appear in Levick's published papers. Concerned by the graphic content, he only printed 100 copies of Sexual Habits of the Adélie Penguin *to circulate privately. The last remaining copy was recently unearthed providing valuable insights into animal homosexuality research. But forays into animal homosexuality research long predate Levick, with observations published as far back as the 1700s and 1800s. More than 200 years later, research has moved past some of the taboos those early researchers faced and shown that homosexuality is much more common than previously thought. Same-sex behaviour ranging from co-parenting to sex has been observed in over 1,000 species with likely many more as researchers begin to look for the behaviour explicitly. Homosexuality is widespread, with bisexuality even more prevalent across species.*

— Juanita Bawagan, "Scientists Explore the Evolution of Animal Homosexuality," Imperial College London, May 2, 2019

♌

Leo Uranus Shadow

Creator

Birth Uranus: Aquarius ♒
Revolution: Self-expression

This shadow expression of Uranus involves artists movements and the ability for the creativity of a group of individuals to form a movement. The birth Uranus in Aquarius needs community, while the shadow demands self-expression through artistic means, so the two come together here in revolutionary artistic communities. Expressionism, cubism, futurism, art deco, dadaism, surrealism, constructivism, De Stijl, Bauhaus—all occur within the range of Uranus in this shadow placement. We can see the value of this shadow Uranus simply in the names of the movements listed above. Can you imagine human history without these movements of artists, grouping together and supporting each other? Neither can I.

The danger of this Uranus shadow is that society favors an individual artist over the movement that the artist is a part of. Through social acceptance of one artist, that artist is placed ahead of the others in the group, and his artwork (and it is almost always a male artist) becomes well known and commodified, while the others remain in the shadows, even though it took a village to form the ideas behind the art movement. The solution to this Uranus Leo shadow is to include all the individual egos in the group and acknowledge how they fed one another and resist singling out an individual artist, whose artwork is then commodified, printed on posters and mugs to be purchased. The counterforce to artistic movements of self-expression is cherry-picking egos who provide the most monetary value. Resist this, and you do not feed the shadow.

Example in Nature

Scientists are still baffled by what prompted the elephants to leave their home at the Xishuangbanna National Nature Reserve, bordering Laos.

Since setting off in spring last year they have pilfered shops and trampled crops worth over $1 million, and thousands of residents have been evacuated from their path.

"For some reason these elephants felt that their traditional home range was no longer suitable . . . and then they just left to find somewhere else," Ahimsa Campos-Arceiz, an elephant specialist . . . told AFP.

"But they didn't have a destination in mind. They are just moving around trying to find a place that will work for them. . . .

"What has surprised me the most is that these elephants are very healthy and look very happy despite roaming in densely populated, unfamiliar areas," Campos-Arceiz said. "These elephants are very playful, which tells me that they are fine," he added.

— Poornima Weerasekara, "March of the Elephants: China's Rogue Herd Spotlights Habitat Loss," phys.org, June 26, 2021

♍

Virgo Uranus Shadow

Purification

Birth Uranus: Pisces ♓
Revolution: Conservatism

This shadow of Uranus in Virgo values perfectionism and seeks to eliminate unwanted influences and purify groups. This may seem to be a good, clean, wholesome endeavor, but in fact it can be responsible for more violence and bloodshed than almost any other Uranus shadow. In passing judgment on those who have not adhered to a puritanical system, this Uranus shadow provides society with a rationale to shame and eliminate those it deems unworthy.

Prohibition, which happened from 1920 to 1933, fell under this Uranus shadow. All this shadow of purification did was drive drinking into the basement literally, that is speakeasies, and fuel organized crime. It made no progress whatsoever in eradicating alcohol use. The rebellion here was spearheaded by women's rights activists who were appalled by the fallout of alcohol abuse, which mainly affected women, who suffered from male violence and domestic abuse. These activists attempted to appeal to higher values and curtail the debauchery, but did so from a place of judgment and virtue. A shamed shadow strikes back; the shaming does not heal. This rebellion and revolution didn't have much luck and may have perpetrated even more violence.

The shaming and repression of violent behavior seems to have little effect on individuals perpetrating violent acts. It turns out that having the death penalty as a consequence for murder has not stopped people from murdering each other. We obviously have to attempt to deal with these shadows and with violence, but perhaps we can find new strategies since shame and punishment aren't having the highest efficacy. The tail end of this Uranus placement was followed abruptly by World War II.

Example in Nature

You may have seen the story earlier this week of the drunken Swedish moose (or elk, as they call the antlered behemoth in Sweden) that got stuck in a tree. "I thought at first that someone was having a laugh. Then I went over to take a look and spotted an elk stuck in an apple tree with only one leg left on the ground," Per Johansson, who spotted the inebriated mammal in the garden next door to his house in Särö, told The Local. *The moose likely got drunk eating apples fermenting on the ground and got stuck in the tree trying to get fresh fruit. "Drunken elk are common in Sweden during the autumn season when there are plenty of apples lying around on the ground and hanging from branches in Swedish gardens,"* The Local *states.*

— Sarah Zielinski, "The Alcoholics of the Animal World," *Smithsonian Magazine*, September 16, 2011

♎

Libra Uranus Shadow

War Pigs

Birth Uranus: Aries ♈
Revolution: Systemic justice

The shadow Uranus in Libra creates rules, regulations, and peacekeeping forces to regulate corrupt authorities and bring them to justice. Often, it seems, the creators and holders of the justice systems, namely governments, also need an oversight committee to maintain truth and avoid corruption in the systems that execute "justice" on larger levels. Sometimes nations have to come together to assist if entire governments behave unfairly to their people. Whenever totalitarian values or unfair circumstances become dominant, the need for justice will come back around to this shadow, which will create a revolution against those forces that abuse the execution of justice by saying they deserve to take away human rights of life, liberty, and happiness.

Attempts to impose accountability arose during World War II, and even before, under this influence in the early thirties after the First World War (there were shifts in time due to retrogrades of Uranus extending the duration of this transit to cover both time periods), nations responded to check balances against forces of war, and thank goodness.

This shadow was prevalent in World War II and the shadow of the god of war appeared in full force through this Uranus revolution whose shadow chose justifications rather than justice. Rather than true justification, this shadow can encourage those who try to make war falsely to justify themselves against their enemies. Cain justifies killing his brother Abel because he broke the rules in Cain's eyes, but God was quick to reprimand Cain, letting him know that that was not his jurisdiction or call to make. Cain was not justified to take the life of Abel, regardless of his own personal views of what justice should be. The Nazi forces felt vindicated against other groups, such as the Jewish people, claiming the "stabbed in the back" narrative; they felt "justified" in their retribution of exterminating a race. This is obviously incorrect and shadow—pure, simple, and awful. Even if you think an entire nation is your enemy, to be clear, eradicating them from the face of the earth is not the solution; it is not just, it is not vindicated—it just isn't, ever.

Retribution rather than reciprocity took over, as this shadow was cast over the land. The shadow of all war is blame and projection onto the other, which falsely justifies destruction. This was taken to a revolutionary level through projecting projectiles in the largest way ever seen in history under this influence. In World War II, one side tried to kill everyone and was then met with a force that also sought total extermination in the form of bombs. Two wrongs did not make right here, and it was a shadow lesson we need to learn well by deeply gazing into its depths. The level of retribution upon innocent Japanese citizens was also unwarranted, and falsely justified.

In order to transmute this shadow, the difference between justice and justification must be clearly defined, and the way through needs to include everyone, not one party over another, or using means to justify the eradication of the rights of others. Perhaps we still haven't come to terms with this shadow, but each of us can learn the lesson as individuals, even if nations cannot seem to neutralize their antagonisms through attaining equity, which serves as an antidote here.

If someone commits genocide, we must not genocide them in return; but we also have to find a way to not allow genocide to occur, and to not let someone kill us. I have no lack of humility in making these statements; I fully see the difficulty. If someone murdered my whole family, Goddess bless me, I would probably kill them all. I am not that strong. We must help each other navigate such crimes and digest and shift this shadow. Whoever has been victimized by it will understandably not be able to do it alone, and I have no judgment, only contemplation. This is a difficult shadow. Please, everyone take a bite of it and help digest it—it will take all of us to work through. This is a madness shadow, to be certain; any progress made is an addition to the progress of humanity.

Example in Nature

Reciprocity can evolve if there are repeated encounters between the same individuals (in an iterated Prisoner's Dilemma game), and if an individual has the ability to vary its strategy according to its partner's previous actions. The maintenance of a cooperative bacteriophage evolving at a low multiplicity of infection (ensuring clonal populations) during long-term selection experiments (Turner and Chao, 2003) can be interpreted as a player changing strategy to dominate the game (e.g., Chen et al., 2012). One successful game strategy is "tit-for-tat," in which an individual responds toward its partner with the same action the other player performed in the previous round (Axelrod and Hamilton, 1981). In Pseudomonas aeruginosa *colonies growing on solid substrate, the costly secretion of pyoverdin, an iron chelator, is maintained in the population by tit-for-tat trafficking between contacting cells (Julou et al., 2013). . . . This local exchange modulates the growth of individual cells thereby preventing a long sequence of retaliation because local patches of non-producers are outcompeted by the faster growth of producers.*

— C. J. Rose and P. B. Rainey, "Cooperation and Public Goods, Bacterial," *Encyclopedia of Evolutionary Biology* 1 (December 2016): 374–80

♏

Scorpio Uranus Shadow

The Pied Piper

Birth Uranus: Taurus ♉
Revolution: The mighty microorganism

Shadow Uranus in Scorpio is a micro-revolution of disease-spreading organisms. We are currently experiencing this shadow, and in keeping with history, we experienced a pandemic under its influence. In the mid-1850s, under this influence, the bubonic plague spread at a disastrous rate, affecting millions of people. There were several iterations of this plague, which was also known as the black death. The plague spread again under this Uranus shadow in the 1930s and 1940s around Asia, specifically China, India, and Africa.

In response to this shadow, revolutions often occur in science and medicine, driven by demand from the public, who must shift social behavior, or avoid it all together in some cases. Increased awareness of these dangers and of how germs spread can affect our communal behavior, resulting in more solitary activities and isolation. Here, the Uranus shadow reminds us of the potential dangers nature can conceal within anyone at any time. It is important to maintain good mental health during such times.

The word *influence* is related to the word *influenza*, as in a contagion, and in olden times astrology, the influence of the planets, was consulted to predict plagues or determine when they would be over. Historical astrologers felt there were correspondences between the planets in heaven and the microorganisms crawling around in our Earth-bound forms. The bubonic plague, for example, also resulted in a revolution of astrology as the masses sought answers through the depths of the misery of the disease.

> Located at the intersection of medicine and mathematics, astrology was once a promising methodology for monitoring the health of the people. Astrologers made annual predictions about the diseases that would predominate in particular regions, disseminating their forecasts widely alongside advice on what should be done in response. Their ability to think in terms of relatively standardized "populations"—alongside their attempts to correlate the incidence of disease with external factors—made astrologers prime candidates for developing novel approaches to epidemics. Before the epidemiologist there was the astrologer, who looked to the stars to find patterns between celestial configurations and major health events, using their findings to model the rise and fall of epidemics.*

*Michelle Pfeffer, "Astrology, Plague, and Prognostication in Early Modern England: A Forgotten Chapter in the History of Public Health," *Past & Present* (17 Feb 2023).

I have to say, I researched much of the statistical experts' mathematical predictions regarding the coronavirus pandemic early on, as it was unfolding, and compared them to many of our modern astrologers' predictions, and it was quite fascinating to view them side by side. In hindsight, the majority of the most popular mathematical predictions ended up being false as things played out in reality. The mathematical predictions tended to be severely inflated while the astrological views were more conservative and closer to the end result. I wasn't sure why the scientists were condemning astrology and supporting models that used scientific means but ended up wrong. Perhaps no one deserved insults and looking at both systems in an objective manner clear from shadow projections—rather than defending one side over the other like a sports team—could have actually yielded some insight.

Example in Nature

Five counties in Florida remain at the mercy of the weather and water currents as a "red tide" algae bloom continues to choke their waters, marine life and economies. . . . Manatee County has picked up 164 tons of fishkill so far this August. Sarasota County, just south, has picked up more than 149 tons. But those counties pale in comparison to Fort Myers' Lee County, about 50 miles further south. Since August 2, contractors hired by Lee County have picked up over 1,700 tons of dead sea life. That number doesn't include marine life collected by the county's parks and recreation department, nor does it include counts on the islands of Boca Grande and Captiva. The overall total also does not include dead fish collected from the extensive network of privately owned canals throughout the five counties.

— Paul P. Murphy, "Florida's Red Tide Has Produced 2,000 Tons of Dead Marine Life and Cost Businesses More Than $8 Million," CNN, August 23, 2018

♐

Sagittarius Uranus Shadow

The End of Dogma

Birth Uranus: Gemini ♊
Revolution: Reform the church

The natal placement of Uranus in Gemini thrives on sharing information, and this placement, in the search for higher truths, rebels against religion and dogma. A major corruption of most churches is a tendency to begin limiting other ideas, information, and data to control what people think in order to keep everyone in unified agreement. When information flows freely through a congregation, members have room to question dogma, test its truth, and determine if it matches their own personal spiritual experiences. Here is the spiritual revolutionary who does not find peace in the pews but in her own heart. This is the revolution of the wandering sage; the high priestess who lives in a cave.

Uranus will be entering into this shadow in 2025, so we can certainly expect to see some major shifts in dogmatic religions at that time. The shift will be in the form of a rebellion against religious institutions and an increase in the practice of individual spirituality. More power will be placed into religion for the people rather than a systemic dogma promulgated by a religious body.

The detriment of this shadow is a tendency to isolate, to be the lone sage, rather than sharing the spiritual experience. You may have an enlightened realization, but others will never know or benefit from it unless you tell them. If a tree falls in the forest and only you are present to hear it, you must share the experience, or it will be as though the event never happened and no sound was made. Tell a couple of people even though it may be risky, especially if they are devoted to a dogma that your experience contradicts.

Example in Nature

"Since only humans are capable of language that can communicate the richness of spiritual experience, it is unlikely

we will ever know with certainty what an animal subjectively experiences," Kevin Nelson, a professor of neurology at the University of Kentucky, told Discovery News.

"[I]t is still reasonable to conclude that since the most primitive areas of our brain happen to be the spiritual, then we can expect that animals are also capable of spiritual experiences," added Nelson. . . .

A Neurology journal study, for example, determined that out-of-body experiences in humans are likely caused by the brain's arousal system, which regulates different states of consciousness.

"In humans, we know that if we disrupt the (brain) region where vision, sense of motion, orientation in Earth's gravitational field, and knowing the position of our body all come together, then out-of-body experiences can be caused literally by the flip of a switch," [Nelson] said. "There is absolutely no reason to believe it is any different for a dog, cat, or primate's brain."

— Jennifer Viegas, "Animals Said to Have Spiritual Experiences," NBC News, October 8, 2010

♑

Capricorn Uranus Shadow

The Repressor

Birth Uranus: Cancer ♋
Revolution: Conservative backlash

Those born with natal Uranus in Cancer seek to rebel against their emotional needs to avoid being controlled by them; the shadow Uranus in Capricorn rebels against corporate control of business and government intrusion into our lives. Business owners turn against larger governing bodies and regulations and form groups of their own to litigate against the oppression. Conservative values can also often arise from labor as people feel the need to defend and protect their jobs and hard work. Often this drive to ensure economic self-sufficiency can devolve into scapegoating groups, such as immigrants, and constructing a strong defensive boundary.

This isn't necessarily a bad thing, to discourage dependency, especially when we see how many people are dependent on government programs. However, we must also acknowledge that much dependency is caused by racism, ageism, sexism, disease, disability, and other factors having nothing to do with an individual's choices. The Social Security Act of 1935 began during this Uranus shadow, and was upheld by the Supreme Court despite much of the New Deal facing backlash from conservatives. The danger of this rebellious Uranus shadow is that we forget how much we depend and rely on others for our survival and hoard resources, causing damage to others. Influenced by the mind-set of this shadow, we may feel like everything we have labored for can be taken from us, and so we develop a scarcity paranoia and become overprotective and aggressive toward assisting others and are critical of welfare programs, public services, and humanitarian donations.

Example in Nature

The expansion of Homo erectus *out of Africa into Asia around 1.6 million years ago appears to have been caused by the need to find more large scale grasslands. . . . All archaic species adapted slowly to new opportunities for settlement and were often deterred by environmental and climatic barriers. Dr Spikins argues that betrayals of trust resulting from moral disputes were a significant reason for such risky dispersals into apparently unwelcoming environments with a desire to avoid physical harm from disgruntled former friends and allies being a key motivation. Offenders and any allies within their social network would feel driven to get out of harm's way. . . .*

[Dr Spikins says:] "Moral conflicts provoke substantial mobility—the furious ex ally, mate or whole group, with a poisoned spear or projectile intent on seeking revenge or justice, are a strong motivation to get away, and to take almost any risk to do so.

"While we view the global dispersal of our species as a symbol

of our success, part of the motivations for such movements reflect a darker, though no less 'collaborative,' side to human nature."

— University of York, "Betrayals of Trust: Human Nature's Dark Side May Have Helped Us Spread across the World," Science Daily, November 25, 2015

♒

Aquarius Uranus Shadow

Idolatry

Birth Uranus: Leo ♌
Revolution: Technology

Uranus in Aquarius's shadow causes a creation energy for the sake of creation rather than self-expression or communication of higher values. This becomes an assembly line of robots making more robots. The shadow of Uranus in Aquarius seeks to create fake communities, fake ecosystems, and fake technologies that serve only to make more of themselves. The energetic of this Uranus shadow is like a virus replicating simply to make more viruses. The birth placement of Uranus in Leo is meant to cause a revolution in artistic creation of the self, like the sun. Here we see one seeking to be a sun who only makes more ego, a damaging shadow that can essentially create waste. Here there is overproduction, overconsumption, and pollution; garbage placed in giant piles. It may seem like making millions of cans of soda is creative and productive, but then there are a million empty cans to deal with as waste. Advancements for the sheer sake of making more advancements will always cause this shadow of Uranus to take over and "recycle" itself. The idea of recycling itself belongs to Uranus, as nature always shall find ways to take things produced back into her breast. If we are constantly creating more waste than fits into her cycle, nature herself shall force us to do her labor when we discover that there is no "garbage" in this world. Everything is made from the body of Earth and returns to the body of Earth. Even you shall be recycled.

Be cautious to balance what you create and what you waste. Think about the purpose of your creations. Are they only fulfilling your need to be noticed or do they serve? How long do they serve, and what do they leave behind? There is much for humanity to learn from this shadow archetype to attempt to counter this show. During the 1950s and 1960s, pollution legislation arose under this shadow influence, as awareness was raised about the amount of waste coming from our "creativity," and attempts were made to counter it.

Example in Nature

> *Every now and then a disease becomes so dangerous that it kills the host. If the disease is able to spread to another host before the first host dies, then it is not too lethal to exist. Evolution cannot make it less lethal so long as it can still spread. If a hypothetical disease eradicates its only host, both will indeed go extinct. The strain of the Black Death plague (*Yersinia pestis*) from the 14th century was too virulent and is now extinct, with modern strains [subspecies, like breeds of dog or varieties of crops] of the bacteria producing less devastating symptoms (although nothing is stopping another deadly strain from appearing again). Extinction is a part of evolution. There is no goal in evolution, so if a creature evolves a trait that drives it to extinction, so be it.*
>
> — Matan Shelomi, "Why Did Some Diseases Evolve to Kill Their Hosts?," answer on Quora, *Forbes,* May 26, 2017

♓ Pisces Uranus Shadow

Subculture

Birth Uranus: Virgo ♍
Revolution: Psychonaught

The shadow Uranus in Pisces rebels against all rules, regulations, and proper conduct. This is the Uranus shadow that ruled the sixties and the psychedelic revolutions of liberating the mind and sexuality on large cultural levels. Rebellions against what was seen as societal norms were shaken, as freedom of expression made massive breakthroughs and individuals began seeking their paths instead of following acceptable pathways laid out before them. The birth Uranus in Virgo seeks to repress and restrict, and this shadow says no way, rejecting all that is prim and proper and heading toward sensuality and an increase in the ability to perceive things for itself.

In typical Pisces fashion, spirituality plays a large role in this rebellion, and interest in places where spirit is made perceivable become attractive under this influence. It is no coincidence that psychedelics would be involved as they blow open the senses and allow individuals to make huge strides in a short amount of time to see past their own limits into the great unknown. The danger of this shadow is in the formlessness of Pisces. Because this shadow goes into the ocean, there is no organization or rules, so things that are seen peter out if no one is able to catch hold of them and provide some kind of structure. Quite a few of the movements formed during this time didn't last, although they did mutate and morph into other ideas and groups. To catch the fire of this zeitgeist, place the dissolution of ego through culture that this shadow provides within some kind of structure so that the insights aren't wasted, dissolving in oblivion. At least consider writing down the revelations you and your peers are able to obtain under this influence.

Example in Nature

Scientists found three new species of fish in one of the deepest parts of the ocean, and these animals are so soft and squishy that they disintegrate if brought to the surface. Researchers captured remarkable footage that shows the fish in their alien home environment. . . .

In the conditions present about 4.7 miles (7.5 kilometers) below the ocean surface, a squishy body is helpful in withstanding cold and extreme pressures, Linley said. So, the hardest objects in the snailfishes' bodies are their teeth and the bones in their inner ears, and the creatures have only minimal structural body parts.

— Rafi Letzter, "This Squishy Deep-Sea Fish 'Melts' at the Ocean Surface," Live Science, September 11, 2018

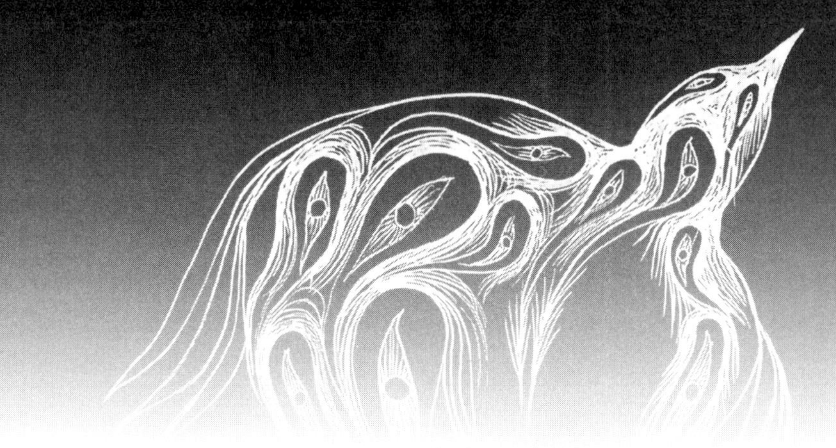

Neptune Shadows

Sleepwalker

In astrology, Neptune embodies the principle of passive receptivity displayed equally in inspiration, intuition, mediumistic powers and paranormal faculties as in unworldliness, madness, aberration and irrational fears. . . . This planet rules the subconscious and brings on mental illness, depression and neurosis. Neptune is the archetype of universal integration or dissolution. It may comprise lack of differentiation from the group or attachment to superior order.

JEAN CHEVALIER AND ALAIN GHEERBRANT,
A DICTIONARY OF SYMBOLS

THE PLANET NEPTUNE, ruler of the oceans in mythology, is the archetypal embodiment of the depths of the subconscious in astrological traditions. Qualities belonging to Neptune are dreams, illusions, and spirituality. Some shadow sides of these realms are delusion, folly, and addiction. Many traps are present in the deep underwater realms, which are too dense to receive light and are under immense pressure formed from the surrounding substrate. The shadow action of Neptune is the

sleepwalker, the daydreamer, the one who enters, or is trapped inside of, the subconscious while waking. This sounds creative and fun, but when our subconscious is driving the car, we become overwhelmed by influences of all kinds. Addiction often accompanies this shadow because of the total loss of boundaries; everything passes in and out of the consciousness, which is not conducive to remaining in integrity and tends to reach a breaking point or limit. People under the influence of the Neptune shadow can easily come under the sway of a guru or preacher; substances enter them, as do the stars themselves, and influence them. Their awareness wanes, and they are overtaken as if by a virus. Rather like an immune system that fails and lets in diseases, when our consciousness drops, the archons descend to fill the empty space.

The unconscious self is in the realm of unconsciousness itself, like a deep sea fish, lost in the darkness of the ocean, your unconscious floats adrift within the collective unconscious, which is full of who knows what. Beings that exist in the dark places of the world have some surprising coping mechanisms. Deep sea creatures and some cave dwellers are bioluminescent: they produce their own light and do not need the sun; perhaps we have more to learn from them than we think. The lifeforms that live in nature's darkest shadows make light in their bodies in a miracle of chemistry. How remarkable! What more proof of "enlightenment" could we ask for than these creatures who have evolved the ability to glow in the dark?

The outer planets move slowly, so Neptune is generational as well as personal. It takes nearly 165 years for Neptune to orbit the sun, as it gradually traverses through all the signs. This means you won't live to see all the Neptune shadows and occultations. These are collective shadows that each individual must navigate, and the energetics of them are important to see, recognize, and come to know. I encourage everyone to study these larger generational shadows to identify them in oneself and in others, rather than leave them enfolded in the skirts of darkness so that we respond to them unconsciously when we confront them in other people, nations, or institutions.

♈

Aries Neptune Shadow

The Poseur

Birth Neptune: Libra ♎
Wake-up Call: Put the mask down

Delusions of grandeur enter the ego with this Neptune shadow. Having high aspirations and ambitions is most likely helpful and can lead to growth. However, being completely disconnected from the reality of your abilities and who you are is dangerous. You will need to eventually take some action, and you cannot just sit around daydreaming all day. When we hold fast to illusions about our ego, we will do ourselves and others a disservice. Say for example we dream of being a pilot, and instead of learning how to fly a plane and developing the skills and discipline, you just hop into the cockpit and try it out. Sometimes we can fake it till we make it, but being grounded in who we are is the key to authenticity, and it completely eludes this Neptune shadow.

Arrogance won't help you live the dream. Be realistic about what it takes to accomplish something so that you can come to completion. *Know thyself* are wise words, and do not let Neptune-based delusions caused by this shadow prevent you from being all you can. It is important to dream big and see our potential past the reality of what we might think we are limited to, but try not to let it go to your head.

Example in Nature

They're known for their extravagant courtship techniques involving a spectacular plumage display and dancing. But while these maneuvers may be enough to attract the attention of a female, further tactics may be required to secure a mate. The male superb lyrebird therefore resorts to a more unpalatable technique: lying. These birds are known to be able to imitate the calls of more than 20 other species in their local environment, and in certain courtship situations, they imitate the mobbing alarm calls of multiple species. . . .

[T]hey'd also enhance the illusion by imitating the sounds of small birds' wingbeats. They pulled this trick only when females attempted to exit male display arenas or during the long copulation period. This Machiavellian mimicry aims to prevent females from prematurely leaving.

— Kayleen Devlin, "Meet the Fakers of Nature," BBC Earth, no date

♉

Taurus Neptune Shadow

Parasomnia

Birth Neptune: Scorpio ♏
Wake-up Call: Your body has more control than you know

This Neptune shadow contains the energy of the sleeping physical body that the conscious awareness cannot reach. In this shadow placement, the body does what it wants while the consciousness sleeps. Technically speaking, the body is constantly doing things we are not aware of, from beating our hearts to fighting infections.

Usually when we go to sleep, the body enters into a state of paralysis, and our subconscious mind gets to come out and up into our awareness through our dreams, for our memory to play with or expand. This Neptune shadow permits rulership of the body in this realm, when otherwise it should be still. The effect of this shadow is that we are compelled by instinct. Often there is sleepwalking, sleep eating, and other activities that our body seeks to express, regardless of our conscious awareness. Horrifying though it may be, there are quite a few cases of individuals murdering people in this state as well.

To work on transmuting this Neptune shadow, we will need to raise the subconscious functions of the body into waking awareness. Though this sounds impossible, many disciplines work toward this, including yoga, which manages the breathing and heart rate, qigong, the work of Wim Hof, and many others, who are actively seeking ways to be more involved in this typically hidden portion of our lives. If you suffer from this shadow form, it might be worth investigating.

Example in Nature

It is commonly assumed that flying birds maintain environmental awareness and aerodynamic control by sleeping with only one eye closed and one cerebral hemisphere at a time. However, sleep has never been demonstrated in flying birds. Here, using electroencephalogram recordings of great frigatebirds flying over the ocean for up to 10 days, we show that they can sleep with either one hemisphere at a time or both hemispheres simultaneously. Also unexpectedly, frigatebirds sleep for only 0.69 h d−1 (7.4% of the time spent sleeping on land), indicating that ecological demands for attention usually exceed the attention afforded by sleeping unihemispherically. In addition to establishing that birds can sleep in flight, our results challenge the view that they sustain prolonged flights by obtaining normal amounts of sleep on the wing.

— Niels C. Rattenborg et al., "Evidence That Birds Sleep in Mid-flight," *Nature Communications* 7, no. 12468 (August 3, 2016)

♊

Gemini Neptune Shadow

Sleeptalker

Birth Neptune: Sagittarius ♐
Wake-up Call: Mind your words

Subconscious talking rules this shadow placement. Words said from our shadows create problems in the world. In the beginning was the word, and what we say matters. When our shadow realm creates speech, these can be lies, rumors, gossip, or simply fantastical imaginary beings that are unrooted in the world. They can play a big role in expanding the mind and our lives by expanding our abilities, but they can also cause harm.

This Neptune shadow creates illusions through words; to transmute it we must practice telling the truth, or at least be able to discern the truth from lies so that we can tell the difference between the two. A tendency to make up illusions rules the day here. For one person this can be manageable, but when entire nations or time periods succumb to such false thinking and speech, we make realities that can be deceptive and unsustainable. Watching the tides of words said and testing them against what we can perceive as real help keep this Neptune shadow in check. This can mean speaking up for truth against a strong tide of illusion, and you as an individual might not be able to accomplish it. Try and spend some time looking into current trends in the narrative; measure it against objective reality and investigate others who are doing the same to keep everything grounded. In this way, the words you say yourself at least won't participate in spreading illusion around. This Neptune shadow is akin to the radio broadcast of *War of the Worlds* when everyone believed that there was an alien attack because they didn't know it was just make-believe.

Example in Nature

> *Deception has evolved multiple times in the context of antagonistic interactions between species. Members of the "deceiving species" transmit misleading information ("fake signals") to members of the "deceived species" which respond in a way that is detrimental for them, but beneficial for the deceiving species. The costs paid by the deceived species generate selection pressures that could start antagonistic coevolutionary races. For example, many palatable insect species have evolved morphologies, odours and colour patterns that make them similar to toxic or dangerous species (Batesian mimicry) and help them deceive potential predators.*
>
> — Yara Maquitico et al., "*Photuris lugubris* Female Fireflies Hunt Males of the Synchronous Firefly *Photinus palaciosi*," *Insects* 13, no. 10 (October 8, 2022): 915

♋

Cancer Neptune Shadow

The Nightmare

Birth Neptune: Capricorn ♑
Wake-up Call: Process negative emotional energy

This is the shadow of the emotional nightmare. Repressed feelings and emotions creep up out of the depths to pinch anything they can get their claws on. This is the epitome of the moon tarot card that shows the crayfish emerging to the surface in the false light after lurking in the muddy water. If there have been traumas, or even just negative experiences that you are not responsible for, they will nestle down into the bottom of your depth and show up in a big juicy nightmare that grips you in sweat in the heart of Earth's shadow of night. This is a healthy way to process them, and it needs to happen, as unpleasant as it is. Sometimes these nightmares can become too much, and it is necessary to seek assistance rather than be the victim of constant night terrors.

The difficulty with this Neptune shadow is that it can drain you of your emotional energy. The incubi and succubi might be real, or they might not, but what is real are the influences that visit us in the night and give us terrible visions, as this shadow does. The subconscious does not forget anything, and even if we lose awareness of something, that does not eliminate it from our sphere of memory. The unconscious depths run deep and hold a lot of shadows; the nightmare brings them up to be viewed. Work on them with lucid dreaming, dream journaling, and saltwater baths.

Example in Nature

Anglerfish are the stuff of nightmares. National Geographic *called the otherworldly terrors from the deep "possibly the ugliest animal on the planet," and they're definitely not wrong. Everything about them is creepy, from their maw full of razor-sharp, translucent teeth to their dead eyes, and yet, we're still fascinated by them because they're so mysterious. Anglers engage in parasitic mating, where male anglers, which are typically much smaller than the females, become permanently fused together. Females eventually absorb the males, who lose organs, such as their eyes, during the process, until the male becomes a sac with sperm, which the female uses at her leisure to procreate. Female anglers may carry six or more males on their bodies at a time according to* National Geographic.

— Daisy Hernandez, "Why the Anglerfish Continues to Haunt Our Dreams," *Popular Mechanics*, July 30, 2019

♌

Leo Neptune Shadow

The Impossible Dream

Birth Neptune: Aquarius ♒
Wake-up Call: Don't lose the ground

The shadow Neptune in Leo creates an illusion of unattainable goals based in heroic intentions and the need for acknowledgment. The incredible achievements of those who reach for the stars propel us as a species, and we would certainly be further back without them. The damage that comes when we disconnect entirely from pragmatics is that our dreams belly flop into failure, making it difficult to reach out for them again. The precious, creative power and the striving of the shadow Leo when combined with the dreams and illusions of Neptune is as cute as a Care Bear. My observation here is to state a warning in order that we do not lose more of our precious dreamers whose hearts often just fly too far away on the wings of their dreams. Please dreamers, precious ones, be safe; do not lose heart in the darkness of the big ideas you have making you feel small. Don't give up. The world is not ideal and neither are you, but your worth is good as gold.

The danger of this shadow placement is that our dreams are too big to fit in this world. When we come into confrontation with this, we tend to give up and not understand the limits of this reality. Please don't quit. Instead, work hard to bring reality closer to your dreams, one thing at a time. Even if all you do is make reality more like your vision in one way, it's better than it was before.

Example in Nature

> *Sometimes, some penguins just head on to the middle of the icy desert, far away from the nourishing water and their feeding and breeding grounds, where they could only meet their doom. It seems unlikely that they just get disoriented, because if you take a penguin and put it back in one of its familiar places, even inside its colony, it just goes back to the same place again. It's like the mountains are calling to them. I couldn't find any peer reviewed study for this, and for now, this remains just an observed behavior—with no proposed underlying mechanism, with no theory behind it. The penguins seem to experience some sort of depression-like state.*
>
> — Mihai Andrei, "Some Penguins Commit Suicide, Walking Away from the Sea, Alone, towards Their Demise," ZME Science, July 3, 2014

♍

Virgo Neptune Shadow

The Buzzkill

Birth Neptune: Pisces ♓
Wake-up Call: Lighten up and relax

Shadow Neptune in Virgo is the opposer of Neptune and Pisces itself; its nature is the Antichrist of Neptune. This is a very uncomfortable placement for the Neptune shadow because the Virgo wants to spend so much time trying to make sense of something that is utter nonsense. This Neptune shadow creates a scenario akin to a mathematician being subjected to the Mad Hatter's tea party. The secret to navigating this Neptune shadow is to just shut up and join the party. The damage and detriment of this Neptune shadow is the party pooper who is powerful enough to drag down everything within a perimeter. Human beings can't work all the time, and nothing is perfect. Neptune shadow in Virgo is the Debbie Downer who creates a miasma that follows her like dust follows Pig-Pen, the *Peanuts* comic strip character.

Material means and being real about what is needed to eat to live came to the forefront in the thirties with this shadow placement being prominent during the Great Depression. Realistic Virgo had to come into Neptune's fantasies and had to deal with them directly. When everything becomes materialistic in this way, humanity becomes malnourished in its spiritual pursuits and the things that give life meaning. There must be an equal amount of the material and spiritual to be productive, otherwise territorial resource hoarding will follow, as became the case in the Second World War. As I write this book, Neptune is currently in Pisces and so this shadow is being cast. Try not to focus only on material concerns and survival even if the prevailing narrative is trying to force your mind into thinking constantly about your resources. The great toilet paper scandal of the coronavirus pandemic is an example of this shadow.

Example in Nature

The koala has one of the lowest ratios of brain to body mass of any mammal. Even though koalas are dumb, they have survived because their brains use minimal energy. Using the least amount of energy possible appears to be a key adaptation to surviving on a nutritionally poor, low-energy diet of toxic eucalyptus leaves. Let's be honest; koalas are not too bright. They expend as little energy as possible, spending roughly 18–20 hours per day sleeping. They move slowly and deliberately from sleeping spot to food source and back again. Sadly, they don't seem able to adapt very well to moving cars or the dangers of crossing highways. Mortality rates are high close to populated areas. Thankfully, they can learn to take advantage of underpasses designed to facilitate wildlife travel.

— George Sranko, "Koala Brain—Why Is the Koala the Dumbest Mammal? How Being Dumb Can Be Smart," Animals FYI, 2022

♎

Libra Neptune Shadow

Rationalization

Birth Neptune: Aries ♈
Wake-up Call: Righteousness is an illusion

Illusions influencing social justice are many. In social justice we have two predicaments, people who have truly been mistreated and victimized by the system or others and those who falsely claim they have. This Neptune shadow shows up when people use social justice erroneously for their own gains. This is a T-shirt company that makes free Leonard Peltier shirts and keeps all the profits for themselves. In the forties this shadow Neptune was cast. Many of the atrocities committed came in the name of justice and reciprocity manufactured by illusions in the perception and the inability to tell the difference between being rational and rationalizations.

We can learn much from shadow Neptune in Libra. The birth placement is in Aries, which is selfish and seeking to defend the self as a victim, so the shadow will seek to implement punishments and reciprocities based upon its ego's decisions of who is guilty. The justified delusion of violence used to support fraudulent imaginations ran rampant through the Second World War where the harsh reality had to come into focus in order to reconcile this Neptune shadow. The best way to transmute this Neptune illusion is to stare deeply into rationalizations that you deserve to live more than others and question tactics you may engage to take out people who are threatening to you. It is one thing to have to deal with those violently attacking you, it is another to rationalize why they do not deserve to exist. In the Bible, Cain kills his brother for violating a law he projected on him, and when God disagreed, Cain tried to claim he was the victim, classically holding this ancient shadow.

Example in Nature

Scientists have witnessed chimpanzees killing gorillas for the first time in two shocking attacks caught on video at a national park in Gabon on the west coast of Central Africa, a new study finds.

The researchers, from Osnabrück University and the Max Planck Institute for Evolutionary Anthropology in Germany, were following a massive group of 27 chimpanzees . . . when they first observed the chimps attack a party of five western lowland gorillas—three adult females and one infant, led by a male silverback. "The silverback was really throwing some of the chimps in the air, so he was really trying to protect himself and his group," study co-author Simone Pika, a cognitive biologist at Osnabrück University, told Live Science. Despite injuring three chimpanzees, the silverback was overwhelmed and the chimps ultimately captured the group's infant and beat it to death.

— Patrick Pester, "Chimpanzee Troop Beats and Kills Infant Gorillas in Unprecedented Clash," Live Science, July 22, 2021

♏

Scorpio Neptune Shadow

Dream Warriors

Birth Neptune: Taurus ♉
Wake-up Call: Manipulation is an illusion

The shadow Neptune in Scorpio can create an illusion to the holder that the ways they have manipulated reality are reality; in other words, they can believe their own lies. This is a different situation than the gaslighter who is trying to fool the victim into believing a false reality; here, they really think their distortion is real.

Everyone appreciates someone who is able to make changes, especially beneficial ones, but no one likes to wake up from a total dream world they have been made to believe by following someone holding this shadow placement. Reality can get shoved into a mind-set here and can have consequences when the party is over. The illusions may become so severe that the individual under their influences is acting as though they are real and true.

This was the Neptune shadow placement during the 1960s when

arguably more people were introduced to hallucinogens en masse than at any other time. There are many benefits to psychedelics for humanity, and they are an important medicinal resource. It is important to place awareness on the dissociation caused by them as well and make sure grounding and integration are cycled into their use to prevent illusions from annihilating the individuals seeking a perceptual cleanse. If psychedelics were what it took to heal humanity, all of Burning Man would be our saviors, but it turns out, it is not so. Many individuals peddling this solution have taken on shadow behaviors such as seeking to be gurus, sexual abuse of their followers, and self-destructive delusions of grandeur. No one in all the festivals contributed to the legalization of any of those substances they so loudly lauded, instead that was carried through by the hard work of a couple of individuals filling out the paperwork who did real things in the world. Stay grounded, dreamers; you will go farther.

Example in Nature

National Public Radio's All Things Considered *considered Lady, a cocker spaniel spending a suspicious amount of time down by the backyard pond. "Lady would wander the area, disoriented and withdrawn, soporific and glassy-eyed," Laura Mirsch, Lady's owner, told NPR. Then there was that one night when Lady wouldn't come back. Eventually, she staggered back from the cattails and opened her mouth like she was going to throw up. She didn't throw up. Instead, recalls Mirsch, "out popped this disgusting toad." The toad was* Bufo alvarius, *a Colorado River toad whose skin contains two different tryptamines . . . and licking Bufo produces heady hallucinations. And toad tripping dogs are just the beginning. . . . Bees stoned on orchid nectar, goats gobbling magic mushrooms, birds chomping marijuana seeds, rats on opium, also mice, lizards, flies, spiders and cockroaches on opium, elephants drunk on anything they can find—usually fermented fruit in a bog hole, but they're known to raid breweries in India as well—felines crazy for catnip, cows loco for loco grass, moths preferring the incredibly hallucinogenic datura flower, mandrills taking the even stronger iboga root.*

— Steven Kotler, "Animals on Psychedelics: Survival of the Trippiest," *Psychology Today*, December 29, 2010

♐

Sagittarius Neptune Shadow

Head in the Clouds

Birth Neptune: Gemini ♊
Wake-up Call: Resources are needed to go to outer space

Dreaming of the cosmos, the Sagittarius Neptune shadow seeks to escape the world and explore the stars. Perhaps many of the early astrologers had this placement and preferred to tilt their eyes to the skies rather than watch their step. The natal Neptune is in Gemini with this shadow, and it tries to articulate and map the imagination, gathering data and knowledge about wonders and the numinous. The nature of wonder deplores and defies these cold constraints, and the Neptune shadow in Sagittarius will blow through these boundaries like a mustang busting out of its pen.

While gathering data is an important part of any exploration, in order to safely navigate, this Neptune shadow teaches us to prepare our minds and our hearts to be open to the unknown, to the unexpected. The negative aspect of this shadow occurs when we make no preparation for anything and try to live on wonder alone, sailing from place to place with nothing and no one. Every Pollyanna seems to need some grounded friend to rescue them, but they could avoid this by being more practical. The illusions that are dangerous for this Neptune shadow make it a burden for others to carry when it cannot consider its own needs and take care of its own survival while it follows its trails into the sky.

Example in Nature

In 2012, Dani Rabaiotti began tracking the whereabouts of a red fox. . . . Other students involved in the scientific study followed their assigned foxes all over the English city of Bristol. But Rabaiotti's fox never seemed to go anywhere. "He was just chilling under this bloke's shed" for six weeks, she says. So she named him Lazy Geoff. Rabaiotti, now a researcher at the Zoological Society of London, found herself reminiscing about Lazy Geoff last March and recounted the story in a Twitter thread. The response was stunning. Thousands of retweets and replies, many from other animal scientists who had similar experiences: tunas, tarantulas, sea lions, bears, and frogs, all aberrantly lazy—or so it seemed. But in the harsh natural world where only the fittest survive, how can wildlife be lazy?

— Dean Russell, "Lazy Foxes, Bold Mice: How Wildlife Personalities Shape the World," WBUR-FM, Boston, October 14, 2022

♑

Capricorn Neptune Shadow

All That Glitters Is Not Gold

Birth Neptune: Cancer ♋
Wake-up Call: We cannot live on bread alone

The shadow of Neptune in Capricorn is the alchemist who tries to make gold instead of forming their immortal spirit, the real goal of the alchemical process. The illusion present in the Neptune shadow in Capricorn is that money can buy you happiness. The natal Cancer placement of Neptune is emotionally driven and knows happiness when it feels it. If it is lacking in feeling fulfilled, rather than face these negative emotions, the Neptune shadow will step in and replace it with ambition to try and fill the black hole of dissatisfaction.

Disappointment and a lack of fulfillment can create feelings of depression and ennui on a deep level within the individual. It can be easy to get caught up in their Neptune shadow and seek to replace it with money-making schemes and illusions of being important. It is true that we need to be and can be happy here. I can say in all my years of providing assistance to people that billionaires are just as unfulfilled as those who are impoverished; unhappiness does not discriminate based on wealth, it just takes different forms. I learned early on in my life that people can have everything and still have nothing at all, and those with very little can be quite fulfilled and happy. Transmute this illusion by feeling joy regardless of your level of success or failure.

Example in Nature

> *An account of animal religion must be inaugurated by diagramming the possibility of invisible systems of bodily affect animating the distinct geographies of animal experience. These geographies emerge directly out of the vast variety of animal bodies and can take observable forms in practices, such as burying of the dead or waterfall dances, or non-observable forms—embedded in the subtle dynamic between bodies and worlds. The chimps at the base of the waterfall, the fox burying her mate, the snow monkey in the hot spring: what do they feel? . . . Animal religion, then, supplies us with what must become the maxim of material religion: Religion affects animal bodies no less than human bodies, and animal religion affects humans no less than the bodies of animals.*
>
> — Donovan O. Schaefer, "Do Animals Have Religion? Interdisciplinary Perspectives on Religion and Embodiment," *Anthrozoös* 25, no. 3 (August 2012): 173–80

♒

Aquarius Neptune Shadow

Utopia

Birth Neptune: Leo ♌
Wake-up Call: There is no perfect community

The idea of utopia is an old one and has been prevalent in every human culture throughout millennia. The prospect of everyone living together in harmony and prosperity remains a worthwhile dream. Some leaders have focused on achieving utopia and held it above reality. Ignoring the negative aspects that can arise when we live together, they seek instead to fantasize about a perfect society, even if their fantasy doesn't quite pan out when tested.

To find the perfect balance to live in this world, we must include both nature and humans. Much literature is surfacing recently analyzing and criticizing ecofascism, which blames the degradation of the environment on overpopulation and immigration, with the consequence that it tends to target the marginalized, suggesting that certain people are entitled to survive while others need to be eradicated. Some green activists arguably go too far by proposing that nature is pure and perfect and humans are corrupt and little more than a deadly virus on the planet, while others seem to care nothing for nature, place themselves above it, and see nature and other life-forms as only resources to exploit. Maybe our minds will be able to hold everything together someday. Perhaps the best way to transmute this Neptune shadow is to integrate human nature within our own hearts and then extend outwardly, as we digest our shadows and become more natural life-forms.

Example in Nature

Thomas More's Utopia *(1516) has not received a great deal of serious ecocritical attention, despite its representation of a purportedly ideal environment in which nature and society exist in perfect harmony. This can be explained in part by the preindustrial character of an early modern economy, which did not have to contend with large-scale exploitation of natural resources, nor with the pollution of air, water, and soil that troubles ecocritics today. . . . Concepts such as the Great Chain of Being, based on a set of correspondences between nature and human society, although interrogated vigorously by Marxists, feminists, and new historicists to the point that many feel they are now permanently discredited, offer ecocriticism a model for ecological kinship between a widely used early modern set of metaphors and the real. One could say that if Marxists, feminists, and new historicists worked hard to denaturalize nature, then ecocritics are trying very hard to renaturalize nature, and, in the process, to naturalize aspects of human society.*

— Ivo Kamps and Melissa Smith, "Utopian Ecocriticism: Naturalizing Nature in Thomas More's Utopia," in ed. Thomas Hallock, Ivo Kamps, and Karen L. Raber, *Early Modern Ecostudies: From the Florentine Codex to Shakespeare* (New York: Palgrave Macmillan, 2009), 115–29

♓

Pisces Neptune Shadow

Release the Kraken

Birth Neptune: Virgo ♍
Wake-up Call: Here there be monsters

When the subconscious is completely ignored, it will rise from its depths to attack us at inopportune moments, often without realizing what it is doing, and usually in front of other people. In this placement the kraken, a giant sea monster from Scandinavian mythology, rises from the prison it has been locked away in and shoots up like a weapon to defend us and take a sacrificial victim. The Greek mythological counterpart to the kraken is the *ketos* or *cetus*, a sea monster. An oracle tells King Cepheus and Queen Cassiopeia to sacrifice Andromeda to the cetus to appease an angry Poseidon. According to the myth, Perseus, upon hearing of her plight, rides in on Pegasus while holding the head of Medusa, whose gaze turns the cetus into stone. But all Medusa's gaze does is force the cetus to look into the depths of its own soul, which freezes its justifications and allows it to understand itself, revealing self-knowledge. We benefit greatly from instances when our deepest subconscious fears arise, but only if we can see them.

Reflecting upon something allows us to see these deep forces for what they are, in the form they are, rather than how we want them to be or how we imagine them to be, which links us deeply into their world. In this way we learn to respect them. Sometimes our own krakens or cetuses are too much to behold, so it may be we can only experience them vicariously or observe our monsters or those of others or nature at a safe distance. Sometimes all we need is a good friend to confide in. This is a very healthy way to integrate, as long as our friend is not taken by a judge's shadow in the process and condemns us for our krakens.

Example in Nature

Many deep-sea species, including squid, have monochromatic visual systems that are adapted to blue [light] and blue bioluminescence rather than long wavelength red-light. . . .

The researchers also used the squids' attraction to blue light to their advantage, outfitting the Medusa with a custom lure that they called the E-Jelly. This small, spinning ring of neon blue lights sat on the end of an outstretched arm, mimicking the movement and glow of a bioluminescent jellyfish. The lure worked, drawing A. dux *out of the darkness in both 2012 and 2019. In fact, the giant squid spotted in the Gulf of Mexico was a little too convinced by the E-Jelly's display; as footage of the encounter shows, the giant squid tried to attack the Medusa's camera arm with its tentacles in the hope of taking home a nice jellyfish meal. . . . That's a handy trick, as there is much to learn about the kraken's behavior that can only come to light in the darkness of its natural habitat.*

— Brandon Specktor, "How Scientists Caught Footage of 'the Kraken' after Centuries of Searching," Live Science, April 30, 2021

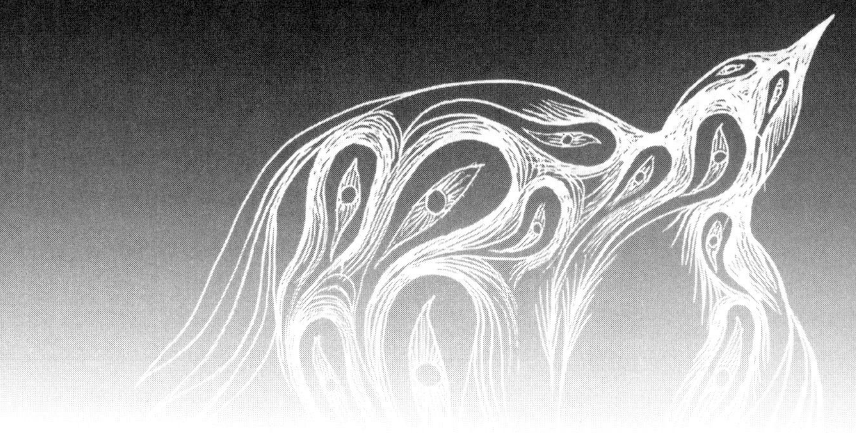

Pluto Shadows

The Underworld Overlord

> *In the Pagan context, a shadowless man was not a demon, a werewolf, or a Schlemhil but one whose soul had gone into eternal bliss. Plutarch said at the end of the world, the blessed ones would be happy forever "in a state neither needing food nor casting a shadow."*
>
> Barbara Walker, *The Women's Encyclopedia of Myths and Secrets*

Pluto moves very slowly, taking 248 years to move through all twelve signs of the zodiac. In 2006, Pluto was demoted to a dwarf planet; but some argue it should be reinstated as a planet. I realize many readers will only read a fraction of this section, but I suggest reading all the placements to familiarize with the shadow forms for archetypal purposes.

Who is the lord of the shadow? Since some of the interpretations of the shadow itself are intimately connected with the dead and the underworld through the shade, the ruler of the underworld plays a role in our shadow book. The lord of the underworld is Pluto. In the underworld and, specifically, in the depths of Earth are gemstones, diamonds, rubies, and emeralds, and precious metals, rhodium, platinum,

and gold. The name Pluto means "lord of wealth," specifically referring to the jewels and precious metals that are wrought in the depths of the underground. These rare and shiny objects are lights in the darkness. What is your gem that lights your way through the shadow realms? We are all given a candle in the dark through Pluto.

In the Pluto placements we see where we have mastered a shadow or perhaps the shadow of another. Look in your birth chart to see what your innate ability is to own the shadow. Though slow-moving Pluto is generational in its influence, we interact with many generations in our lifetimes and can come across a variety of Pluto shadows. The Pluto placements we see show the underworld shadows in the faces we meet.

Here perhaps is Pluto's biggest lesson. Pluto asks of you: Where are you lord? What do you own? What belongs truly and only to you? What identifies your core shadow? Being the lord of a shadow isn't necessarily a good thing; it is just where we wield it deftly. Familiarizing yourself with tales of Pluto and Hades in the myths might be helpful to understand the lessons contained here. In many cultures, the rulers of the underworld are female, such as Hekate, Santa Muerte, the fairy queens of the grave mounds, and the underworld goddesses of Demeter and Cybele. There is a lot of interplay in the myths and cultures in terms of identities of underworld deities and Pluto is by no means the only one; it is used here as an archetypal representative only.

To be lord of our shade requires that we see and know it, first and foremost, so see if you can identify the following shadow forms. These shadows can also be seen when planets hit them by transit, meaning the real time location of the planet, or transiting Pluto interacts with these shadows.

♈

Aries Pluto Shadow

Birth Pluto: Libra ♎

Pluto in Aries is a master of the ego. This might not seem like much because we tend to shame ego, but really, this is a celebrity. They have owned their ego and use it to help themselves. The Aries Pluto shadow is attractive to individuals who have not mastered this archetype, and so they can tend to attract many who are seeking this same level of ego achievement. The danger of being lord of this shadow is that the master can also manipulate the egos of others and draw them into serving the master's power. Being the head of an identity cult sounds like fun but has never ended well throughout history.

♉ Taurus Pluto Shadow

Birth Pluto: Scorpio ♏

Pluto's shadow in Taurus is the master of Earth. The creative arts, food, and agriculture are some of the talents these individuals wield well. Affinities with animals can also be found and tend to be rather like Saint Francis of Assisi. Pluto in Taurus shadow individuals are challenged to free the nonhuman life-forms from slavery. Here, there is an opportunity for the human to evolve by giving assistance to the nonhuman life-forms and caring for their root needs. This is handing out food to animals and watering plants; it's domesticating beasts and taking care of them in sustainable rather than factory-farm ways. The danger of this shadow master is that they lapse in their responsibility to Earth and use lazy ways to care for the flora and fauna, thereby causing them harm.

♊ Gemini Pluto Shadow

Birth Pluto: Sagittarius ♐

Pluto shadow in Gemini is a master of words and communication. Wielding words is no small gift, for through communication, nations form. Words have meaning, and that meaning can be conveyed through analogy, relationship, and language. Where we create language we use it, and we find the place where it connects us to others. This Pluto placement is not just a lord of words, but also a creator of languages, making culture through the use of internal meaning. This gives the lord of this shadow the ability to make words, to find nuanced ways of communicating, and possibly shedding light on the study of language itself.

♋ Cancer Pluto Shadow

Birth Pluto: Capricorn ♑

Pluto in Cancer is the master of emotional manipulation. Though the word *manipulation* has a decidedly negative connotation, it can be used for benefit; just ask any parent who has had to coax or trick a child into eating vegetables. Most of society involves manipulation at some level, and these individuals master it. The holders of this shadow lord can sometimes be found working in advertising or as lawyers. They usually exhibit an immunity to being manipulated and resist being drawn into drama themselves.

♌ Leo Pluto Shadow

Birth Pluto: Aquarius ♒

We will be entering this Pluto shadow as I write this book. The Leo Pluto shadow is the master creator. Here we find artists and the emergence of the master of the arts who does so from the depths of personal experience and breaks free from artistic influences to create for the self. The birth Pluto in Aquarius brings influences from society and art history, but here the individual is able to master a unique individual style, whether that is music, painting, or any art form; finding pure ego expression rather than just copycat mimicry, which so many creatives fall victim to. The danger of this shadow is being ahead of one's time: the artist's unique expressions can alienate the creator from society so that many may never see the art. As Pluto enters Aquarius we have artificial intelligence threatening artists and writers by being able to cheaply create from the collective rather than the living soul; it will be interesting to see how it turns out.

♍
Virgo Pluto Shadow

Birth Pluto: Pisces ♓

Pluto in Virgo is the master analyzer, the solver of puzzles, the creator of systems, and the one who will crack the case. Pluto mastering the Virgo shadow enables the possessor to see the minutiae under the microscope, to go into the small, the particulars, to see the devil in the details. No bit is missed when the eyes of this shadow Pluto take a look at something. This master can become lost in this ability and form an obsession with the solutions, being driven to madness until the discovery is made, but rest assured, the answer will be found. Someone who points out the faults in everything can be very annoying, or that person can be a well-paid consultant, finding patterns of error in larger systems.

♎
Libra Pluto Shadow

Birth Pluto: Aries ♈

The Libra Pluto shadow has mastered reciprocity. For this karma master, things always turn out even steven. This is the incorruptible judge and the master of justice. The Avengers, comic-book superheroes from Marvel Comics, are famous because we admire them for being so fair and serving justice. They are balancing the scales without needing anything in return. Vigilantes are not for sale, and you cannot buy them; their heart is ruled by a purity of justice that belongs to this Pluto master, and you can't persuade them with ideology or sophistry. The scales determine their value system, and it is clear in all the choices they make.

♏
Scorpio Pluto Shadow

Birth Pluto: Taurus ♉

Scorpio Pluto shadow is the master of sex and death. This can take a few different forms, such as someone who works in a hospice and assists people to pass away or a sex worker who is skilled in the sexual arts and in general works with the root chakra. The root needs of reproduction and death cause major fear for the majority of the population, but this placement is free from these types of worry and can manage to focus on other things.

♐

Sagittarius Pluto Shadow

Birth Pluto: Gemini ♊

The Pluto shadow in the location of Sagittarius gives the holder the ability to distill wisdom from the darkest behaviors of others. This position can assist the lord of this shadow to teach others about personality, psychology, and spirituality in a way that takes some of the power out of our worst behaviors and enables us to gain some understanding of human nature from a higher perspective. This Pluto shadow lord can educate and teach others about personality itself on a transpersonal level and enable us to unify through the collective experience of our shared ego traits.

♑

Capricorn Pluto Shadow

Birth Pluto: Cancer ♋

The Pluto Capricorn shadow is the master of real estate. This is the ability to become a large landlord. Quite an enviable position. But if the tenants are not taken care of, this mastery can quickly become shameful, such as when wildlife preserves or arable land is bought and sold for profit, subdivided into building lots, instead of preserving habitat for wildlife or farmland for growing food. How quickly our needs can no longer be met when all we have is money but no shelter or food. If we are a master of land, that means we are stewards of a place where things need to live. Shall you be responsible for their needs? Being master of the land is lordship, and if we are lord of people and animals who live in misery and want, what a dire kingdom indeed.

♒ Aquarius Pluto Shadow

Birth Pluto: Leo ♌

The Aquarius Pluto shadow is the lord of technology. The Leo birth Pluto is adept at creating, and with this lordship placement, there is an ability to invent and utilize technology. This is the energy of the hacker, the innovator, and the code breaker. Being master of this shadow creates important discoveries but also opens the door to wielding abuse over others. To make sure being master of this shadow does not corrupt you, do not use it to control the data of others, as some social media companies have done, for example.

♓ Pisces Pluto Shadow

Birth Pluto: Virgo ♍

Pluto's shadow in Pisces, birth Pluto Virgo, is the ruler of the dead. Here the Pluto shadow is the possessor of the dead through owning an estate or the rights to the creative works of the deceased. This is the ruler of the name and reputation of a dead celebrity. To me this is a bit like shrunken head collecting, but to each their own. Profiting off the fame of the dead is really a type of necromancy, but if I were to call the Walt Disney Company a necromancer, I might ruffle some feathers. This placement is a shadow lord archetype. If the wealth garnered from these estates is not shared with the heirs or the ancestors, negative karma can accrue through this vulture-like behavior.

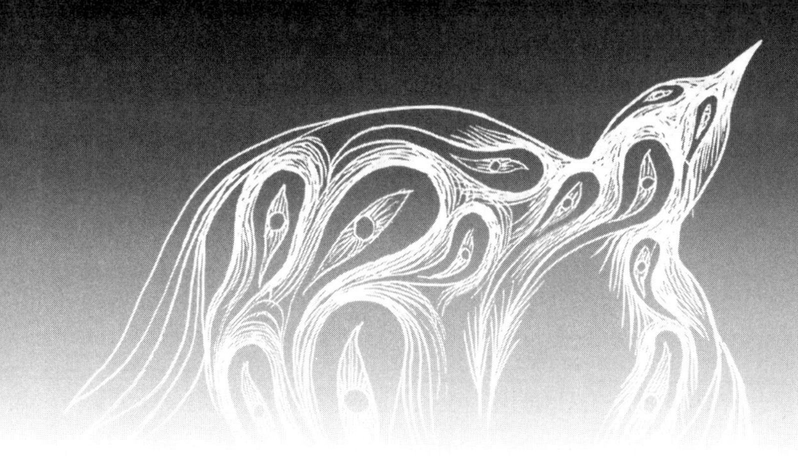

Ophiuchus Shadows

The Venom Master

In Greek mythology, the constellation of Ophiuchus represents Asclepius the healer, and the serpent he is holding probably represents the snake of legend from whom Asclepius learned to raise the dead. Asclepius strangled a snake, but when he discarded the body, another snake slid up with an herb in its mouth and administered it to the dead snake, resurrecting it. Before the second snake could escape, Asclepius snatched some of the herb from its mouth and used it to revive the dead.

Fred Watson, *Astronomica*

Ophiuchus is the thirteenth zodiac constellation and remains hidden below the ecliptic for much of the sun's travels throughout the year, making it a hidden sign in general—and its shadows deserve some attention. You likely will be unable to find Ophiuchus in your birth chart because it is left out of modern astrology. Ophiuchus is located between the Sagittarius and Scorpio constellations. That means that shadows are cast into Ophiuchus by planets placed opposite this location, which will be in the constellation of Gemini. We can examine the effect on each of the

planets casting a shadow in this location. Ophiuchus is a healer and a handler of serpents, and so we look to the serpent bearer to find our venom.

If you have a birth planet located in Gemini, near the constellation of Orion, it is casting an Ophiuchus shadow. If you have a birth planet located in Ophiuchus, you can read for Gemini shadow positions found in this text in the planetary locations. Placements here are the venom masters and poison artists, usually studying plants, healing, and medicine. Those with an Ophiuchus shadow prominent in their charts should familiarize themselves with the type of venom their nature is offering them. We can also look at transits of planets through Gemini for opportunities to heal during the active time of the Ophiuchus shadow.

Sun Ophiuchus Shadow: This venom is an ego popper and is a good placement for teachers of the martial arts, enabling them to break down people's egos and, especially, their own. Practice some ego-death techniques and get comfortable with them; the venom here dissolves ego.

Moon Ophiuchus Shadow: Emotional stings are arguably the worst. Once we are masters of emotional venom, we cannot be manipulated by people who would use our feelings against us. The healing here is much needed, and the ability to withstand poisonous emotions may be more valuable than the finest gems.

Mercury Ophiuchus Shadow: Mind poison is the actor here. This venom has a stabilizing effect on mental health and makes you immune to gaslighting from another poison mind. The venom can withstand assaults on the mind and help you heal or simply endure mental illness and mental abuse.

Venus Ophiuchus Shadow: Love poison is the brew here. The venom is immune to romantic ideations and the drama that accompanies the game of love. Be careful how much of this shadow's poison you ingest; it could be your undoing. This venom will have a strong attraction on others, and they may work as performers.

Mars Ophiuchus Shadow: The art of war is a game of risk, and the venom here is the ability to do battle. This is a sip from the warrior's cup and is not for the faint of heart. Coming into an awareness of sport and strategy without being overcome emotionally is the gift of this venom; we could all use some.

Jupiter Ophiuchus Shadow: Here we have the venom of authority. The path to self-mastery is to not let someone else control you even if you do not have any control over your life. Becoming self-sovereign is a gentle balance of being healthy about your boundaries without being abusive to others. Coming into authority means executing decisions for yourself and expanding your freedoms.

Saturn Ophiuchus Shadow: This is the venom of no. It takes a lot to be immune from the word *no*, as rejection is one of the toughest pills to swallow. Respecting people's no takes a unique kind of medicine, which is found here. Some people have no problem setting boundaries or respecting other people's boundaries; others constantly trespass boundaries. Use this venom for boundary transgressions.

Uranus Ophiuchus Shadow: The poison here is society; the venom developed is the ability to separate from it and break off to investigate the self and the nature of the larger dynamics occurring. This is the one who has triumphed in self-sufficiency and can withstand isolation. This is the venom of the hermit who does quite well on his own.

Neptune Ophiuchus Shadow: Imagination venom is a special commodity for artists. Access to the subconscious and dreams powered the surrealist movement, who lived on this venom. Once we can remember our dreams and become lucid, we can feed this healing medicine to others in the form of art. We must extract poison from these realms to assist our travels here in the mundane world.

Pluto Ophiuchus Shadow: Death venom is hard to swallow. We have no control of death, and once we have passed through its gates, we come back more powerful. This venom is acquired through a near-death experience. Coming back from the dead is a special experience and holds a potent medicine that can assist those who are dealing with grief and the loss of loved ones.

Destiny Shadows

The Role of the Moon Nodes in Our Evolution

The relic from before birth
Enters one's heart one day.
Be as careful as if you were holding a full vessel,
Be as gentle as if you were caressing an infant.
The gate of earth should be shut tight,
The portals of heaven should be first opened.
Wash the yellow sprouts clean,
And atop the mountain is thunder shaking the earth.

Sun Bu'er, *Immortal Sisters: Secret Teachings of Taoist Women*

There is quite a bit of speculation as to what the north and south moon nodes mean in astrology charts and what purpose they serve, with some variations in interpretation. They appear in your birth chart as horseshoe-shaped symbols: the north node opens downward and the south node opens upward. Generally, people agree that the moon nodes tend to be involved in our life's purpose, our destiny, or our driving purpose. The north node is tied to the present, whereas a lot of astrological

scholars and Vedic astrologers tend to think the south node is tied to past lives, our previous incarnations, or our ancestors, implicating a kind of inheritance or karma that is carrying over into our present incarnation.

Many people talk about past lives as literal lives they led in the past, with an individual identity and ego, and I certainly can claim no expertise on the matter to say that this is incorrect. For me, I view past lives as memories from our ancestors, stored in our physical bodies, in our DNA. When we remember lives we have lived before, it could be possible that these are some kind of memory we are holding in our flesh. You could imagine, as the spirit workers do, that we could conceivably remember, technically, to the beginning of DNA itself, since it is a storage system. But this is only one way to look at it, and in this work I will approach the destiny shadow as an inheritance from what came before.

We must do ancestral work to break free from past patterns from parents and extended family. This does not mean leaving or abandoning the family, but we must see what patterns we have inherited from our parents, become aware of them, and integrate them in order to move forward. Nature demands that we, as spiritual initiates, must perform this task first before we can move forward and evolve as individuals.

> *Nature in her truth and simplicity is the true "mother," ever kind and gentle, wounding only to save. When insulted by wilful neglect she becomes a "step mother," and when violated she becomes the most inexorable of masters, wearing the terrible face of a tyrant.*
>
> Ethan Allen Hitchcock, *The Red Book of Appin*

I was thinking about the phenomenon of identity and how some individuals become consumed with identifying their ego with some notable figure from the past, latching onto it. I was once verbally assaulted by someone claiming they had been Madame Blavatsky in her past life, and she was angry that I would not acknowledge her identity. To be honest, I would be more impressed if someone claimed to be nebula 456789 rather than some notable human being.

Essentially, the shadow of your north node placement is the south node. The south node belongs to the past, and the past belongs to the dead. The south node is where you are from, the seed you grew out of. If it sounds strange that this could form a shadow, it can manifest as difficulty individuating from your parents and family. A large part of shadow work is also ancestor work. Even if you master your own personal shadow, you still have to come to terms with what has given birth to you and the human beings you come from. Maybe your ancestors were victims of terrible crimes; maybe they perpetrated them. The south node shadow is where you can illuminate some of this and grow into your own purpose, which is directed through the north node. Individuation requires ancestor work no matter where you are from. We cannot accomplish our spiritual liberation without including everyone first, a big job. To be one we must, first, be all.

To look into your shadow node, find your north node in your chart and then look directly opposite from that location. This is your shadow south node sign. Below are descriptions of each shadow node placement.

♈

Aries Shadow Node

Shadow node in Aries places the north node in Libra (♎). Here we descend from warriors, from aggression, and from placing the self first. The lesson is the ancestral need for isolation and selfishness. This is a survival tactic and deserves recognition. Perhaps your ancestor was a soldier, or had to somehow defend their life in a way that required separation from others. Learn how this served in the past and release the tendency to avoid moving into relationships, as your north node path is to be in relationship. You must fight your shadow that wants to be alone.

♉

Taurus Shadow Node

Shadow node in Taurus places the north node in Scorpio (♏). In this shadow node the ancestors were made to work the land. Farmers and food show up in this shadow node, as well as sensual pleasures, addiction, and attachment. The sensual focus can also give the ancestors a disposition toward art and music. Things to integrate from the past will encompass earthly delights, and the movement should refocus on emotional labor and discipline. We do not need to go into detriment from earthly values but rather simply avoid excess. The power of the Scorpio north node is to withstand almost anything, so you might be surprised that you can do much more than you think and let go of almost everything.

♊

Gemini Shadow Node

The Gemini shadow node places the ancestors in a social context, seeking status, and as expert communicators. This shadow node places the north node in Sagittarius (♐). The challenge to overcome with this shadow destiny is to form deep relationships that are not seeking social climbing. You must be very careful about your communication and avoid gossip and flattery used in vain to sway people. The habit of relying on status is very hard to break because self-reliance is required, which is hard work. Throughout your life, work on finding out who you are and joining others who you sincerely click with rather than making superficial connections. Sagittarius north node will gift you with the inner connection to your higher self, making the need for social status melt away as you enter authenticity of self.

♋

Cancer Shadow Node

The Cancer shadow influence on destiny focuses on matriarchal influences and emotional behavior. You need not relive the life of your mother or grandmother, especially if they had to sacrifice much of their personal pursuits in favor of raising families. You can also, if they are still living, encourage your matriarchs to still seek their destiny. You can release influence from the matriarchal side of the family by offering a sacrifice of sincere devotion to the aims they were attempting to accomplish. The north node in Capricorn (♑) is trying to pull you to career success, so perhaps spend some time on this focus. An easy way to honor the matriarchal shadow is also to work with energies of Earth and give back to what you have received from her, perhaps make donations to a nature reserve.

♌

Leo Shadow Node

In the Leo shadow node, your ancestors are attempting to overshadow your ego with theirs. They want to be remembered, honored, and seen as heroic. The ancestor work needed here is to make altars to the ancestors, acknowledge them, and tell the tales of those who came before you. Sometimes writing a book about your forebears is a good way to transmute this destiny shadow; publishing tales of your family can satisfy this need. A good story told around the fire to friends or others can also suffice. What is needed are memories of the antics of the ones who came before you told orally in a jovial fashion. Then you will be able to move forward and create stories of your own. The north node in Aquarius (♒) assures you will create or invent something all your own that will be utilized by an entire community. North node Aquarius is gifted with unique thoughts, why not remember the thoughts of those who came before you in order to find balance?

♍

Virgo Shadow Node

With Virgo placed in the position of the shadow node, the roots are analytical and service oriented. If your predecessors committed their lives in martyred service to others, you have no obligation to emulate this behavior. There can be a tendency for guilt to be passed along through this ancestor shadow for not being a certain way or doing certain things. You will break through and find your Pisces (♓) north node when you shed these expectations and permit your ancestors to have their values while you have yours, which are probably more open and less rigid. Pisces north node will expand with a breaking or dissolving of certain rules, so try not to focus too much on the grammar and permit yourself to be a little messy.

♎

Libra Shadow Node

Libra shadow nodes tend to throw shades of run-ins with the law or imprisonment that may have occurred within the ancestral heritage. Work or involvement in the judicial system could also be indicated: maybe your parents want you to be a lawyer, but you have no interest, or you make a choice of becoming a lawyer simply because your parents went to jail. Both of these show pressure and a path that does not belong to you. With the north node in Aries (♈), you will need to choose your destiny yourself. Help your ancestors to come into reciprocity and justice, but practice your own path, regardless. If you get lured into some kind of legally challenging mess through family, make sure you keep your own boundaries and resist giving over to that influence.

♏

Scorpio Shadow Node

The presence of a Scorpio shadow node could show sexual abuse or poverty your ancestors experienced. There might be some long shadows of inequity, or perhaps there were no resources left to support you. The placement of this shadow will try and drive you down into your root to seek security through force, but do not worry. Your Taurus (♉) north node will get you to comfort and safety if you follow its lead and experience your own delights and joys; this is the path for you to take. If your ancestors were starving, you might be a chef, or if there was no money, you might be a banker. If sexual trauma is there, perhaps you will become liberated in your sexual expressions as a result of their trials. Honor them in their suffering and feel into your path of well-being. Avoid questioning your worth and value with this placement, and encourage others to grow their self-esteem.

♐

Sagittarius Shadow Node

Overcoming the shadow node in Sagittarius will require staying in one place and mastering the art of commitment. Here the influence is pulling you to quit, to try other things, to be spread out and explore. This is not your path. Your path will be to consolidate, to stay in one spot, and to work on articulating and gathering research before acting. If your ancestors were nomadic or had difficulty settling down, know that you do not need to follow in their footsteps and that you will be perfectly happy sitting in one place. The Gemini (♊) north node is trying to find a friend who will last and make things meaningful; someone who enjoys your conversations. Gemini north node will help you publish or broadcast your words so that they last for a long time and go the distance—as long as you don't keep chasing adventure for the sake of avoiding staying still.

♑

Capricorn Shadow Node

The Capricorn destiny shadow will make you feel like you must be successful with work and career. Perhaps your family demands this of you. You might have other plans, though, and want nothing to do with being a banker or something traditional at all. Maybe you are more of an entrepreneur who wants to find your own way. To work with this ancestral energy, remove yourself from financial dependency on the family. This could be very difficult, but the first step will be to end the influence of their finances over you in order for you to set out on your own path. The north node in Cancer (♋) will direct you to caring for others or providing nourishment and employment for an entire group of people, either as a parent in a family or through innovating a new corporation.

♒

Aquarius Shadow Node

Aquarius shadow node suggests your ancestors were inventors with unique mental gifts, maybe even geniuses. Creativity of mind is present: perhaps an ancestor invented a machine or patented an idea. You may be the beneficiary of these intellectual properties and their results, but your journey is to head toward the north node Leo (♌) and make sure your reliance on this ancestor does not stop you from creating something all your own. This shadow makes shoes for you to fill and step out of. If the ancestor's invention has not been put to use, it could be helpful for you to honor your ancestor by attempting to put it forward, if it could be useful for the community at large.

♓

Pisces Shadow Node

Shadow node in Pisces places north node in Virgo (♍). The ancestors of the Pisces shadow node were perhaps under the sway of a cult, a group mind-set, or some kind of spiritual group. Abandonment of the ego altogether here could indicate communal living, servitude, slavery, and other things like this. If you belong to a church just because your family has always gone there, perhaps you could do some field trips and check out what other practices are out there. It could be that you find your own belief system, which may deviate from the religion you always were part of through family ties. Virgo north node wants you to do service for the community, and comes into its purpose through helping others, but not at the expense of your identity, or your survival. For example, you could be a nurse and earn income for your service, making a win-win rather than a total sacrifice.

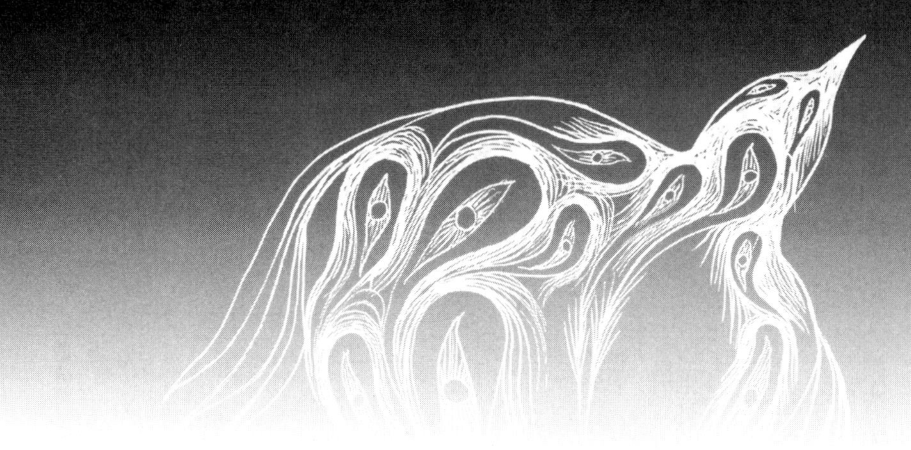

The Power of Oppositional Identities

The Shadow Chart and Its Implications

For counter movement is the bringer of stillness. Now the planetary spheres are moved in the opposite direction to the fixed stars. They are moved by each other in opposition. They are moved round their opposite by a point which is fixed and it cannot be otherwise. Those two Bears (the constellations which you see) neither set nor rise and are turned about the same point, do you think they are moved or are fixed?

-A- They are moved O Trismegistus.

-H- With what kind of movement, Asclepius?

-A- With movement that turns around that point.

-H- The circular movement is a movement about that point governed by that which is still, for revolution round that point prevents any digression; digression is prevented, if the revolution is established. Thus the movement in the opposite direction is stabilizing and is fixed by the principle of counter movement.

Clement Salaman et al., trans., *The Way of Hermes*

When we combine all the placements of the entire chart in their shadow placements, the equal but opposite chart is the shadow chart as a whole. This mirror image of the natal chart forms an in-depth persona of shadow that can also be read in the totality of the chart, just as we do with a birth chart. Both the birth chart and the shadow chart can be broken up into their individual aspects and then looked at as a whole to see larger patterns and aspects. I encourage you to look up the shadow placements in totality, in the circle of the birth chart, and view the oppositional placements next to each other, as well as in isolation. What patterns do you see? What side of the chart does it lean on? Is it well distributed? You may need to do this by hand, drawing a circle split into twelve pie slices, or just print out a blank chart and fill it in. I also recommend seeing what friends, lovers, and relationships you have with people with the astrological placements that fall in your shadows to investigate if those patterns are playing out with them.

> *If we are uncritical we shall always find what we want: we shall look for, and find, confirmations, and we shall look away from, and not see, whatever might be dangerous to our pet theories. In this way it is only too easy to obtain what appears to be overwhelming evidence in favor of a theory which, if approached critically, would have been refuted. In order to make the method of selection by elimination work, and to ensure that only the fittest theories survive, their struggle for life must be made severe for them.*
>
> Karl R. Popper, *The Poverty of Historicism*

Being able to see the polar opposite of your astrological identity can be expanding, even in looking at the chart, especially if you are versed in astrology and have gazed upon your chart often. The shift in perception caused by the opposition is palpable. Why must we deal with counterforce? We live in a universe that contains opposition as a physical law of reality; nature is always seeking to reach homeostasis and equilibrium. We find peace not by destroying opposition, for this imbalances the scale, causing the weights to swing wildly; we must only equalize and neutralize. This is the system of the Taoists and the alchemists, who do not take a separational oppositional stance but instead seek to neutralize it. It is not for everyone; you might not be able to come out of opposition. Please understand the middle path of equilibrium does not mean toxic positivity, where we let destruction happen. The labor involved is much more nuanced than simply trying to destroy destruction. It turns out that destroying destruction doesn't work energetically to reach peace and equilibrium. Is it a logical fallacy to assume you cannot deal with it either, for then that path leads to destruction as well. So what really do we do? Meeting it with positive force isn't always wise, though sometimes, depending on the situation, it should not be discarded as an option. You can't positive-attitude your way out of crimes and destruction that reach offensive levels; you just can't. We need more ways to deal.

I feel like we can use astrology to investigate because—much like a retrograde planet whose orbit goes in reverse when in reality its faster orbit around the sun makes it appear to go retrograde from our rotating planet Earth—the enemy, too, is a matter of misperception. True, there are real crimes and trauma committed against each other—there is no denying that—but to take those occurrences personally and view them as something done against you, resulting in a vendetta, requires a certain perception that may or may not be true. Yes the person did something, yes it affected you, but was it really against you specifically? Was it much larger than the individual, who may have been caught up in a repeating form of an archetype that is affecting and influencing many people? The more we are able to see clearly past the oppositional stance, the more unbiased we become and the more data we are able to take in. As soon as we are able to see past the forces opposing us and gauge the nature of those forces and how they impact us, we can reach a greater understanding of the forces themselves. This liberates and frees our minds from combating those forces, and we can then form a strategy for properly dealing with them. The difference here is in the expenditure of our energy, emotions, and spiritual freedom.

The Caduceus, Jacob and His Angel, and Evolving through Opposition

I was meditating upon the meaning of the caduceus, and the story of Jacob wrestling the angel kept popping into my head. I didn't know why, so I looked up the story of Jacob in the Bible and contemplated some more. Through a series of synchronistic events, I came to a realization about an important meaning of the caduceus, which I had not seen before, regarding the power of opposition.

In the image of the caduceus, we see two snakes intertwined around a staff, or sometimes only around each other. The two serpents are opposing each other, engaged in a face-off, equal and opposite to each other. At each point up the staff, where the bodies of the two snakes touch, there is a confrontation, a contact. In this contact the two serpents impact each other, mingling their essences in the intimacy of battle. Because neither snake is bested, a growth erupts, and the snakes are able to continue rising. Each snake would have remained on the ground had each not had an enemy, the other, to lift it up. By engaging in friction, they are able to rise up from the ground. If one or both snakes had attempted to destroy each other in battle, neither snake would have been able to make the ascent; each one was in fact dependent upon the other to grow, though I doubt the snakes would take this news kindly. As the serpents use each other's bodies to climb up, they grow wings, as both evolve, as long as they do not kill each other; this growth is symbolized by the wings at the top of the staff of the caduceus. The danger in dealing with opposition is always death, but where there is no destruction, there is growth.

The story of Jacob in Genesis 32 depicts an obscure and metaphor-laden tale of a brother confronting his brother. But according to Jewish scholars, on a deeper level, the tale depicts an individual confronting a double or shadow, or as the Hebrew traditions call it, the *yetzer hara*. In Kabbalah, and according to rabbis, this simple tale reveals huge implications for shadow work and the oppositional identity.

> The Degel Mahane Efraim states that Esau and Jacob, the twins struggling in Rebeca's womb, symbolise the struggle of the *yetzer tov* and *yetzer hara* in each and every one of us, a struggle that we engage in every day of our lives. Judaism teaches us that a person has two inclinations: the *yetzer tov*, the good inclination and the *yetzer hara*, the evil, often understood as the selfish or self-protective inclination. In our tradition as well as in other religious paths, human beings are seen as being a battle ground between these two seemingly opposing inclinations. We are often taught that the *yetzer hara* is a negative force which needs to be subdued by the *yetzer tov*. However, many sources in Judaism speak not about the destruction of the *yetzer hara* but of the necessity for us to transform it for the performance of good in the world. Our tradition teaches that we have been given the ability to choose the moral path even when we are under the influence of the selfish/self-protective inclination. We have the capacity to use our *yetzer hara* for the greater good. The Degel expresses this powerfully when he states that the word *yitrozzetzu* (struggling) . . . is related to the word *ratzutz* (broken) in Hebrew. These two inclinations are always struggling within us, breaking us in half, tearing us apart. Sometimes the selfish inclination subdues the good and sometimes the good triumphs over the selfish/self-protective, but these two voices within us are in continuous struggle.*

Simultaneously depicting both Jacob's battle with his brother, who is possibly his shadow, and his battle with his higher mind, or higher self, represented by the angel, the story is extremely important.

Throughout their lives, Jacob had constant problems with his elder twin brother, Esau, who bullied and terrorized him, even from the womb, much like some species of shark who eat and kill their womb mates to make sure only they are born. Jacob receives news that his

*Rabbi Cantor George Mordecai, "Drash on Parashat Tol'dot 2021," Union for Progressive Judaism website.

brother is coming to visit him and is told to prepare gifts, but secretly Jacob prepares to do battle, evacuating the town and getting his arms ready. That night, according to King James translations of the Bible, he is approached by a man. In more traditional texts, such as the Rashi Chumash, this "man" is either an angel (possibly Esau's guardian angel) or Jacob's own conscience (a bit like Jiminy Cricket and Pinocchio) and it could possibly symbolize his libido as represented by the location of the injury he receives while wrestling. The entity asks Jacob, What are you doing? Jacob explains his case to the angel, justifying why he needs to get ready for his evil brother. The angel argues he needs to prepare food to greet his brother and welcome his brother into his home. Jacob does not want to do this. He and the angel lock arms and begin to wrestle. The word *wrestle* is interesting, here especially, as it relates to the two serpents in the caduceus. In the Rashi Chumash the word used is not *wrestle* per se but rather *intertwined* or knotted together, much like the two oppositional serpents. Some scholars state the caduceus is a reference in fact to two serpents when they mate. The angel wins the "wrestling match," causing Jacob an injury, which symbolizes that when a good sporting competition ensues, if things go too far, someone will get hurt.

> As the commentary in *Etz Hayim* indicates, this admittedly strange story and the change of name that accompanies it have been variously interpreted. The "man" in Gen. 32:25 or the "divine being" (*Elohim*) in Gen. 32: 29 and 31 is interpreted in most of the classical commentaries as a spirit bent on doing Jacob harm. It could be Esau's guardian angel (Genesis Rabbah 77:3) or, as in more anthropologically based commentaries, the demonic guardian of the river he was about to cross. Yet again, it might be Jacob wrestling with his own conscience, for he emerges as a changed man who is whole (Gen. 33:18, *shalem*) in that he now contends with God and people instead of avoiding or manipulating them. And the whole story may just be an etiological myth to explain why Jews do not eat the *gid ha-nasheh* of even a kosher animal, translated in the Jewish Publication Society translation as the "thigh muscle" (Gen. 32:33),

interpreted as the sciatic nerve in Rabbinic law, and probably referring to the animal's genitals in its original meaning.*

The site of the injury is important too for shadow work, as it is the loins, specifically the cut of filet mignon, and could symbolize castration of the libido. The injured Jacob agrees to the angel's recommendation, being forced into submission, which in esoteric Jewish texts symbolizes the submission of the ego to spirit, or the humbling of the inclination to do evil through force of good. The angel then honors him by giving him an angel name, Israel, recognizing his evolution, much like the serpents rising up the caduceus (and an esoteric reference to Jacob receiving a title of Ba'al, an honorific title as described in the Saturn shadow chapter).

Spirit showed me through this story that an Israelite is one who is doing shadow work, who is engaging and advancing, like the serpents up the pole. Israel is a title of honor for one who engages this battle of shadow, the battle with hara, the battle with spirit. Of course I can't speak for Jewish folks; this is just what I saw in the story and from my research into the rabbinic Jewish literature.

Example in Nature

Conflicts between animals of the same species usually are of "limited war" type, not causing serious injury. This is often explained as due to group or species selection for behavior benefiting the species rather than individuals. Game theory and computer simulation analyses show, however, that a "limited war" strategy benefits individual animals as well as the species.

— J. Maynard Smith and G. R. Price, "The Logic of Animal Conflict," *Nature* 246 (November 2, 1973): 15–18

We see opposition constantly, every day, and the tendency is to see the opposition as an enemy, as someone or something to fear and hate.

*Rabbi Elliot Dorff, Ph.D., "Wrestling With God," American Jewish University website, December 4, 2011.

Look at the oppositional stances in the media, in politics and in sports. It's as if society treats each other like WWE wrestling opponents in a ring, in sensationalized drama. Look at them. There is a law in thermodynamics that states for every force there is an equal and opposite force; for every action there is an equal and opposite reaction. These things exist together, simultaneously. This is the physical reality that we exist within. If we see "enemy" as an oppositional counterforce, rather than something threatening us, we will have grown closer to truth in that moment and will rise to the occasion.

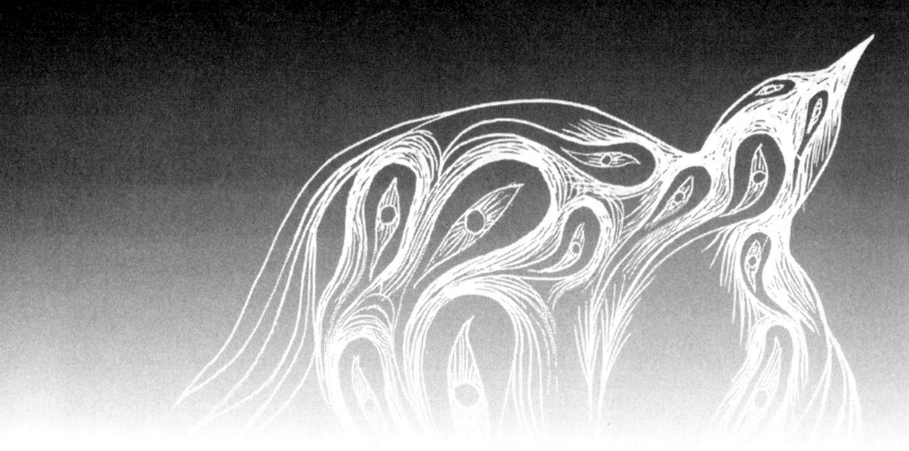

Epilogue

Revelations of Eclipses

> *At the same time the seasons changed with the sound of thunder. Observing the oppositional forces that worked to bring about change in the natural world, nature demonstrated productive growth through friction. Without this oppositional energy, the ancient taoist recognized how life would lose its vitality to become stagnant. Therefore a sage was always a student of nature. When obstacles became insurmountable, one simply emulated the way of nature.*
>
> Kari Hohne, *Tao Te Ching: The Poetry of Nature*

An eclipse is a very important natural occurrence for a human being who is trying to understand shadow work, astrology, and the occult. The eclipse is the physical manifestation of occultism. A lot of people associate the word *occult* with something evil, but the word simply means hidden. In astronomy, an occultation happens when object A is hidden from an observer when object B passes between A and the observer; for example, when the moon occults the sun, it passes between the sun and Earth and blocks our view of the sun. During an

occultation, something is hidden behind another thing, which is essentially what all of us are. This is the nature of shadow work itself. Our blind spots contain deep insights, and one of the best opportunities to see reflections of meaning is during an eclipse. The definition of eclipse is very closely related to the definition of the occult. We are hidden behind this other thing, and we can only emerge under certain conditions. You are hidden behind your body, which Earth itself represents. Interestingly enough, eclipses mark an important beginning of science as they were one of the first events to occur proven by a theory based upon astrological findings.

The importance of an occultation or an eclipse is that it shows opposition through contrast, and through an oppositional contrast you can gain knowledge of the thing itself. Through a totality of the thing *and* the no-thing, the inverse of the thing, we must come up against the night, against what we are not, to gain knowledge. Embracing the light *and* the dark brings knowledge through that definition; we are made somewhere in between polarities.

One of the main reasons that astrology is such a great tool for shadow work is due to occultations providing a time period, an envelope or a portal, to reveal the thing that has been hidden and bring it up into the light. Ironically, this is done by casting a shadow, providing an opposition. A bit like using our hand to make a shadow puppet on a wall, the shadows cast from the planets during occultations and eclipses are special times where gnosis may be revealed. Occultations can happen with celestial objects other than the sun and moon, and they are windows into shadow energy that are vitally important to our consciousness. My advice is to raise awareness to these influences and feel into them.

Eclipses arrive in pairs; there are two that couple and double together based on the relationships of the sun and moon. One eclipse is of the sun, and one eclipse of the moon. They form together in time periods, and it is important to look into the shadows they cast to see what energies are present. If you discover an eclipse is occurring, you can look up the shadow of it in this book, under the sun or moon shadow placement in the zodiac, to gain a deeper understanding of what to look for.

During a solar eclipse, we are given information regarding our ego. We are also given information regarding the ego itself, what it is and its nature. We are more likely to see ego in others and not ourselves because the nature of the ego is to project itself; our ego tends to deflect, to hide, and only see the evil in others rather than in ourselves.

The ego, like the sun, has a powerful ability to eclipse all else in view. When the sun is out during the day, it steals your view of all the other stars in heaven. You cannot see the stars when the sun is shining. The ego, similarly, blocks the view of everything else in its blinding need for adulation and attention.

I had an experience, when I was still active on the toxic entity that is social media, that assisted my understanding of this. I had made a post attempting to draw awareness to bigotry toward witches. In the post, I shared an article by *US News and World Report* about Lady Gaga. After I shared the post, which I felt was straightforward, it was quickly overwhelmed with commenters discussing Lady Gaga, rather than the subject I had brought up. The post was sidetracked and derailed simply because it involved the name and ego of Lady Gaga, which took over the entirety of the post, eclipsing everything else I said. It was quite a phenomenon, which I observed with great interest.

If you are now wondering what gossip I was sharing about Lady Gaga, perhaps you too are under the sway of the ego; no shame here for that, as it is a phenomenon that deserves recognition. The *US News and World Report* article was a fact check, stating that Lady Gaga was not a witch. The article referenced a long string of smear campaigns that had attempted to besmirch the reputations of many, claiming they were witches and ate babies. My point was *US News* failed to clear the name of witches and point out that witches don't eat babies; the article simply focused on clearing Lady Gaga's name from the accusation of witchcraft, rather than righting the wrong of accusing witches of baby eating. No one reading the post seemed to understand this, and all of them proceeded to make comments on the ego presence of Lady Gaga, insulting Lady Gaga with many less-than-gracious troll remarks. It was a revelation in ego shadow work, as I realized I could have said anything at all, and all people would cling to was the name Lady Gaga, her ego presence totaling eclipsing everything else.

The Significance of the Solar Eclipse for Shadow Work

The solar eclipse provides an ability to witness and perceive individuals' egos coming to the surface to become visible. Look at others and yourself at this time for revelations on the ego—who has what mask on and what response it elicits from you. Look up in this book the placement of the eclipse in the zodiac according to when it occurs and compare and contrast trends you observe, feelings you experience, and things your friends and loved ones might bring up at this time. The solar eclipse also offers a rare opportunity to observe collective trends of events that unfold in the news and actions taken by notable people or celebrities, who receive a great deal of attention. What are some desires that arise within your ego at this time? Who are you jealous of during these events? It might seem odd to focus on your jealousies, but they can communicate a large amount of information about your desires. Focus on what they are telling you about yourself, and don't target anyone with them.

There is a passage in the crucifixion of Jesus the Christ when he laments and cries out to God, which is uncharacteristic of Jesus, because like Job, the Christ does not usually complain to God. Here the passage is:

> *My God, my God, why have you forsaken me?*
>
> Matthew 27:46

The translation is controversial among both Christian and Jewish scholars concerning the word *forsaken*. Christians tend to view it differently because it seems uncharacteristic that God would abandon his son. We see, though, that in the rest of the passage the whole sky went dark, which, to most, strongly indicates a solar eclipse.

Jesus Christ would have most likely spoken Aramaic, and his words would have been *Eloi, Eloi, lema sabachthani?* The authors of the New Testament wrote, however, in Greek, and the passage in Matthew was originally: *Thee mou, thee mou, hinati enkatelipes?* The Greek word *enkatelipes*, also spelled *egkataleipo*—which is usually translated as "forsaken"—also means "to leave behind" and has an etymological connection to the English word *eclipse*. The Greek root for eclipse is *ekleipsis*, which in turn derives from *ekleipein*, a Greek word that means "to leave out, to abandon." It was revealed to me through my personal spirit guide that the crucifixion of Christ is a metaphor for our own ego's suffering, of being harmed by others and punished, humiliated, and shamed in front of a crowd. Esoteric schools also characterize Christ's crucifixion in this way, and it is common for initiates into esoteric traditions to undergo trials and tribulations, mimicking the trials of Christ, the death of the ego.

These words appear elsewhere in the Bible, for example in Psalm 22.

> *My God, my God, why have you forsaken me? Why are you so far from saving me, so far from the words of my groaning?*
>
> Psalm 22

The seeming betrayal of Jesus Christ by God somewhat mirrors the betrayal of Abel by Cain, who, motivated by hate and jealousy, commits the first murder by killing his brother. The Hebrew name Abel means a few things: it can mean a void, like an empty space, and also a thing created to be destroyed. Something created to be destroyed might not ring many bells for most of us these days, but if we time-travel we know that such sacrificial idols were made for the grain gods and the agricultural harvests; another word for them is *straw dogs*. Jesus mentioned that his fate is only to be created for destruction, which is a lament on the fate of Abel and a critique of his murder, a murder that Jesus also underwent.

The ego wants to be acknowledged, to not be abandoned in its time of need. The ego wants all to know, love, and honor it, to have a gravestone memorializing it and not be left as a pile of bones on Golgotha. However, by undergoing humiliation the ego grows through and past this state into an ego death, where it undergoes a transmutation. The eclipse provides us a window into our ego wounds and demands that we confront and deal with it within ourselves. Christians argue there is no need for this now, as Christ accomplished the end of the straw dog. I wish that were true, but daily news stories indicate we seem to replay this story over and over again, sacrificing one another.

When my doppelgänger was revealed to my consciousness during a solar eclipse, I saw it completely. It kept repeating "What about me?," as if it had been forsaken. It was after this event that I was led to the quotes above from Matthew and Psalm 22. As I was typing this on my computer, the text dropped out to white, although I did not select this type face, so I decided to leave it. My shadow is speaking through the pages, inverting the paper to turn it dark.

The Significance of the Lunar Eclipse for Shadow Work

The lunar eclipse allows us a glimpse into the hidden nature of our emotions and fears. Every time there is a lunar eclipse, pay special attention to what creeps forth from the shadows. My advice is to track closely how you feel, to note negative emotions in yourself and others that may surface at this time. In my work I have noticed themes and patterns of breakups, fights between couples and in families, and public outbursts during lunar eclipses.

The lunar eclipse is especially good at revealing our core defense response. The basic core responses are: fight, flight, freeze, hide, and fawn. These responses are our defenses, and so during this time, mind how you go to your default position during an altercation with someone. What is your go-to, fallback core defense? What core response do your loved ones express? Try and just watch it and identify it; learn about yourself and others by seeing which kind of creature is present at these times.

The lunar eclipse grants us a precious opportunity to reveal our emotional darkness and transmute some of it. Here we are given an opportunity to raise into awareness the darkest, most unaddressed aspects of our moon shadows. Chances are you will certainly see the emotional moon shadows of others during this time, and I have found that if I am able to keep in mind that what is occurring is shadow work, it helps me loosen my reaction to it and shepherd others through it, or at least offer some insight afterward so they can see what happened from another perspective. If I hold an awareness of the eclipse energy and how it affects me, I find I am also able to avoid some missteps myself by feeling through my emotions rather than projecting them. I don't always win, but in paying closer attention, I can see the growth won by the attention paid.

So many of our interactions with each other never touch or make any contact, though we may shout directly into each other's ears. Shadow makes ways to use the other to display the self so that we can see ourselves with our own eyes, but often we miss the picture. We don't get through in our relationships when shadow is thick because it is coating our glasses: we project our shadow selves on the other and so see neither the other clearly nor ourselves for who we are. The mutual projection of ourselves upon the other leaves us stuck in a cycle of isolation and alienation. The betrayals and shadow behaviors we throw upon each other cause pain, suffering, and a feeling of not being human, not belonging, schism upon schism of not feeling human. For how could behaving this way be human? Why can't I be seen? We feel insane when we think we have explained ourselves, communicated, poured out our hearts, only to witness the other completely distorting what we have said, like some kind of tabloid media interpretation of a person or event, skewing it to fit a certain lens or narrative. The truth is shattered, like a mirror broken into pieces, each shard mirroring a separate view. The suffering caused by shadow is one of isolation—creating aliens, preventing touch, preventing love, understanding, and compassion.

Be cautious in your approach to inform another of the presence of shadow when you see it, friend. The first thing that will happen when you try to illuminate a shadow is that it will attack you, as though it were fighting for its very life.

> *Consciousness is knowledge and life; unconsciousness is ignorance and death. If we are conscious of the existence of a thing, we know that a relation exists between ourselves and that thing. If we become unconscious of its existence, neither we nor that object ceases to exist, but we fail to recognize its relation to us. As soon as we begin to realize that relation, the character of the object perceived in the sphere of our mind becomes a part of our mental constitution, and we begin to live in relation to it. We then possess it in our consciousness, and may retain it there by power of our will.*
>
> Franz Hartmann, *Magic White and Black*

Resources

For free astrological charts, I recommend the website **Astro.com**.

For information on astrological chart readings and consultations with me, Maja D'Aoust, as well as more of my writings, art, and other projects, visit **Witchofthedawn.com**.

For readers interested in continuing their shadow work, I also recommend the following books.

Bastian, Simon. *The Way of Demons: Shadow and Opposition in Taoist Thought, Ritual, and Alchemy.* Keighley, England: Hadean Press, 2020.

Hollis, James. *Swamplands of the Soul.* Toronto, Canada: Inner City Books, 1996.

Meador, Betty De Shong. *Inanna, Lady of Largest Heart: Poems of the Sumerian High Priestess.* Austin: University of Texas Press, 2001.

Naydler, Jeremy. *Shamanic Wisdom in the Pyramid Texts: The Mystical Tradition of Ancient Egypt.* Rochester, VT: Inner Traditions, 2004.

Read, Jason. *Fox Magic: Handbook of Chinese Witchcraft and Alchemy in the Fox Tradition.* Oxford, England: Mandrake of Oxford, 2021.

Starhawk, and M. Macha NightMare. *The Pagan Book of Living and Dying: Practical Rituals, Prayers, Blessings, and Meditations on Crossing Over.* San Francisco: HarperOne, 1997.

Wang, Winnie Chan, and Ji W. Choi. *Honoring Darkness: Embrace Shadow Work to Nourish and Grow Your Power.* Toronto, Canada: Soulfully Aligned Publishing, 2022.

Wolkstein, Diane, and Samuel Noah Kramer. *Inanna, Queen of Heaven and Earth: Her Stories and Hymns from Sumer.* New York: Harper Perennial, 1983.

Zweig, Connie. *Meeting the Shadow on the Spiritual Path: The Dance of Darkness and Light in Our Search for Awakening.* Rochester, VT: Park Street Press, 2023.

Index

Books of Related Interest

Familiars in Witchcraft
Supernatural Guardians in the Magical Traditions of the World
by Maja D'Aoust

The Occult I Ching
The Secret Language of Serpents
by Maja D'Aoust

Astrology for Mystics
Exploring the Occult Depths of the Water Houses in Your Natal Chart
by Tayannah Lee McQuillar

The Path of Elemental Witchcraft
A Wyrd Woman's Book of Shadows
by Salicrow

Meeting the Shadow on the Spiritual Path
The Dance of Darkness and Light in Our Search for Awakening
by Connie Zweig, Ph.D.

Shadow Animals
How Animals We Fear Can Help Us Heal, Transform, and Awaken
by Dawn Baumann Brunke

The Nature of Astrology
History, Philosophy, and the Science of Self-Organizing Systems
by Bruce Scofield

Soul Journey through the Tarot
Key to a Complete Spiritual Practice
by John Sandbach